Inside the Brotherhood

T0056554

Inside the Brotherhood

Hazem Kandil

polity

First published in 2015 by Polity Press

Polity Press
65 Bridge Street
Cambridge CB2 1UR, UK

Polity Press
350 Main Street
Malden, MA 02148, USA

ISBN-13: 978-0-7456-8291-4

A catalogue record for this book is available from the British Library.

Library of Congress Cataloging-in-Publication Data
    Kandil, Hazem.
    Inside the Brotherhood / Hazem Kandil.
      pages cm
    Includes bibliographical references.
    ISBN 978-0-7456-8291-4 (hardcover) – ISBN 0-7456-8291-X
(hardcover)   1. Jam'iyat al-Ikhwan al-Muslimin (Egypt)   2. Islamic fundamentalism–Egypt.   3. Islamic fundamentalism. I. Title.
    BP10.J383K36 2014
    320.55'70962–dc23

                                                        2014019107

Typeset in 10.5 on 12 pt Sabon
by Toppan Best-set Premedia Limited
Printed and bound in the United Kingdom by Clays Ltd, St Ives PLC

For further information on Polity, visit our website: politybooks.com

To those Brothers who found the strength to climb the walls
and look beyond

– Support your brother, whether he is the oppressed or the oppressor.

– O Prophet of God, support him surely if he is oppressed, but what if he is the oppressor?

– Restrain him or prevent his oppression; this is how you support him.

Prophet Muhammad

Contents

Contents

Introduction

A reputation established over eight decades collapsed in less than eight months. Islamism, an ideology that carved its name from Islam, had always been synonymous with it in the minds of many. And the Egyptian Muslim Brothers, who have invented and embodied this ideology since 1928, had been merely perceived as fervent believers who went beyond practicing religion to propagating and defending it. But a gathering rebellion against the country's first Brotherhood president changed all that. On the eve of the 2013 popular uprising against Muhammad Morsi, Brothers organized preemptive sit-ins in several locations around the country. The biggest crowd camped around Cairo's Rab'a al-'Adawiya mosque. For 40 days, unsuspecting Egyptians tuned in (some even strolled in) to witness for themselves what Brothers said and did.[i] It was a rare opportunity to eavesdrop on this exceptionally discreet group. And what the people saw and heard was somewhat different from what they were used to from the normally polished Brothers: political competitors were religiously condemned; images of Prophet Muhammad's epic battles were conjured; biblical stories, from David and Moses to Armageddon, were invoked; claims that Archangel Gabriel prayed at the Islamist

---

[i] The myth that there was a media blackout on Islamists during the sit-in is a powerful one, especially outside Egypt. But in fact Al-Jazeera Egypt managed a live, non-stop broadcast from the sit-ins, and the speeches made on stage were recorded and uploaded daily on YouTube and other social media. Furthermore, hundreds of Egyptians, including the author, could move in and out of the sit-in freely and anonymously.

campsite were flaunted; and sacred visions were relayed on stage night after night. This was not the vocabulary Brothers typically employed in their public interactions. Almost overnight, many Egyptians panicked. Who were these strangers, they wondered?

Little did they know that many Brothers were equally confused. Popular hostility was certainly frustrating after decades of successful promotion of the Islamist image. But there was more: Brothers were visibly shaken by the absence of divine intervention. In their mind, everything was set in place for their divine empowerment (*tamkin*); and God would never desert His soldiers. The fact that the sit-in coincided with the holy month of Ramadan, which featured Islam's early victories, was quite suggestive. Brothers held constant vigils, fasting during daytime, and praying from dusk till dawn to make themselves worthy of divine favor. As the political showdown approached, the daughter of the Brotherhood's effective leader was caught screaming on television: "God will part the sea for us! Just wait and see!"[1] She was echoing one of many prophecies circulated during the sit-in: that the soldiers of Pharaoh had trapped the Brothers just as they had done with the ancient Hebrews, and if the Brothers kept faith with Morsi, as their predecessors did with Moses, a miracle was shortly at hand. Brotherhood preachers even determined the date (some random Friday) for the metaphorical drowning of the soldiers.[2] But the sea remained as calm as ever, and the cornered believers were mercilessly slain. Those who saw their campsite laid to waste muttered in shock and denial: why would Heaven forsake us?

This book attempts to answer these two questions: Who are the Muslim Brothers? And what sort of relationship do they believe they have with the divine? My search for an answer began in 2006 with a handful of interviews with leading Islamist figures. Responses were typically longwinded, insubstantial, and ultimately unsatisfactory. Resisting the temptation to abandon the project, I decided to revisit the Islamist literature I had ploughed through years before. This was supplemented by six years of regular attendance at a Brotherhood mosque in California, and hours of audio/video indoctrination materials. But immersing myself in Islamist rhetoric raised more questions than answers.

Then something unexpected happened. A mutual friend asked me to lecture informally to a group of Muslim Brothers on secular ideologies. This was the summer of 2008, and Islamists were concerned that their poor grasp of secular platforms hampered their strategy to unite opposition under their banner. Weekly lectures were organized at a Brother's house (during the months I spent in Cairo) with 30 male attendants on average, from a variety of age groups and backgrounds. We bonded over discussions on the origins of Western ideologies and their history in the Muslim world, and I was allowed over the next five years to observe group members closely in their 'natural habitat,' amongst themselves and their families, rather than 'in action' (teaching, providing welfare, campaigning), as other researchers had done before.

Our relationship was dramatically enhanced by the truly singular experience of revolution. As the 2011 revolt unfolded, I saw different members of my study group resign from the Brotherhood in disillusionment; rise to fame as independent activists; assume posts in the Brotherhood's first political party and presidential team; and sacrifice their lives in horrific street battles. This trying episode encouraged them to open up and inspect their beliefs and actions more than they would have normally done. It was also during this time that a series of tell-all memoirs and published testimonies began to trickle out. Months into Morsi's presidency, it became obvious that the Brotherhood's days in power were numbered. So, in March 2013, I returned to Egypt to conduct interviews and focus group sessions – some with members of my original crowd, and others with Brothers and Sisters they knew. I was also granted access to crucial movement documents from their personal archives, such as training manuals for group prefects, the all-important cultivation curriculum, questionnaire samples, internal memos, resignation and prison letters, and daily correspondence. Equally important was the opportunity to witness Brotherhood exchanges first-hand on the street, through social media, and in private meetings during the turbulent summer of 2013. These observations, complemented with dozens of memoirs and unpublished writings, allowed me to define the three-sided process that goes to the heart of any attempt to understand the Brotherhood: how individuals are recruited and socialized; how their social networks are constructed and sustained; and how their governing ideas are formulated and imbued.

This is an entirely new approach to studying Islamism. Past accounts have often been fettered by partial access – which mostly involved interviewing spokesmen and handpicked members. Research, therefore, remained limited to interactions between Islamists and their environment, rather than extending to the relationship between movements and their own members. Intellectual historians and discourse analysts pored over published texts and other public utterances. Social movement theorists examined how Islamists served their communities, garnered votes, framed and disseminated ideas. The politically inclined evaluated Islamist strategies regarding the state and the economy. Even anthropological accounts centered on the constituencies of Islamism rather than Islamists themselves. This book shifts focus from what Islamists say and do to who they really are – not in terms of social background, but as ideological subjects. Applying this new paradigm to Egypt, the book provides the first in-depth study of the Brotherhood from the inside: how Brothers are cultivated; how they interact; and what goes on inside their heads. These three interrelated processes are discussed in the first three chapters. The following two chapters then apply this new knowledge to reinterpret the history of the movement, before and after assuming power, and compare it to other Islamists (including Brotherhood affiliates) around the Muslim world.

Two notes are in order, however, before we proceed. First, this book does not attempt to reduce the Brotherhood to what it is from the inside – implying somehow that its exterior is a façade. Like any other organization (and, indeed, like any individual), the Brotherhood is the sum total of its interior and exterior facets. Brothers are both the public activists we have long recognized, and the closed ideological subjects that we will encounter in this work. Second, although this research partly draws on ethnographic fieldwork, the aim is not to understand the Brotherhood on its own terms, as a conventional ethnography would do. This is a political sociological study of how the movement's ideology contributed to its downfall. The chief focus, in other words, is on how ideas both empowered and restricted Brothers in their political power struggle. Needless to say, my purpose is not to judge the Muslim Brotherhood. This research was inspired, above all, by personal curiosity. It is simply an attempt at understanding.

1

Cultivating the Brother

One cannot choose to join the Muslim Brotherhood; one has to be chosen. Fayez, a lawyer who was recruited in his village mosque when he was only 11, said he did not remember embracing the Brotherhood like one would embrace an intellectual faction or a political party. It was the movement that decided (2013: 12). Mahmoud (2013), a hot-blooded Alexandrian journalist who had dwelt in Brotherhood circles since he was five, remarked with some amusement: "I was actually born to find myself a Brother." And even though Rida (2013), a shopkeeper and lifelong Cairo resident, made it to the ranks a bit later (at elementary school), he did not remember making a conscious decision to join: "You simply slid in."

Brothers constantly vet relatives, neighbors, colleagues, and – the most yielding pool – mosque attendees[1] for potential recruits. Candidates pass through an average three-year probation period, typically without their knowledge, before being invited to join. They are encouraged to pray regularly at the mosque and participate in its activities, especially Qur'an-reading groups (*maqari'*). They are also advised to limit their interaction to pious individuals of their own age and gender. After this exceptionally long screening period, nominees are finally informed that they are being considered for Brotherhood membership. Only a tiny fraction refuses to play along after this extended courtship. And in that case, they are asked to support the cause without official membership. As for the willing majority, the recruitment process concludes with invitations to Brotherhood day-trips and informal gatherings for inspection by more experienced eyes. Those who receive the stamp of approval are designated as devotees (*muhibin*) and assigned to apprentice groups to test their diligence and familiarize them with the organization. Successful devotees are next enrolled on a grueling three-month induction course (*dawrat tas'id*), which provides a brief introduction to the founding history of Islam and Islamism, followed by qualifying exams (mostly in the form of questionnaires). If all goes well, devotees are asked to swear an oath of allegiance (*bai'a*) to the general guide (*al-Murshid al-'Am*) – an oath historically reserved for caliphs, but temporarily appropriated by Brothers as the provisional leaders of the community of the faithful until a new caliphate is established. This intensely ritualized oath transforms a devotee into a Brother.

Still, elevation to entry-level membership is only the first step in another long journey through the five ranks of membership.[2] Promotion from novice to full member is subject to a complicated set of monitoring mechanisms centered on the process referred to as cultivation (*tarbiya*). When 'Umar al-Telmesani, the third general guide (1974–86), was invited to join the organization in 1933, his recruiters were curious to know how he spent his spare time. "I breed chicks," he replied. His recruiters smiled knowingly and retorted: "There are creatures more in need of breeding than chicks ... There are Muslims who have turned away from their religion" (Telmesani 2008: 56). One of the first lessons imprinted on the mind of Muhammad Habib, who joined in 1969 and rose to become the general guide's first deputy (until 2009), was that cultivating the right type of Muslim is what will eventually bring Brothers to power (2012: 115). It is no coincidence that the Brotherhood's first and second founders, Hassan al-Banna and Sayyid Qutb, were educated at the Cairo Teachers' College and graduated as primary school-teachers. In their writings, cultivation is treated more meticulously than anything else. For while this process might strike the casual observer as simple indoctrination with a religious flavor, it is actually an elaborate activity that borrows from at least four different schools: it instills a transformative worldview in the minds of members, as communists do; it claims that converting into this worldview is contingent upon a spiritual conversion, as in mystic orders; it presents this worldview as simple, uncorrupted religion, as in puritan movements; and it insists that this worldview cannot be readily communicated to society because it is not yet ready to handle the truth of the human condition, as in Masonic lodges. The ultimate aim, therefore, is not to win over more believers, but to produce a new kind of person: the Muslim Brother. This is a person striving for a new world through a spiritual struggle that reproduces the experience of early Muslims.

Practically speaking, cultivating requires frequent group meetings in which an experienced prefect (*naqib*) guides members through a detailed cultivation curriculum (*manhaj tarbiya*) under the careful gaze of the cultivation committee, and with regular intervention from higher administrative circles. Initially, Brothers attended a cultivating school, which opened its doors in 1928 with 70 students. As members multiplied, Banna organized them into small study groups. Brothers were now expected to meet on a weekly, monthly, quarterly, and biannual basis – though security restrictions sometimes disrupted this ambitious schedule. The nuclear group, the family (*usra*),[i] is composed of five to ten Brothers who meet every week (usually on Tuesdays) in the house of one of the members. With the prefect acting as moderator, Brothers share personal and professional concerns, worship and dine together, recite and comment on devotional readings from Qur'an and Prophetic pronouncements (*hadith*), and discuss the writings of the movement's founders, and, less frequently, other Islamist authors. At the end of the meeting, leadership instructions are circulated and organizational tasks allotted. Every few meetings, the prefect administers a questionnaire designed to measure the spiritual condition and religious performance of family members, with questions varying from how many times a Brother missed dawn prayers at the mosque, to how he negotiated his way through various moral dilemmas.

The family is considered the Brotherhood's "cultivation uterus" and canonized by members as "the brilliant method that God has guided Banna towards" (Habib 2012: 117). In the "Order of Families" ("Nizam al-Usar"), the founder has in fact expounded at length the practical steps needed for Brothers to become familiar with one another (*ta'aruf*); come to understand each other (*tafahum*); and support one another (*takaful*). For example, he ordered Brothers to confess their sins to one another, so they could encourage each other to repent – an interesting combination of Catholicism and psychoanalytic therapy – and decreed that those who persist in their sinful ways for a whole month must be reported to the prefect (Banna [1949] 1993: 324). That being said, intimate family bonds are prevented from solidifying into narrow, clique-like attachments by the annual redistribution of members. So, while families remain essentially divided according to residence or occupation, members are

---

[i] To make sense of the Brotherhood's structure in terms of other ideological movements, *usra* has usually been translated as 'cell.' I retain the literal translation ('family') because it reflects the Brotherhood's intention for *usra* meetings to replicate those of the nuclear biological family.

reshuffled, making sure that a Brother does not report to the same prefect for more than four years in his organizational career ('Eid 2013: 48).

At the same time, family members are incorporated into broader organizational networks. A cluster of families (varying in number according to region) forms a branch (*shu'ba*).[3] Once a month (preferably on a Thursday), branch members (40 on average) participate in a 'battalion training' (*katiba*), which involves fasting until sunset; breaking fast over a communal banquet; attending inspirational lectures by movement doctrinaires throughout the evening; praying together until daybreak, before heading home. Banna described these larger meetings as the Brotherhood's "spiritual cultivation academies," which synergize group energy to enhance each Brother's inner strength ([1949] 1993: 189). Every quarter, several branches come together in a weeklong camp (*mu'askar*) in some isolated location, where they add martial arts and athletic training to lectures and worship. Camps can take place anywhere from Brotherhood-owned apartment buildings to deserted public beaches. The important thing is that they must allow Brothers to simulate the harsh experience of military barracks. Brothers are instructed to refrain from joking or idle chat, and try to recreate the spirit of *jihad*. Finally, there is a biannual fieldtrip (*rihla*) for recreation, to which Brothers are asked to bring along their wives and children to socialize ("Turuq" 2002: vol. I, 472; vol. II, 336). Rida (2013), a seasoned Brotherhood cultivator, summarized the value of these multilayered meetings as follows: the family deepens personal relations; the battalion elevates spirituality; the camp fosters teamwork and a martial attitude; and the fieldtrip creates a sense of community. In addition, these overlapping activities enable senior leaders to interact with members from all levels, rather than relying exclusively on prefect reports ('Eid 2013: 35).

Female members are enrolled in a parallel structure, the Muslim Sisterhood, often described as 'an order not an organization' (*nizam la tanzim*), to keep them out of harm's way, since membership in an illegal organization warrants arrest. They do not perform the oath of allegiance or participate in battalion trainings and camps, but they do meet on the level of family and fieldtrips, and devote the rest of their time to mosque activities (recruiting women and indoctrinating children) and charity work. And a similar hierarchy, grounded in weekly family meetings, characterizes Brotherhood affiliates around the world.[4]

The guiding light for all these meetings emanates from the cultivation curriculum, which is composed of several edited volumes, running from basic to advanced levels. Each volume contains lessons tailored to weekly family meetings. A typical lesson comprises carefully selected extracts from the Qur'an, *hadith*, and the life of the Prophet and his Companions, followed by excerpts from the writings of Banna, and sometimes Qutb. This deliberate pairing of revelation and movement literature conflates the divine and the temporal, presenting the Brotherhood as a faithful application of Islamic teachings and history. To aid prefects, each lesson begins with pedagogical goals and concludes with a short exercise to ensure their accomplishment. Prefects also undergo a special training course (*dawrit nuqaba*) to learn, among other things, how to iron out differences in understanding and keep Brothers on the same page. More importantly, prefects cultivate the talent of matching the fixed curriculum lessons to the movement's varying policy positions. The best prefects are those who can conjure the suitable verse or sacred story to justify whichever policy the movement adopts.

The masters of this art, of course, are the heads of the cultivation committee. Among all the Brotherhood's specialized committees, those selected for this sensitive role must have specific qualities: they must be staunch loyalists; they must be able to tame spirited Brothers with a paternalistic attitude; and they must not have a busy working schedule. Because cultivating is almost a full-time job, senior cultivators are often retired professionals, absentee landowners, shop owners, or rent collectors. A central cultivation committee receives regular reports from branch-level committees, and *en mission* veteran cultivators roam through family and battalion meetings to offer advice and mete out reprimands. Constant vigilance is justified by the fact that cultivation mistakes are quite taxing. For example, Brothers claim that former President Gamal 'Abd al-Nasser, the 1952 coup leader, was their recruiting lieutenant in the army in the 1940s, and when he complained that the moral criteria for cultivating members were unattractive to officers, who were not very observant by nature, the Guidance Bureau succumbed and relaxed the requirements. Hassan al-'Ashmawi, his Brotherhood contact, blamed this flexibility for the Free Officers' subsequent betrayal of Brothers ('Ashmawi 1985: 26). Along similar lines, morally questionable actions by today's senior Brothers are attributed to the lenience of the third general guide, 'Umar al-Telmesani, who incorporated "un-cultivated" Islamist activists *en masse* in the 1970s to reinvigorate the decaying Brotherhood (Farghali 2013).

But if cultivation – which is defined in article 3(b) of the Brotherhood's General Order (*al-Nizam al-'Am*) as endowing an entire generation with a "unified Islamic view" – is to succeed, the question that immediately arises is: how could hundreds of thousands of members from different backgrounds subscribe to the same version of something as complicated and personal as religion? Similarly, how could a movement as large as the Muslim Brotherhood suffer no major dissent in its eight-and-a-half-decade existence? The answer must be sought in the general spirit that drives the whole cultivation process – what I refer to as the Brotherhood's 'anti-intellectualism.' This pervasive attitude towards those who, in Collini's (2006: 37) description, relish "complicating the simple and obscuring the obvious," manifests itself, firstly, in privileging sentiments and practice over enquiry; secondly, in the methodical censuring of arguments; and finally, in an aversion towards those with a background in the social sciences. These three strategies work together to curb members likely to foster disagreements among Brothers. Let us consider each separately.

The Pedagogy of Praxis

Those nominated to join the Brotherhood are typically young men and women with a kindling passion and a humble knowledge of history, politics, and religion. It helps that many are either born into Brotherhood families, or recruited as children. Their modest knowledge is considered an asset. As Mikkawi (2013) explained, "It is better to come with an empty glass. You learn faster. This is why Banna frequented coffee houses and popular neighborhoods not mosques and intellectual salons."[5] 'Abd al-Mon'iem Abu al-Fotouh, the leader of the 1970s Islamist students who later formed the backbone of the Brotherhood, confessed that he and his colleagues had "little [religious] heritage or political tradition to draw on. We did not know much about the logic and philosophy of the state, and made do with very primitive ideas" (2010: 70). Even more striking is the fact that those invited to join are not terribly familiar with the Brotherhood literature itself. Shatla (2013) and Tariq (2013) recalled their surprise at discovering during their induction course that none of their educated, middle-class comrades was acquainted with the writings of Banna or Qutb. What drew them in, mainly, was a crude passion to support Islam.

This emphasis on sentiments is central to the Brotherhood's pedagogy. Banna once wrote: "Our primary concern is to arouse the spirit, the life of the heart, to awaken the imagination and sentiments. We place less emphasis on concrete ideas . . . than on touching the souls of those we encounter." He recounted how he and his companions would spend their nights "drowned in tears" over the state of the nation, while intellectuals, who were supposedly better equipped to come up with solutions, wasted their time on idle chatter ([1949] 1993: 135, 180). As a child, Banna's role model was Muhammad Zahran, his primary schoolteacher, who demonstrated how creating "spiritual synergy and emotional bonds between pupil and teacher" pushes the former to work tirelessly without complaint ([1948] 1990: 16). This is probably why the Brotherhood's primary source of Qur'anic exegesis is Qutb's "In the Shadows of the Qur'an" ([1966] 1980), which captures the emotional state of the Companions upon receiving revelation rather than dwelling on jurisprudential and theological debates.

With this state of mind, little wonder that someone like Muhammad Habib, who had been on the Guidance Bureau since 1985, attributed the movement's recent blunders to the fact that leaders had become "cruel at heart, rugged in emotions, and dry in sentiments" (2012: 128); or that Mahmoud 'Ezzat, the acting general guide since 2013, would press the hands of his listeners so hard so that his words would "travel through their veins into their hearts" (Mahmoud 2013); or that Muhammad Sa'd Tag al-Din, the movement's contemporary doctrinaire, would boast that management sciences have just caught up with Banna's brilliant appreciation of 'psychological capital', which links superior performance to emotional satisfaction (2013: 79–80); or that the Brotherhood's leading cleric, the world-famous Sheikh Youssef al-Qaradawi, would ask "What value is someone with knowledge in his head, if his soul was steeped in sin?" and proclaim his preference for Brothers with "little knowledge and deep faith" (2000: 103) – though, curiously enough, some of his own books were removed from the cultivation curriculum because of their excessive rationality ("Istiqala" 2012).

As with everything else in the Brotherhood, this general philosophy was faithfully translated into mundane cultivating tasks. Prefects would regularly fill out forms ranking their apprentices on a scale from one to five on "emotional presence" and "spiritual elevation" during family meetings ("Madkhal" 1997: 25). Questionnaires are also handed out to young Brothers at the beginning of every month so they can rank themselves (Sabbagh 2012: 183). All group sessions, according to the cultivation curriculum, must be designed to help Brothers relive the psychological state experienced by the Prophet and his Companions ("Madkhal" 1997: 136). Lectures and sermons are infused with stories of the heroism of early believers and the glories of the caliphate. And the children of Brothers and Sisters are directed to express these themes in plays, songs, and other artistic forms.

Malik (2013), a young Brotherhood businessman whose father belonged to the founding generation and whose brother had become one of the most prominent leaders, fondly described how group meetings "recharged one's religious batteries," and substantiated this vivid metaphor with a personal story. On a short trip to Seattle, Malik felt so emotionally drained that he had to inquire frantically whether there were any family meetings being held in the area. He was directed through a Brotherhood mosque to a family meeting headed by a Pakistani, with an Egyptian, a Sudanese, and an American convert in attendance. Malik recounted with amazement how this meeting replicated the ones held back home to the last detail, and how those Brothers, whom he had just met, greeted him as warmly as those he had known all his life. This was a sign of divine grace, since no human being could forge such emotional bonds, as in the Qur'an (8: 63): 'If you had spent all that is on the earth, you could not have brought their hearts together; but God brought them together.' Malik's experience is quite common. Emotions play a major role in keeping Brothers attached to the movement. As Mikkawi (2013) conceded:

> It is personal affection not ideas that attracts you. I was quite ignorant about Islam when I began attending mosque activities. 'Love in God' was the essence. You meet pure and devout Muslims; people you would like to hang out with, and for your wife and children to spend time with. They accept you with all your flaws. Unlike fundamentalists or traditional clerics, they do not ask you to read books or judge you for smoking or talking to girls. But being around pious people eventually rubs off on you. After a few years they tell you: do you see all those good people you've been mingling with, they are Muslim Brothers. So you naturally say: count me in. I am sure this is what happened to 90 percent of Brothers.

The individual experience Mikkawi described could be replicated on a much larger scale. In the 1980s, the veterinarian of Kafr Ghatati introduced Islamism to his village. A decade later, hundreds of the village's 20,000 inhabitants joined the Brotherhood, principally because its members were perceived as good people: leading prayers; attending weddings and funerals; organizing football tournaments; tutoring children and showering them with toys; and so on (Fayez 2013: 38–40).

Of course, sentiments and practices must go hand-in-hand. This is translated in the cultivation curriculum through a pervasive stress on practicality. Brothers are asked to focus on the "executive operations" of the Prophet through a table dividing his life into 51 practical lessons ("Turuq" 2002: vol. I, 23–4). Sections on Islamic history end with summaries of the lessons learned. The Qur'an is treated in the same manner. In every family meeting a few verses are recited, and Brothers are asked to derive practical lessons from them. For example, lesson 15 in the first volume of the advanced cultivation curriculum starts with the verse: 'And remember the favor of God upon you, when you were enemies and He brought your hearts together and you became, by His favor, brothers' (Qur'an 3: 103). Prefects verily conclude that faith and brotherhood are the twin pillars of Islam, and that one's faith remains lacking unless it is combined with service to one's brothers ("Turuq" 2002: vol. I, 103–6). Tag al-Din recalled proudly that, when he was a group leader, he helped Brothers derive a list of 50 attributes and 30 remedies for hypocrisy from one chapter of the Qur'an (2013: 150).

Even in terms of spiritual elevation, the curriculum provides Brothers with a list of "procedural goals" to help them attain the "morality and behavior of true believers," including night-time prayers, modesty in outlook and attitude, venerating one's parents, and accepting one's fate without complaint. It then instructs prefects to divide each procedural goal into tangible tasks that could be measured and evaluated, and to assign Brothers one or two tasks a week ("Turuq" 2002: vol. I, 27–8). For example, the principle of devotion to God (*ekhlas*) requires Brothers to attend burial washes (*ghusl*) frequently to witness man's helplessness after death ("Madkhal" 1997: 36). To foster compassion, the curriculum instructs a Brother to smile when he meets other Brothers; to initiate greeting; to "squeeze their hands in a way that transmits love"; to tell them how much he misses them; and to call them by their favorite nicknames. A Brother is also required to think about Muslims' plight in warzones until he is moved to tears – and if his eyes remained dry, he should resort to audio and visual aids ("Mabadi'" 2003: vol. III, 213–14, 244).

When a Brother fails to perform these tasks, then he must be afflicted with "a heart disease," which – predictably – requires even more tasks to overcome, such as visiting the sick, dwelling in grave-yards, helping the weak, and so on. A Brother's frustration with the movement is most likely a reflection of his own spiritual shortcomings. Indeed, the most serious of all the heart's diseases is vanity. And its main symptom, according to the curriculum, is the belief that one surpasses others in "intelligence, experience, analysis, and knowledge of the art of politics and its [worldly] means . . . and [such a Brother] therefore looks down on his Brothers . . . despite their [religious] preeminence. These [afflicted Brothers] think they could better serve the cause through their [intellectual] ability and downplay divine grace" ("Turuq" 2002: vol. I, 451–5). The cause of this fatal disease is excessive attachment to knowledge. And this is why the curriculum warns against those who fall victim to the "sweetness of knowledge and the fun of reading and research . . . to the point where they weigh men according to how much they have read rather than how much faith they have" ("Turuq" 2002: vol. I, 495). Beginners, in particular, are told that whatever objections they find in their hearts to Brotherhood policies are symptoms of conceit, self-adoration, bad faith, and prejudice, rather than superior knowledge ("Mabadi'" 2003: vol. III, 258).

The worst form of vanity is the conviction that you need to raise others to your standards, rather than humble yourself to theirs. For example, when Sharif (2013), a Brotherhood university professor, submitted a proposal in the 1980s offering to design a political crash course to alleviate his Brothers' inexperience, he was immediately rebuked: "I was advised to teach children Qur'an at my local mosque or do something useful, since I obviously had too much time on my hands." A similar fate awaited another reform document, drafted in 1986 by a group of young Brothers. The gist of this pertinently titled Organizational Crisis in Cultivation and Administration Report is that Brothers cannot aspire to govern Egypt when they are wholly consumed with cementing their emotional ties rather than learning about the people and country they intend to lead (Abu-Khalil 2012: 23–4).

More than two decades later, the Brotherhood's attitude had changed little. When Jamal (2013) asked for permission to take religious courses to expand his knowledge, he was instructed to devote his time to practical tasks: "Instead of immersing yourself in complicated interpretations of the Qur'an, teach beginners how to read it; instead of reading several volumes on the life of the Prophet, read the prescribed portions [in the curriculum] and relay them to others; instead of studying theology, raise funds or distribute charity. Action is more rewarding in Islam, they would say." Shatla (2013) was likewise directed to "live Islam, rather than learn about it." Cultivators would frequently repeat that: "Islam is a lived religion. We are merely incubators. Islam lives through us." And prefects constantly invoked Banna's famous axiom: "Duties are more [numerous] than the [available] time (al-wajibat akthar min al-awqat)" to reprove those who insist on wasting their time pursuing extra – understood here to mean 'unnecessary' – knowledge. To reinforce the message, Ahmad al-Bialy (2011), the head of the movement's office in the Nile Delta province of Damietta, and future governor under Morsi, stated in a widely circulated article that: "The Brotherhood's house is one of worship and toil . . . not a house of arguing philosophers." In this same article, Bialy claimed that Brothers do not need to immerse themselves in religious sciences to be able to interpret the Qur'an, as traditional scholars did, for once they successfully relive the emotional atmosphere of the first generation in Mecca and Medina, the Qur'an will automatically "reveal its treasures . . . and secrets."

Particularly restive Brothers are often loaded with administrative duties to absorb their excessive energy (Samir 2013). Sameh 'Eid, for instance, was saddled with 13 group meetings a month, to the point where he had no time to think (2013: 51). One way of keeping the Brothers' hands full is to oblige them to monitor their actions scrupulously. General Guide Telmesani advised his followers to spend at least an hour before retiring to bed revising their actions during the day (1981: 66). This procedure was justified in the cultivation curriculum with reference to how the Prophet's Companions interrogated their souls every day. Before long, the process was extended and institutionalized. Newcomers learn to begin their day with 'condition making' (*musharata*), which takes place right after dawn prayers, and involves a self-imposed contract to obey God and devote one's day to Islam. The second step is 'surveillance' (*muraqaba*), which continues throughout the day to ensure fulfillment of that contract. Finally, there is 'accountability' (*muhasaba*), which occurs after night-time prayers, when each Brother holds himself accountable "as a merchant would question his partner, or an employer would query his workers." These morning and night-time sessions should ideally take place in a dark room to help one concentrate. A Brother is then expected to punish himself, and consider means of rectifying any devious behavior before the start of a new day. At the end of the month, the results are recorded in questionnaires and handed back to prefects ("Madkhal" 1997: 58–61; "Mabadi'" 2003: vol. II, 137). Needless to say, this whole process provides group leaders with a regular stream of information about not only the actions, but also the innermost feelings, of every Brother.

Overleaf is an example of one evaluation model (from "Turuq" 2002: vol. II, 136–7). Most models are longer and more detailed (such as the eight-page template in "Turuq" 2002: vol. II, 235–52). There are also questionnaires with more psychological angles, containing questions such as: "Does your heart ever whisper to you to abandon the cause? Do you secretly consider yourself a free rider? Does your heart urge you to embark on *jihad*, at least once a week? Do you ask God to bless you with martyrdom everyday?" ("Mabadi'" 2003: vol. III, 251). Others concentrate on one's relationship with one's Brothers, asking, for instance: "Do you think about your

Characteristic	Weak (<50)	Pass (50–74)	Good (75–89)	Excellent (>90)
First: Worship				
1 Night-time prayers				
2 Reading the Qur'an daily				
3 Mosque attendance				
4 Daily remembrance				
5 Daily supplication				
6 Voluntary prayers				
7 Voluntary fasting				
8 Almsgiving				
Second: Ethics				
1 Polite conversation				
2 Punctuality				
3 Calmness				
4 Sincerity				
5 Modesty				
6 Acceptance				
7 Generosity				
8 Cheerfulness				
Third: Sociability				
1 Rights of wife				
2 Rights of children				
3 Rights of parents				
4 Visiting relatives				
5 Supporting Brothers				
6 Rights of neighbors				
7 Rights of colleagues				
8 Role modeling				
Fourth: Commitment				
1 Commanding virtue, forbidding sin				
2 Initiating charity				
3 Winning popular opinion				
4 Obedience				
5 Recruitment				
6 Membership fees				
7 Organizational discipline				
8 Positive attitude				
9 Dismissing rumors				

Brothers in their absence? Do you miss your Brothers and pay them personal visits? Do you tell your Brothers that you love them? Do you ask your Brothers to help you evaluate your piety?" ("Turuq" 2002: vol. II, 325, 334).

Those who still find time to read after all this homework are presented with a list of reading priorities, starting with the Qur'an,

Prophetic traditions, sacred history, then jurisprudence, theology, and mysticism, and, at the very end of the list, Arabic literature, followed by secular studies. Moreover, the list is complemented with a Saudi-published pamphlet on *Books [Islamic] Scholars Warned Against*, which includes a handful of books by Brotherhood clerics, such as Youssef al-Qaradawi and Muhammad al-Ghazali (Fayez 2013: 111–12). Even so, avid readers are not indulged for long. Jamal remembered how his prefects turned a blind eye to his eagerness for knowledge when he first joined, dropping hints here and there about the importance of action. When he persisted, they explicitly discouraged him from dabbling with anything beyond the carefully chosen excerpts in the curriculum and other certified books (Jamal 2013). The criterion behind these prescribed works is that they are all action-driven, i.e., they supply Brothers with the amount of knowledge needed for practice.[6] Remarkably enough, this approach to reading applies to Islamist literature itself. When Fayez, the son of a manual laborer, rushed to the village's only bookstore to fetch anything written on the Brotherhood, he stumbled across a paper-thin hagiographic account of the life of Hassan al-Banna, and carried it back to his recruiter, hoping to impress him: "What happened was the complete opposite. The sheikh scolded me, and asked me to return the book and never read this type of literature. He spoke so harshly that I thought al-Banna was his personal enemy." When Fayez matured, he realized that his recruiter did not want to encourage this sort of attitude: relying on books to validate what one hears during group meetings (2013: 27). The Brotherhood's motto here is "Hear from us. Do not read about us" (Tariq 2013). Fortunately, this policy does not elicit much opposition in a country where "only 1 to 2 percent of the population read books regularly," and where opinion is usually formed through word of mouth (Eickelman in Hefner 2005: 39–43).

Banna himself, assassinated at the age of 42, left his followers two relatively short tracts: a sketchy memoir, and a collection of epistles (*rasa'il*): a patchy compilation of memoranda, public speeches, organizational propositions, and a handful of homilies. Among these, Brothers are mostly required to familiarize themselves with the ten-page Epistle of Edification (*Risalat al-Ta'alim*) – usually shortened to the Teachings – which lays down the ten pillars of the oath of allegiance (*arkan al-bai'a*).[7] Banna justified his economy with pen and paper – and advised Brothers to follow suit – by claiming that if he wrote too much, his words might be subject to misinterpretation and therefore cause friction between Brothers. It was better, he sensed, to communicate his message verbally to people he was acquainted with (Banna [1948] 1990: 13, 182). Qaradawi added, with some pride, that Banna was not "a researcher who immersed himself in original sources, but a reformer who sufficed with summaries" (1999: 119).

Tag al-Din, the most recent interpreter of the Teachings,[8] had a more intriguing justification for the brevity of Banna's writings. As with the Qur'an, which the Companions read over and over again throughout their lives, Brothers need to consult the founder's epistles repeatedly. And whereas the Qur'an is far from brief, modern-day Companions (i.e., Brothers) are relatively short of time. He also reflected on why the founder gave his most precious epistle the odd title of *ta'alim* (Teachings), rather than the more commonly used *ta'limat* (Instructions), and concluded that Banna wanted to highlight the sanctity of this specific text (Tag al-Din 2013: 84, 64–5) – just as he chose for himself the title of *murshid* (guide), which had never existed before in the Muslim world, rather than *emir* (leader). No wonder that Banna famously prefaced his short manifesto by asserting that "These brief statements are not [just] lessons to be memorized, but instructions to be followed," and ended it with a list of 38 instructions, varying from devotional readings, to performing regular health check-ups, observing hygiene, avoiding tea and coffee and smoking, and not laughing too loudly ([1949] 1993: 303, 315–18). Evidently, Banna's attitude colored the entire cultivation curriculum, which was conceived as a school syllabus to be studied and tested in (through exercises as basic as fill-in-the-blanks and connect the columns), not an ideological platform to be discussed.

Should an issue become particularly pressing, the leadership would remedy the plight of inquisitive minds with carefully sifted knowledge. Rida (2013) recalled that Brothers became anxious, for some reason, about sectarian differences between Sunni sects. A senior Brother was entrusted with cutting-and-pasting the non-controversial parts of a book by the eminent scholar Sheikh Muhammad Abu-Zahra, and reproducing them in book format. This slim volume not only played down sectarian differences, but was published by the Brotherhood's own publishing house under the name of this older Brother, without reference to the original source, to dissuade members from pursuing the matter further. Likewise, controversial topics in Islamic history, such as the successive wars between the Companions, known as the Great Dissent (*al-Fitna al-Kubra*), are addressed exclusively through works that adopt a conciliatory view (Sameh 2013).[9]

When objections to this overprotective attitude arise, Brothers are reminded that the purest form of knowledge is the one handed down to them by pious movement figures through lectures and written commentaries. Non-Islamist sources either spring from a distorted understanding of Islam, or dwell endlessly on inconsequential philosophical topics (Shatla 2013). However, a veteran Brother calculated that the time Brothers spent discussing history and politics with group leaders does not exceed 100 hours a year (Abu-Khalil 2012: 32). When some invoke Banna's demand for a Brother to be 'intellectually cultured' (*muthaqaf al-fikr* – a odd adjective in Arabic as much as it is in English), group leaders say they could get by with reading newspapers, though Brotherhood newsletters and circulars are more reliable ("Madkhal" 1997: 83; "Turuq" 2002: vol. I, 32). In fact, General Guide Mahdi 'Akif (2004–9) confessed that he no longer read newspapers because they depressed him (Gallad et al. 2009).

This eschewing of knowledge in favor of emotions and actions is why someone like Shafiq (2013), who had participated in mosque activities for years alongside Brothers, and saw many of his friends get hooked, was never invited to join. His eager pursuit of religious education, especially jurisprudence, kept him beneath the Brotherhood's radar. Recruiters, however, do make mistakes, such as the time when they cast their net around Rami (2013), a serious Qur'an student, whom they had been observing for years in a suburb mosque. Rami's recruiter invited him to join Brothers for ten days of 'secluded worship' (*'etikaf*) during the holy month of Ramadan, and pilgrimage (*haj*) a few weeks later. Rami emerged quite disillusioned. The Brothers' treatment of the Qur'an, in his view, "was fit for kindergarten." Rami ended up exchanging heated words with some senior Brothers and never went back.

Taking account of all the above, it appears that Brothers are expected to be passionate and active believers, but not ones too keen on learning. The principal justification for this is that Islam is a practical religion. Life is short, and would be better spent loving and serving God and His creatures. A second, though no less important, justification is that the independent pursuit of knowledge invites arguments, and arguments poison the peace between Brothers. Banna had, in fact, paired these two justifications in his well-rehearsed maxim: "Be practical not argumentative" ([1949] 1993: 171). Unfortunately, the Brotherhood might have gone too far. Longtime cultivator and Azhar-trained scholar,[10] Sheikh Muhammad Sa'id 'Abd al-Bar, complained in a report submitted in 2007 that the present leadership had compromised the founder's standards. Cultivators were originally conceived as modern-day Sufi saints, who were superior to their followers in knowledge and spirituality, and were responsible only for a handful of students in order to be able to penetrate and influence their lives. In Sufism, dozens could participate in rituals, but only a limited few struggle for real spiritual purification (*tazkia*), and a handful are eventually selected for divine grace and become saints (*awliya*). In today's Brotherhood, tens of thousands are supposed to become quasi-saints through standardized *tazkia* sessions presided over by amateur prefects, who are usually younger and more ignorant than those they are supposed to guide. More troubling still is that many prefects do not even read Banna closely enough, so that when seasoned cultivators, like 'Abd al-Bar, alert them to this or that concept in the founder's epistles, they would deny its very existence, and, by the same token, they would invent new concepts *impromptu* during sessions to calm opposition. Likewise, some of today's cultivators would scorn past and present Islamic scholars if they perceived their writings to contradict Islamism. In 'Abd al-Bar's estimate, this is the real reason why prefects nowadays are so adamant about preventing Brothers from pursuing independent knowledge; they are afraid of being challenged. The result is that both cultivators and cultivated are deprived of the opportunity to learn and develop ("Taqrir" 2007).

In a rare occurrence, the high-handedness of cultivators and the meekness of the cultivated were captured in a play that circulated among Brothers in January 2010. The author, an old cultivator frustrated with the mediocrity of the present cultivation process, thought that presenting his critique in the form of biting satire might get more attention – though he was sufficiently prudent to publish it anonymously. "Sallimli 'ala al-Manhaj! Kartha min Fasl Wahid" (Greetings to the Curriculum! A Tragedy in One Act) portrayed a typical family meeting. The fictional prefect presided over three Brothers: Mutie' (obedient), Wathiq (trusting), and Thabit (constant). He opens up the session by reciting verses from the Qur'an, and then presses his students to offer their reflections (*khawatir*). When the Brothers hesitate, on account of their ignorance of the science of exegesis, the prefect encourages them: "You do not need to read any books. Instead, recite the verse three times with utmost piety; live with the meanings for a few minutes; and then say whatever comes to your mind, and it will surely be the true meaning of the verse." Emboldened, one of the Brothers volunteered: "Turley, these are very beautiful verses. Praise to God! When you contemplate a little, you feel them penetrating your soul . . . as if you were alive when the Qur'an was first revealed, and you find yourself rushing to obedience and acceptance. Praise to God! They are very beautiful." Ignoring the fact that his student did not really offer any interpretation, or even indicate that he understood the verses, the wily prefect congratulates him on coming up with a much deeper insight than a scholar who had spent his life studying the Qur'an. Just like the Prophet's Companions, the young

Brother did not have to rely on dusty books to understand God's words. The prefect then adds playfully: "See! You were going to deprive us of this wise reflection." Next, the experienced prefect embarks on a long speech, praising the Brotherhood's leaders, when he is suddenly interrupted by one of his grateful underlings: "Yes! Praise to God! When one of us shakes their hands, we feel as if we were shaking the hand of an angel or a Companion. How great is it when one of them takes your hand in his – although you are really a nobody that he did not have to greet, or even notice . . . You feel your soul being transformed . . . You feel so close [to God]." Mentioning the Companions prompts another Brother to ask the prefect for a good book on the life of the Prophet. The prefect is taken aback and says: "Not a single book! Religion is not in books. Religion is not in scholarship. I have never read a book on the life of the Prophet, yet I understand it more than those who have memorized it from books." He goes on to say that mingling with virtuous men is the key because it allows you to relive the early history of Islam yourself without having to read about it. This is why Banna, a primary schoolteacher, understood Islam better than any scholar before him had done. The prefect then changes the subject abruptly to warn Brothers not to pay heed to critiques by a leading member who accused his colleagues of violating the Brotherhood's bylaws in the recent Guidance Bureau elections. That disgruntled Brother "had temporarily gone astray," and would soon return to the fold. But until he did, Brothers must refrain from reading anything he published or watching any of his televised interviews, even out of curiosity – "Do not even think about him" – until they were told they could.

Finally, the playwright offers his readers a glimpse of the mind games that cultivators practice nowadays to keep novice Brothers under their thumb. One of the three Brothers in the play asks the prefect if he could leave early because his university professor is holding a revision session early next morning. The prefect turns to him slowly and says, stressing every word:

> Do not deceive yourself . . . You are not excusing yourself to attend the revision because the revision session is tomorrow not tonight. You want to leave early in order to go to sleep. Be clear with yourself . . . Is sleeping more important or the mission [of Islam]? Besides, do you know who the people are who frequently make excuses, as the Qur'an tells us? The hypocrites!

The thoroughly intimidated Brother smiles sheepishly and thanks his prefect for helping him to expose the devil's tricks – and, of course, he oversleeps and misses the revision session ("Sallimli" 2010).

Smothering the Flames of Discord

Censuring extra-curricular reading could only go so far in placating inquisitive minds. Brothers steeped in the art of cultivation must act creatively to stifle critical attitudes before they spread. Their arsenal is fairly diverse; and the first tactic is *preemption*. Even before joining, devotees learn about how opinionated Muslims, with their sophistic attitude, have fractured the nation. Argumentative devotees, like Sameh (2013), find their probation period extended from the usual three years to ten. And Shatla (2013) barely averted this fate because his father-in-law, a veteran Brother, vouched for him. On the eve of the induction course, devotees are warned that quarrelsome individuals will be summarily dismissed. The induction course itself is designed to ensure that devotees have internalized the Brotherhood's version of Islam and history, and have become totally aligned with the movement's way of doing things. In Hani's (2013) words, the course effectively "hammers in the nails that have been positioned in the devotees' minds during the probation period." At the end of the course, those invited to take the oath of allegiance are again reminded of the supreme importance of compliance. Hani remembered how he welled up when his recruiter, 'Amr Khalid, the celebrated televangelist, emphasized how blessed he should feel that God had selected him from among millions of believers to join the privileged few and carry out His work. Sowing discord among the godly elite could only be regarded as a poor repayment (Hani 2013; Ahmad 2013 heard a similar speech from his recruiter). Sameh 'Eid vividly painted the drama of performing the oath itself, when, at the end of the course, the attendees stood in a circle; a verse from the Qur'an (48: 10) was recited: 'Indeed those who pledge allegiance to you [Muhammad] are actually pledging allegiance to God. The hand of God is over theirs'; the pledgers then started weeping and hugging each other (2013: 58). All are finally reminded that through this pledge they have "sold themselves" to God in return for Paradise, and that one who sells himself "could only march on the designated path, without turning, or choosing, or debating, or arguing, or doing anything else other than obeying, exerting effort, and submitting" ("Turuq" 2002: vol. I, 359).[11]

After the devotee is elevated to entry-level membership, family prefects take over from recruiters. Their task is much more daunting:

to dispel critique during family meetings, or, better yet, to anticipate and deflate it before it arises. They are aided by the beginners' curriculum, which overflows with anti-argument exhortations, such as the notion that consensus over a good enough opinion is better than division in pursuit of the best one ("Mabadi'" 2003: vol. III, 274). Brothers are also taught that submissiveness to one's educators is the hallmark of a good Muslim; and are supplied with a ten-point model to help them measure their performance ("Mabadi'" 2003: vol. II, 178):

1. Modesty towards the teacher.
2. Humbleness during education.
3. Following the advice of the teacher.
4. Respecting and venerating the teacher.
5. Not burdening the teacher with questions.
6. Not interrupting the teacher.
7. Listening carefully to the teacher.
8. Fixing one's glance on the teacher.
9. Not repulsing the teacher.
10. Not debating with the teacher.

Needless to say, 'the teacher' here refers to family prefects, who in many cases are younger and less experienced than their students. Still, we find a senior Brother, such as al-Bialy, disgusted with how some Brothers nowadays "get frustrated with their prefects; raise their voices; demand their apology when they make mistakes; and even dare stare them in the eye, regardless of the fact that these are all religiously prohibited actions" (Bialy 2011).

During battalion and camp lectures, moderators take over from family prefects. A moderator is required, as the curriculum states, to flank lecturers, vet queries, and dismiss critical or irrelevant ones ("Turuq" 2002: vol. II, 343). So when Rida (2013), for example, questioned a lecturer on the Brotherhood's jurisprudential position on violence, considering the divergent Islamist positions on this sensitive issue, the moderator asked him to refrain from intellectual hairsplitting. And when Yasser (2013) tried to open a debate with a Guidance Bureau member, during a 2006 battalion training, on the need to divide the political and religious wings of the Brotherhood in light of the movement's demonstrable political ineptitude, he was rebuked with a short lesson in the comprehensiveness of Islam, then asked to return to his seat with a dismissive gesture.

More experienced Brothers, however, preempt debate in a much more nuanced way. In 1999, General Guide Mustafa Mashhur invited Tharwat al-Khirbawi, a lawyer and longtime member, to the Brotherhood's headquarters in Cairo. Once the lawyer entered through the door, the general guide turned to ask whether he had offended him in some way. The startled Khirbawi, of course, denied this. Mashhur then told him that he had learned from his sources that Khirbawi was planning to criticize him in a battalion meeting in Nasr City (a Cairo suburb). Taken aback, Khirbawi explained that his intention was to use one of Mashhur's books in an analytical exercise. To which the general guide retorted sharply: "So my inform-ers were correct?" He then regained his composure and conceded that, while nobody was above critique – except the Prophet – lecturers should be careful not to appear too critical of the general guide because Brothers venerate him so much that they could not bear to hear the slightest remark made against him (Khirbawi 2012: 154–6). Likewise, Sameh 'Eid was asked to lecture at a meeting of 'employee families' – Brotherhood slang for families with members close to retirement age. He prepared a few critical exercises for these supposedly mature men, but was subsequently reprimanded by senior Brothers for puzzling his audience unnecessarily (2013: 50).

Preempting argument also occurs by framing matters in a way that invites consensus, usually through rhetorical questions. A senior lec-turer, for instance, urged his audience to "think openly" about the virtues of the Brotherhood compared to other Islamist groups. This is how he prefaced the discussion: "If we are all traveling from Cairo to Alexandria on the same road, would it be better to walk, ride a bicycle, go by car, or by train?" Everyone shouted back: "By train!" To which the lecturer contently responded: "Islamist movements are similarly all on the straight path to paradise, but the Brotherhood, like the train, is the biggest, fastest, and safest way to get there." Although he never explained why the Brotherhood was the train, not the car or the bicycle, the way he posed the question made those likely to challenge him appear unreasonable (Hani 2013). At times, this required Brothers to fault their own memory – as when group leaders summoned combative or peaceful sections of revelation to justify the Brotherhood's vacillation between confrontation and rec-onciliation, without once failing to preface their comments with: "As we have always said" (Hani 2013). Sometimes would-be dissenters are entrapped and exposed. On one occasion, a lecturer told his bat-talion members that the Guidance Bureau was reconsidering its old stance on the indivisibility of religion and politics. Attendants were urged to express their views freely to provide leaders with feedback. All looked confused and slightly irritated except for Shatla (2013) and another Brother who welcomed the revision. After everyone had a chance to speak their mind, the lecturer revealed – while staring at the culprits with fiery eyes – that this was a test to uncover those afflicted with skepticism. Yet the most brilliant gambit, by far, was when a prefect warned his Brothers during a family meeting that "If I ever leave the Brotherhood, do not believe any critique I make, because I would have been tempted by the devil" – the irony is: he actually left (Mahmoud 2013).

These mind games do not always work. So whenever the tide of opposition is too high to dismiss or deflect, seasoned Brothers shift to the next, and most widely employed tactic: *disinformation*. Examples abound. When the Brotherhood decided to boycott the 1995 parliamentary elections, Brothers from the Nile Delta town of Damanhur wanted to vote for the Leftist candidate to prevent the ruling party candidate from winning. The Guidance Bureau thought otherwise. But rather than being given any tactical reason why the movement was supporting its declared regime enemies, Brothers were told that the Leftist candidate did not pray or fast, and some spiced it up by adding he was a closeted atheist ('Eid 2013: 5). Along similar lines, when a Brother slapped a female protester (Mirvat Musa) outside their headquarters in front of television cameras in the winter of 2013, angry members were placated during family meetings by claims that 'Ali, the Prophet's cousin and fourth Rightly Guided Caliph, once stripped a woman naked to retrieve a letter she was carrying to the infidels – though traditional narrations held that 'Ali merely asked her to hand in the letter or he would have to search her, a request she complied with ('Eid 2013: 164).

In a 2003 battalion training, Hani probed Mahdi 'Akif, the man who was about to assume the position of General Guide, on news reports claiming that the Brotherhood was in contact with the Americans despite the fact that Washington was about to bomb Baghdad. 'Akif snapped back: "How could the Brotherhood negotiate with a country that lists it as a terrorist organization?" Later, of course, it was revealed that the movement was in fact talking to the Americans, and Washington had never placed the Brotherhood on its terrorist list. On another occasion, Hani (2013) asked his family prefect about Qaradawi's denouncement of the Special Order (*al-Nizam al-Khas*), the Brotherhood's militant wing of the 1940s, only to be assured that the distinguished cleric had misspoken, and after being reproached by the Guidance Bureau had agreed to retract his comments – which never happened. Another episode involving Qaradawi was when Ibrahim al-Houdeibi (2013) objected to his prefect's claim that the current rulers of the Muslim world were "un-Islamic." Feeling challenged, the prefect cited a Qaradawi *fatwa*

(religious injunction) stating as much. Unconvinced, Ibrahim contacted Qaradawi's office only to discover that no such *fatwa* existed.
When two senior Brothers (Ibrahim al-Za'farani and Hamid al-
Dafrawi) presented memos accusing the Guidance Bureau of manipu-
lating the bylaws and tampering with the Bureau's 2009 election
results, leading cultivator Muhammad Sa'id 'Abd al-Bar requested an
official explanation from the Bureau. He was told that the two high-
ranking Brothers withdrew their complaints and made peace with the
top leadership. When 'Abd al-Bar contacted them, they categorically
denied any such thing ("Istiqala" 2012).

In a similar experience, Tariq (2013) heard a prominent Brother
defend organizational unity by citing a Qur'anic verse (3: 100) that
stated: 'O you who have believed, if you obey a party of those who
were given the Scripture [Old and New Testaments], they would turn
you back, after your belief, [to being] unbelievers.' The speaker
assured his audience that the term 'unbelievers' here meant
'disunited.'[12] Tariq found this hard to fathom. The speaker responded
confidently that *all interpreters* of the Qur'an adopted this interpretation. When Tariq double-checked, he discovered that *not a single
interpreter* made such a claim. This triggered an extended private
exchange between Tariq and the senior Brother, who explained that,
since Banna said as much in the Teachings and no Qur'an scholar
contradicted him, then one could assume that they all implicitly
agreed. Tariq remained unconvinced since most authoritative Qur'an
interpreters had been long dead before Banna was born, and those
alive did not necessarily read the Teachings.

Besides these ad hoc interventions, Brothers employ a number of
textbook spins to disarm recurrent critiques. The most frequent of
those critiques relates to the Brotherhood's lack of prominent public
intellectuals. Members wonder why clerics of the stature of Qaradawi
and Ghazali, or Islamic-oriented authors, like the columnist Fahmi
Houwaidi, and the lawyer Muhammad Selim al-'Awa, either left the
movement or never joined. The standard answer is: these great thinkers are committed to the Brotherhood, but have been relieved of the
duties of membership to allow them to spread the message without
security hurdles or accusations of partisanship. As Ahmad Samir
noticed, however, during the 2012 presidential elections, al-'Awa ran
against the Brotherhood's candidate, and Qaradawi and Houwaidi
voted for a third candidate (Samir 2013).

Justifying desertions is equally troublesome. When Abu al-'Ela
Madi and 'Essam Sultan resigned from the Brotherhood to create
their own political party, members were told that they were fired for
embezzlement. And when 'Abd al-Mon'iem Abu al-Fotouh broke

ranks to run for the presidency, Guidance Bureau apparatchiks alleged he was an American agent (Mahmoud 2013; Sameh 2013). When asked how an American spy could have been allowed to sit in the Bureau, the response was: "So that older Brothers could keep an eye on him" (Abu-Khalil 2012: 147). In another amusing anecdote, Rashad al-Bayumi, Guidance Bureau strongman, asked a group of young Brothers to go check out a poor old porter a few blocks away from their meeting place, adding that this man used to be an educated and wealthy member, but when he abandoned his Brothers he brought divine punishment upon himself. Those who desert, Bayumi warned, faced similar damnation in this world and the next – the story about the porter proved entirely baseless (Hani 2013).[13]

Organizational *pressure* is also a common disciplining tool. Argumentative Brothers, who do not heed advice, must answer to investigation committees with the power to punish or expel them. Youssef (2013), for example, protested when his prefect excommunicated the Nobel laureate Naguib Mahfouz, Egypt's foremost novelist, despite the Brotherhood's public stance against excommunication. The following morning, a hearing was scheduled, and Youssef had to defend himself against the charge of abusing a Brother because of his inferior social class. Such a horrid accusation, he understood, was meant to tame his opposition in the future. Ahmad Samir (2013) was a more persistent critic. He pressured senior Brothers to articulate their views clearly on a number of issues, such as resurrecting the caliphate, which was too grand an objective to be left ambiguous. Brothers should decide whether they sought to unite Muslims in one big country (like China), or a federation (like the US), or a union (like the EU). Samir had similar concerns regarding the rights of women and religious minorities, and called for the democratization of decision-making within the organization. When ignored, Samir began to publish his views on Facebook and in newspaper columns. After several hearing sessions, in which he was reprimanded for excessive egoism and thirst for the limelight, he had to resign. Brothers take pride in their ability to turn every critique against the critic – as Moses turned the magic against the magicians, they would add – by shifting focus from what is wrong with the movement to what is wrong with the person to think that there might be something wrong with the movement. Every critique therefore turns into a close scrutiny of the "diseases of the [critic's] heart" (Abu-Khalil 2012: 28).

Sameh 'Eid had a few close run-ins with these investigative committees. Although he had been affiliated with the Brotherhood since he was seven, when he began to criticize his direct superiors, his three roommates (also Brothers) were asked to report on his relationship with God. They submitted an incriminating report based on such trivia as the fact that he sometimes used the summer heat as an excuse not to perform noon prayers at the mosque. When called to face a five-member committee, he mocked the report and insisted that the General Bureau respond to his queries. His main concern at the moment was that junior Brothers were not allowed to see, let alone discuss, the movement's bylaws,[14] and that leaders took advantage of this to make up laws – for example, that a Brother must receive permission before changing jobs, making an investment, marrying, divorcing, or even traveling outside Egypt. When told that these rules were all mentioned in the bylaws – which he later discovered was not the case – 'Eid demanded they should be scrapped. The committee leader ended the meeting abruptly by repeating: "May God guide you back to His path my son!" Instead of repenting, 'Eid got himself in trouble again for criticizing Banna for not cultivating a suitable successor. Although this remark was made in a casual chat with a few close friends, a nine-member committee summoned 'Eid for what turned out to be a record six-hour hearing. This time he affected innocence, asking what was wrong with mentioning that the founder might have committed a minor mistake if Muslims believe that some great prophets, like Moses, were not infallible. The committee leader exclaimed that even if Prophet Moses had made a mistake, this did not necessarily mean that Banna had. 'Eid was speechless. Another member censured 'Eid for discussing a historical period he did not live through. 'Eid retorted that Brothers discuss the life of the Prophet and his Companions although they were born centuries afterwards, but the committee thought this was somehow irrelevant. On another occasion, 'Eid was called in as a witness. He was involved in some leisurely chat when a Brother said "We believe ourselves to be on the right path," upon which a more zealous Brother corrected him: "Do you want us to face God and say we were just experimenting? We are absolutely certain we are on the right path." 'Eid did not think much of it, until he was called to testify against the "flaky-faith" of the first Brother (2013: 55–69, 81).

If all else fails, argumentative members suffer *marginalization*, and a few are eventually cut off. To deter Brothers from ever visiting him, 'Eid's apartment was compared to Masjid al-Diar, the mosque built by hypocrites to lure Muslims away from the right path and eventually burned by the Prophet ('Eid 2013: 75). Sharif recounted how he tried to make himself useful to the movement by pointing out that the term 'civil state', which Brothers adopted to appease secular forces, was meaningless, and advising them instead to defend their

'Islamic state' model, which he volunteered to help articulate and promote. Despite his four-decade membership, Sharif (2013) was ignored: "I knocked on all doors only to discover that even when you criticize them to make them better, they isolated you. Instead of seeing their problems, you become their problem." Muhammad Sa'id 'Abd al-Bar complained in his 2012 resignation letter that, after spending a quarter of a century in the organization and assuming some of the most sensitive responsibilities in the cultivation process, his concerns and critiques were routinely ignored. He cited specific examples, including financial and moral problems that made headlines in the national media but remained unaddressed beyond a warning to younger Brothers not to discuss them. In his case, an investigative committee acquitted him, but high-ranking Brothers continued to claim that he was under investigation to dissuade others from contacting him. And when he confronted these leaders, they implied that if he toed the line like before perhaps these rumors might disappear ("Istiqala" 2012).

Radwan (2013) drew on his religious studies at al-Azhar University to object to the use of 'religiously decreed reprimand' (*ta'zir*) by prefects to discipline Brothers. In his view, group leaders were not ordained judges, and therefore could not mete out penalties, such as fines, or corporal punishments. Officials in the central cultivation committee asked Radwan not to waste his time and theirs on trivial matters. Yet a few Brothers did not think this was really trivial. *Ta'zir* was an Islamic right granted to the ruler to penalize criminal offenses not tied to a specific punishment in sharia. The Brothers used it to punish administrative slip-ups, such as showing up late to a meeting, or speaking out of order. There was no rulebook for disciplinary actions: group leaders made them up on the spot. Wrongdoers could be asked, for example, to drink saltwater; eat dust; walk miles on end under the scorching sun; crawl on hot sand; or pay a fine of whatever amount. On one occasion, a Brother was asked to stand for an hour in a smelly toilet during one of the camps. Another was required to walk in the small hours to perform dawn prayers at a faraway mosque ('Eid 2013: 71, 156–8). Yet, despite the gravity of this issue to some, when Radwan refused to let it go, he was banned from lecturing, and thereafter completely marginalized.

Finally, there is the case of Ahmad (2013), who married into one of the wealthiest Brotherhood families; fell out with his in-laws because of what they perceived as intolerable independence; and had his membership frozen. What is remarkable about his story was how he was severed from the organization without the opportunity to discuss his grievances. In Ahmad's words:

I was first relieved of attending any group activities other than the weekly family meetings. Then they tailored a dormant family of old men especially for me, as a sort of reprimand. We would discuss a few mundane issues for a brief time before dispersing. A year later, one of them confessed that he was moved by my predicament and stoic acceptance, and promised to intervene on my behalf and reactivate my membership. He asked me to stop attending this weekly meeting and wait for his call. I never heard from him again.

All these dissidence-preventing techniques constitute the negative aspect of consensus building, the positive aspect being constant *praise of harmony*. General Guide 'Umar al-Telmesani described how the religious atmosphere he grew up in made him naturally disinclined to sophistic discussions:

> I remember that whenever someone inquired about the Brotherhood's philosophy in politics, economics, or society, I would shrink away. I have learned from a few students of philosophy that, in one of its definitions, philosophy is no more than the accumulation of human follies across history. Islam has no philosophy because it is brighter than the sun, and does not require the complications of philosophy . . . philosophers bring us nothing but a headache.
>
> (2008: 198)

'Comprehension' (*fahm*), which is the first of the ten pillars of the oath of allegiance, as presented in the Teachings, is defined as "achieving certainty that our doctrine is purely Islamic, and to understand Islam as we understand it" (Banna [1949] 1993: 305–6). The cultivation curriculum instructs prefects, when introducing the pillar of Comprehension, to emphasize the "necessity of bringing Muslims around a single interpretation of Islam" and the "necessity of reducing the gap between different interpretations by turning away from debate and arguments" ("Madkhal" 1997: 34). In fact, Brothers are presented with the pillar of 'Comprehension' as something they need to memorize, not discuss. They are actually quizzed on the topic. One three-part exam requires them first to define the concept by filling-in-the-blanks; then to cite support from the Qur'an and *hadith*; and finally to present a bullet list of practical ways to implement it ("Madkhal" 1997: 26–7).

Further down, as the sixth pillar of the oath of allegiance, comes 'obedience' (*ta'a*), which Banna presents as a combination of "absolute mystical submission in the spiritual domain, and absolute military submission in the practical domain" ([1949] 1993: 312). In his section on family meetings, Banna states clearly: "There is no place in the family for arguments, harshness, or raising one's voice. This is religiously prohibited (*haram*) in the jurisprudence (*fiqh*) of the family. One can only ask for clarification or elaboration in the most polite manner" ([1949] 1993: 325). Article 7 of the Brotherhood's General Order obliges Brothers to express their opinions according to Islamic ethics. Consultation within family meetings, according to the cultivation curriculum, should be limited to logistics (such as the time and place of meetings) not the content of the discussion ("Madkhal" 1997: 274). The curriculum also introduces the concept of *al-tarbiya al-shuriya*, which means nurturing the right form of consultation ("Turuq" 2002: vol. I, 30). The aim of group meetings, in the words of Deputy General Guide Muhammad Habib, is to help Brothers practice correct Islamic behavior, not to debate it (2012: 118). As always, Brothers are constantly assessed using these standards. One of the forms used for camp evaluations lists 23 criteria to help group leaders rank attendees from weak to excellent ("Madkhal" 1997: 23–4). Three questions relate to a Brother's temperament during group meetings:

No. 3: Whether he accepts comments with goodwill.
No. 4: Whether he responds to questions with respect.
No. 6: How he addresses Brothers inside and outside group meetings.

And five questions assess the friendliness of his attitude:

No. 2: His cheerfulness when meeting Brothers, and concern about those absent.
No. 13: His willingness to socialize with Brothers to facilitate love . . . and solidarity.
No. 14: His magnanimity with Brothers.
No. 15: His modesty with Brothers.
No. 16: His altruism with Brothers.

To counter the fact that not all group leaders are equally competent in the field of human management, individual-level controls are fortified by a number of *structural controls*. For one thing, the Brotherhood has recently witnessed a notable shift in social composition. The Brotherhood had always been socially inclusive, with members from all social strata – though the leadership had historically been confined to urban elements, especially middle-class professionals and merchants. But during the first decade of the twenty-first century, steady 'ruralization' (*tarief*) on all levels had reinforced primal loyalties and paternalism. The aim was to shrink the urban stratum, with its modernist infatuation with debate, in favor of countryside members, who are much more comfortable with traditional hierarchies (Tammam 2012: 77). Recruitment rates in provincial universities trumped those in major cities, reshaping the organizational base, with reverberations at the top. Sameh 'Eid, a native of the Nile Delta province of Behirah, reported that, by the 1990s, his 4-square-kilometer provincial town of Damanhur had 2,000 Brothers (2013: 5).

Amendments to the Brotherhood's bylaws in the 1990s and 2000s adjusted the electoral weights of the provinces regardless of size or population. The 35 million citizens of Greater Cairo and Alexandria, were represented by 11 out of 105 seats in the 2008 General *Shura* Council, the Brotherhood's highest legislative body. So although they represented over a third of Egypt's population, not to mention the wealthiest and best educated, they occupied 10 percent of the council. On the other hand, the Nile Delta provinces were allotted 44 seats. Moreover, on the eve of the council elections, many candidates were asked to move to Cairo or Alexandria to guarantee a provincial presence in these urban quotas. The countryside now dominated, with three Nile Delta provinces (Daqahlia, Sharqia, and Gharbia) controlling a third of the council. Another round of amendments revoked the restriction that 9 out of the Guidance Bureau's 16 members must come from Cairo (Abu-Khalil 2012: 76). As a result, 8 provincial council members secured seats on the Guidance Bureau,[15] notably Muhammad Morsi, Egypt's first Islamist president (a native of Sharqia), and Sa'ad al-Katatni (from Menia), the future head of the Brotherhood's Freedom and Justice Party and its first Speaker of the House. By 2009, the 17-membered Guidance Bureau – the first to be elected since 1995 – was effectively ruralized, with 10 members from the provinces (including the General Guide Muhammad Badei' of Mahala), 4 city dwellers with strong rural ties, and 3 from major cities.[16] Most of these provincials ended up governors and cabinet ministers during Morsi's rule.

The drive towards enhancing conservatism did not just occur through shifting the social composition from urban to rural, but also by shifting the religious temperament in the organization from moderate to fundamentalist (*salafi*). The Brotherhood always had a puritan streak, and overlapped with Wahhabi doctrines in its revulsion towards philosophy. King Saud was a patron of Hassan al-Banna, and hundreds of Brothers fled to Saudi Arabia to escape persecution in the 1950s and 1960s. During the next two decades, exiled Brothers encouraged Riyadh to flood Egyptian university campuses with Islamist literature, distributed almost for free. And when senior Brothers emerged from prison in the mid-1970s, they incorporated the fundamentalist student movement, operating under the rubric of the Islamic Group (*al-Jama'a al-Islamiya*). These students had relied on Gulf-funded mosques and associations to rebuild the Islamist movement after thousands of Brothers had been detained. To absorb this new generation, an estimated 40,000 members, the Brotherhood had to become more conservative in outlook. And the merger had a lasting influence on the Brotherhood. It is true that these puritan young men placed themselves formally under the leadership of Brothers. But, in reality, they now formed the core of the organization. This conservatism became more pronounced after the 1991 Gulf War, when throngs of Brothers residing in Saudi Arabia and Kuwait returned. And with the spread of satellite television, websites, and other forms of communication technologies, Gulf affluence tempted many Brothers to reinvent themselves as fundamentalist televangelists. This inter-fertilization of Egyptian Islamism and Wahhabi dogma produced a bloc of "Brotherhood Puritans" that rose to power and fame on the eve of the movement's coming to power (Tammam 2012: 119). Examples include the Brotherhood's propagandist Safwat Hegazi, who spent years in Saudi Arabia, before resettling in Cairo in 1998 to present religious shows on one of the prime fundamentalist channels, Al-Nas. A more prominent case is Hazem Salah Abu-Isma'il, the Brotherhood's candidate for parliament in 2005, and the future presidential candidate in 2012, also a regular on Al-Nas. There were also the hosts on Al-Hafiz channel who played a crucial role in backing Morsi's election and rule. Of course, this transformation meant that Brothers were now expected to adopt stricter views on everything from music and art to gender. But it was crucial to submerging critical attitudes, since fundamentalism, in principle, snubs debate in favor of a simple creed regulated by religious chiefs.

These social and temperamental reengineering processes went hand-in-hand with another structural shift: the rise of the so-called "Qutbist" wing. Hassan al-Banna had an elitist side (discussed later), but he believed that Brothers should focus on converting and leading the masses. His ideas made sense during Egypt's liberal age (1920s–1940s). By the time Sayyid Qutb joined the movement, in the mid-1950s, the Brotherhood had been dissolved, thousands of Brothers were beginning their two-decade tour in detention camps, and Islamist sympathizers prudently kept silent. Qutb, who was imprisoned between 1954 and 1964, placed all his hope in a vanguard of believers (*tali'a mu'mina*) that would impose the Islamist project through insurrection or a coup. He organized his followers in what came to be known as the 1964 Organization. Qutb was executed two years later, and his followers were imprisoned for another decade.

Nonetheless, they capitalized on their legacy, as the last grain of resistance, and became quite influential. When they were released from prison, these Qutbists preferred to work in the shadows, selecting and nurturing promising candidates to join their ironclad network. By the late 1990s, this network included about 1,000 group leaders, reporting to 1964 Organization member and Guidance Bureau magnate Mahmoud Ezzat – acting general guide after the 2013 showdown. They submitted reports on the activities of regular members and saw themselves as the movement's "temple monks" ('Eid 2013: 186–7). Mahmoud (2013) described how his close relationship with strongmen, like Shatir and Ezzat, made ordinary Brothers assume he was one of the in-group. Doors opened in front of him, and even leaders allowed him to talk to them without reservation. Qutbists were active on all organizational levels: marginalizing hesitant elements, and promoting a regime of iron discipline. Muhammad Badei', who met Qutb in prison and implemented his doctrines when he became the Brotherhood's cultivation supervisor, was elected general guide in 2009. And, afterwards, Qutbists dominated the movement's executive and legislative branches. Brothers now aspired to join this vanguard, or at least not to cross it, and understood that the key was unquestioning deference.[17]

These three structural changes have in fact reinforced each other: countryside residents tend to hold fundamental religious views, and their sense of social alienation attracts them to elitist, confrontational politics. And equally significant to the rise of rural, fundamentalist, and combative factions was the Brotherhood's systematic bias against students of the 'argumentative' sciences.

Snubbing Argumentative Sciences

Discouraging criticism was only possible if the right people were recruited in the first place. One look at members' educational backgrounds reveals that highly educated Brothers (including 20,000 with doctoral degrees, and 3,000 professors) come overwhelmingly from the natural sciences. In addition, 150,000 Brothers – over a fifth of members in some estimates – are schoolteachers.[18] There are also clerics, lawyers, and businessmen: the first necessary to expound Brothers' religious positions, the second to defend them in court, and the third to manage and expand their wealth. One might even find a handful of literature students. Absent, however, are students of politics, sociology, history, and philosophy – a conspicuous structural omission.

This is very obvious at the top. The general guide in 2014 is a veterinarian; his top three associates are an engineer, a geologist, and a medic; the head of the Brotherhood's International Organization is an agronomist; the president of the Brotherhood's first political party and speaker of the lower house is also an agronomist, his deputy is a medic, and the speaker of the upper house is a pharmacist; last but not least, the Brotherhood's first and second choices for the presidency were engineers, and the president's chief policy advisor was a pathologist. This is not a new phenomenon. The six founding members of the Brotherhood were a carpenter, a barber, a gardener, an ironer, a mechanic, and a cycle repairer, led by a primary schoolteacher.[19] The first man to assume the position of deputy general guide was a carpenter. And the six general guides between Hassan al-Banna and today's veterinarian were two judges (a father and son), a landowner, a criminal lawyer, a meteorologist, and a physical education instructor. In fact, article 13(c) of the Brotherhood's General Order states that Islamic jurisprudence is the only type of scientific knowledge required for a member to be elected general guide. The exemplary first-generation Brothers, mentioned in Banna's memoirs as role models, were two carpenters, two small retailers, and a tailor. The man he entrusted with establishing the Brotherhood's militant branch, the Special Order, was a literature freshman. The students who revived Islamism in the 1970s were almost exclusively medics and engineers. Continuity is also evident when comparing the first and last Guidance Bureaus. The former, elected in 1931, consisted of a registrar, a merchant, four government clerks (three in irrigation and one in treasury), a primary schoolteacher, a mosque preacher, and two clerics. And the present Bureau, elected in 2009, is made up of a biologist, a geologist, a social worker, six medics, three engineers, two agronomists, and one cleric. In addition, the most influential men in the organization today are businessmen. Social scientists are almost nonexistent.[20]

So how does the Brotherhood defend this lapse? Sanaa' Farghali (2013), a leading matron in the Sisterhood, remembered asking a senior Brother: "How could we assume the responsibility for leading Brothers and Sisters, when we are not qualified scholars?" He responded: "If a hospital admits a wounded man while there are no doctors around, the nurses cannot abandon the call of duty because they lack training; they have to at least stop the bleeding." Similarly, Brothers have to fill the gap until proper experts are at hand. But Egypt does have social scientists, so why filter them out? Muhammad Sa'd Tag al-Din (2013), an engineer and self-styled social theorist and historian, blamed the poverty of education in Egypt for the absence of professionally trained social scientists. If the country has little regard for such disciplines, why should the Brotherhood seek them out?

There are, of course, exceptions. Ibrahim al-Houdeibi and Sarah Lotfi are two of the very few people who studied political science (at the American University in Cairo, and Cairo University, respectively) before joining the movement. These two young members were probably admitted because of their family backgrounds. Ibrahim's grandfather and great-grandfather were general guides, and Sarah's father was a longtime member. Nonetheless, they soon went their separate ways: the former deserted to become an independent activist, and the other lent her expertise to the Brotherhood through joining a political research unit attached to the presidency. Their divergent paths could be partly explained by their assessment of the organization's motives for excluding social scientists. Ibrahim believed that the Brotherhood favored obedience over analytical thinking, and thus methodically marginalized those who might question its ideological platform (Houdeibi 2013). Sarah, on the other hand, speculated that Brothers might be averse to the Western-inspired curriculums taught in Egyptian universities, and believed that the technical aspects of politics, economics, and social policy could be acquired through ad hoc expert panels, such as the ones she was involved in during Morsi's rule. The fact that secular social scientists might be reluctant to lend their expertise to an Islamist movement when the time came did not cross her mind, since everyone should be loyal to the country (Lotfi 2013).

These are the two most common explanations among Brothers regarding the organization's aversion to social sciences. Critical members, naturally, adopt a line similar to Ibrahim's. Some went as far as accusing Brothers of specializing in the art of "nullifying minds" (Khirbawi 2012: 59). Samir (2013), the activist whose critical attitude forced him to withdraw from the Brotherhood in 2012, believed that the sidelining of social scientists is intended to circumvent dissent: "In social sciences, one learns that someone made an argument; another criticized it; and history validated or disproved it. Questioning received wisdom is welcomed. In natural sciences, by contrast, there are no opinions, only facts. This type of matter-of-fact mentality is more susceptible to accepting the Brotherhood's formulas, which present everything as black and white."[21] So, for instance, when Sameh 'Eid opposed outlawing personal sins (such as gossip or envy), an Islamist lecturer snapped: "You political scientists come up with bizarre ideas you do not fully understand." When 'Eid objected that he was a mathematician not a political scientist, the lecturer responded nonchalantly: "So stick with $1 + 1 = 2$" (2013: 200).

Political science professor 'Emad al-Din Shahin (2013), who is quite familiar with the Brothers, also thought that they probably regarded social scientists as too argumentative. When he was invited, with other political scientists, to help develop the Brotherhood's political party, he observed how the leadership took their suggestions with a grain of salt, and a movement whip was present at all times to prevent extended engagements between Brothers and academics. Another political scientist, Seif 'Abd al-Fattah (2013), who was appointed presidential advisor to Morsi, recalled that his impression upon reviewing the Brotherhood's party platform was that this was not a program, but an assortment of incoherent proposals overflowing with religious sentiments. His critique remained unsolicited. I had a similar experience with the Brotherhood's Political Bureau in 2008.

Loyalists, on the other hand, admire the Brotherhood's aversion to "complicated stuff," as Mikkawi (2013) described it: "When you spend time with older Brothers, you realize that Islam is a simple religion that does not require theorizing and philosophy. The strength of the Islamist project lies in its accessibility and down to earth practicality." According to General Guide Hassan al-Houdeibi (1951–73), the Brotherhood advocates "pure religion; true religion; religion without philosophy; religion without books to study day and night and refer to . . . the religion of correct intuition" (1973: 258–9). The ingrained belief that politics is something that Brothers could master without much studying is quite remarkable. Jamal (2013) remembered signing up for the Brotherhood's first political education committee in 2005. Less than a dozen people showed up, mostly engineers like him, and no social scientists. The instructor, a very prominent Brother, was a medic. He began with a quick survey of Western definitions of politics, only to dismiss them all and announce that he was going to focus on "legitimate Islamic politics" (*al-siyassa al-shar'iya*), which he never defined. After two sessions, instruction was suspended because the instructor had more pressing tasks to handle. In fact, the political section is the only Brotherhood section that does not have provincial branches. Its members rarely meet, and when they do, it is to read newspapers and chat about the latest news (Mahmoud 2013).

Another curious example comes from Brotherhood cleric Sheikh Muhammad al-Ghazali, who published his first book on Islam and economic affairs, followed by two other works on the same subject. His aim was noble: to refute claims that Islam justified social inequalities. But he went on to assess the various economic doctrines of his time according to Islamic standards. Sheikh Youssef al-Qaradawi admitted that his Azhar colleague "never studied economics, nor did he familiarize himself with its [various] schools and approaches," but still held that Ghazali was right to "outline Islam's true position" on secular economic philosophies.[22] And what was this position? Islamic economics, according to Ghazali, occupies a middle ground between "radical Communism and arrogant capitalism": capitalists sanctify private property, communists abolish it, and Islamists respect private property unless it contradicts public interests (Qaradawi 2000: 14–15). Evidently, any good Muslim could teach politics or arbitrate between socioeconomic theories.

But that is not all. Brothers also associate social sciences with Westernization. And well-bred Brothers understand that these sciences were founded on secular materialist philosophies that do not apply to Muslims (Tariq 2013). The perception is that inductive experimental knowledge, such as chemistry, is neutral, but deductive speculative knowledge, such as political theory, is colored by ideology (Mahmoud 2005: 29). The fact that social sciences have become grounded in empirical observations for at least two centuries does not change the belief that Western thought, in general, is imprisoned in the Middle Ages, rotating mostly around the theme of how religion suppresses society and obstructs progress (Abu al-Fotouh 2006). "Thinking in Islam," as one veteran Sister put it, "is meant to intensify belief through contemplating divine wisdom, not provoke skepticism [as in Western social sciences]" (Farghali 2013). Farghali's cultivator, 'Ali 'Abd al-Halim Mahmoud, wrote in his classic interpretation of Banna's Teachings that Islam not only is rich with all the values and lessons preached by sociologists, but is better than these because its principles are derived not from empirical observations that could be corrupted by the devil, but by direct revelation from God (1994: 35). This even applies to history. As first-generation Brother Hassaan Hatthout remarked: "I have never once read history – ancient, medieval, or modern – without my conscience whispering: 'God knows best.' The honesty of history is [measured] by the honesty of its authors. And its authors are normally the mighty. And the mighty normally lie" (2000: 7). This is why Banna chastised those who abandon the natural sciences and waste their time with "abstract philosophies and unproductive, fanciful sciences" ([1949] 1993: 156). He prided himself on the fact that he influenced people not by referring to theories and logic, but by reminding them of God's glory ([1948] 1990: 84). The cultivation curriculum mentions two kinds of knowledge: religious and temporal; and limits the latter to "medicine, engineering, agriculture, etc." ("Madkhal" 1997: 84). When Banna's successor as general guide, Hassan al-Houdeibi, urged Muslim rulers to support education in their countries, he meant "sciences required by Muslims to run their lives, such as agronomy, trade, medicine, engineering, and aviation" (1973: 244). The third general guide rejected claims that Banna discouraged Brothers from pursuing modern sciences when he was in fact fond of "important sciences, such as physics, chemistry, and astronomy" (Telmesani 2008: 316). And today's recruiters are explicitly asked to eschew students of social science (Alfy 2013).

Moreover, Banna had warned in an epistle entitled "Our Call" (*Da'watana*) of the disease of admiring one's enemies to a point of becoming fascinated with them, and wondered why Muslims occupy themselves with examining Western positive theories when Islam has spared them the trouble by determining the right course for every social problem ([1949] 1993: 29, 51). He expressed impatience, in his memoirs, with those Muslims attracted to foreign materialist philosophies, to the detriment of their great heritage ([1948] 1990: 73). Other Islamists warned that times of "cultural wilderness" produce a class of "misleading intellectuals who deceive people with abstract concepts and drive them to the abyss." And it is these "leaders of mischief and professional debaters" who transform the intellectual sphere into a wasteland ('Uwis 2010: 154, 157).

The Brotherhood's most prominent lawyer, 'Abd al-Qadir 'Uwda, who was executed in the 1950s, had to study the philosophy of law at college. He apparently felt so morally indignant that he devoted most of his future writings to denouncing Western-inspired legal systems. 'Uwda described positive laws as pagan idols, and judges and lawyers who abide by them as priests in their temple (1953: 12). A legal philosophy, 'Uwda insisted, must reflect a nation's morality. The French Revolution uncoupled laws and morals, expunging law's spiritual essence. Henceforth, Western codes explicitly contradicted Islamic ones. Sharia "directed people to righteousness and perfection," while positive laws "directed people to evil and aggression, and propelled them to corruption and destruction." Tragically, however, Western legal philosophy "tempted us to discard our refined morals and elevated human virtues, and awoke in us an overwhelming materialistic instinct, shaping our society on the bases of utility and interest, leading us to degradation and debasement ... and turning us into beasts dominated by desires" ('Uwda 1953: 28).

Qutb went further: "The English Magna Carta, the French Revolution, and the so-called American experience all proved unworthy of surviving" ([1953] 2001: 48). In his view, "Americans are no better than the English, and the English are no better than the French.

They are all the children of one civilization, a hateful materialist civilization without heart or conscience . . . a fake civilization because it failed to provide humanity with spiritual nourishment" (quoted in Yunis 2012: 171). "Mankind today are on the brink of a precipice," he declared; "Westerners realize that their civilization is unable to provide guidance for mankind . . . Mankind needs a new leadership," and Islam must compensate for the West's bankruptcy and "seize leadership of mankind" (Qutb [1966] 1982: 5–7).[23]

In the introduction to his multi-volume interpretation of the Qur'an, Qutb added: "I dwelled in the shadows of the Qur'an, watching from above the ignorance that has overtaken the world, and the trivial interests of its inhabitants, and the pride they take in their childish knowledge and childish perceptions, and childish preoccupations, as a sage looks down on a group of absurd children . . . Everything became clear and simple" ([1966] 1980: 11). He later wrote in "Signposts" – the manifesto of militant Islamists – that he had wasted 40 years exploring Western sciences and became an expert in the contemporary face of *jahiliyyah* (pagan ignorance) with "its deviations; its errors; its ignorance; as well as its arrogance" and subsequently returned to the fountainhead of his faith. "Philosophy, history, psychology, ethics, and sociology have all been shaped by *jahili* beliefs . . . and thus contradict the fundamentals of Islam" ([1966] 1982: 92–7).

Qutb advised Islamist youth to trust his judgement rather than waste their time reinventing the wheel. They should devote themselves to uncorrupted knowledge, just as the first Muslim generation got by with a few verses of the Qur'an. They should treat these verses "like a soldier receives instructions in the battlefield," and apply them without argument. And they should steer away from Western philosophies without inspecting them too closely, just as a soldier identifies his enemies by their uniform (Qutb [1966] 1982: 18). Muslims must derive their knowledge exclusively from those with impeccable piety. Western intellectuals are "prisoners of their mentality, their environment, and their civilizational heritage. They are incapable of seeing things as they really are" (Qutb [1953] 2001: 46). In a memorable passage in "Islam and Universal Peace," Qutb stated:

> Our vanity upon seeing the human mind excel in the world of matter has blinded us, giving way to the illusion that he who has invented the airplane and the rocket is capable of designing an appropriate system for human life . . . Muslims [should] rely on God's absolute knowledge – knowledge devoid of ignorance, error, and bias . . . His absolute knowledge opposes our absolute ignorance.
>
> ([1953] 2001: 83–5)

On the surface, Qutb's statements might appear to be a simple repudiation of Western sciences. But, on closer inspection, his attitude seems to reflect a much deeper philosophy – and, ironically, one inspired by the West. Brothers insist that it was Qutb's long and harsh imprisonment that shaped his worldview. But, according to his most recent Egyptian biographer, the Brotherhood's radical prophet had always been a diehard *Romantic* (Yunis 2012). Years before he found Islamism, Qutb had been a Romantic poet, literary critic, and one-time novelist. He resented Egypt's rationalist school for its disregard of sentiment and spontaneity, insisting in a 1948 article that it is "great emotions not great ideas" that leave their mark on history (cited in Yunis 2012: 52). The recurring theme in his work had been the deadening effect of rational modernity and the need to fight back through voluntary estrangement from this hopelessly materialistic world. As a skeptic (or, in his description, a borderline atheist), Qutb was drawn to the aesthetic side of the Qur'an, its artistic images, and published a 1939 piece (expanded into a book five years later) on the Romantic reading of revelation. It took one long visit to America for the Romantic critic to reinvent himself as a Romantic ideologue (Yunis 2012: 67). In a letter to an old friend from America, in February 1950, Qutb wrote: "Passionate belief is what grants life to ideas ... This is why the words of prophets and saints live on, and those of philosophers and intellectuals die" (quoted in Yunis 2012: 168).

From then onwards, his writings anticipated the arrival of a heroic generation that would bend the world to its will, and bring the reign of rational philosophy to an end. He wholly embraced the Romantic doctrine of an indivisible and repressed 'self' struggling to reclaim its rightful place under the sun. A believer's rejection of the world is not based on an objective analysis of history and society, but on a decision to rise above history and society and draw inspiration from an unpolluted self whose image flickers from a distant and glorious past: a self sanctified by God and crusted in legend. A believer only needs to know himself to be able to reshape the world in his image. And by resurrecting this sacred self, the believer brings salvation to humanity (Yunis 2012: 25–6). Transforming life, therefore, becomes no longer contingent on scientific learning, but on the art of becoming. The battle is within: one must revive one's authentic identity and reject any distortion or deviation to achieve spiritual enlightenment. This was a remarkable merge of Islamism and Romanticism – "a mystic positioning of Romanticism" (Yunis 2012: 57). And, sure enough, Qutb instructed his followers during the violent confrontations of the 1960s to tap into their inner strength, and ignore rational calculations of the power balance between them and Egypt's military government (Yunis 2012: 79) – as would occur in 2013.

Making Sense of Constructive Ambiguity

The Brotherhood's suspicion of those inflicted with 'intellectualism' – a compulsive tendency to complicate and criticize – dictated their threefold containment strategy against critical knowledge, debate, and argumentative sciences. But the Brothers might have thrown out the baby with the bathwater. Islamism had become, in fact, an unusual phenomenon: an ideology without intellectuals. And without those capable of formulating new ways of being and doing in a systematic manner, the Brotherhood could scarcely claim to provide an ideological alternative to its secular competitors, who – as mediocre as they might be – rest on well-established Western ideologies, such as neo-liberalism, social democracy, and nationalism. Whether in parliament or in the presidency, Brothers adopted eclectic reform proposals from here and there, without clearly communicating what was distinctive about Islamism as a transformative ideology.

Frustration at the absence of a comprehensive project for change weighed heavily on the minds of some Brothers. Ibrahim al-Houdeibi (2013) cited the movement's intellectual bankruptcy as one of the reasons why he left. He was dismayed, for example, by the fact that their only remedy for Egypt's socioeconomic problems was encouraging moral obligations, such as charity and productivity. When Ibrahim pressed future President Morsi during a 2007 battalion training to present precise suggestions, Morsi lectured him on the importance of producing the perfect Muslim society first. Yasser (2013) had a similar run-in with Morsi, this time on the eve of his presidency in the summer of 2012. A meeting was set up between the presidential candidate and 60 affluent urbanites in a posh resort on the outskirts of Cairo. Morsi's goal was to convince these potential voters that he had clear plans for society: "Instead, he embarked on what could only be described as a religious sermon. It was like he was trying to convert them to Islam." He said nothing specific about gender, freedom of opinion, economics, or anything else. His answers were probably not very different from those of his ideological mentor, Hassan al-Banna. The founder was once invited to Cairo University by a secular audience to outline the Brotherhood's position on controversial issues. When asked whether art was acceptable in Islam, he famously responded: "Acceptable art is acceptable; and forbidden art is forbidden" (quoted in Hatthout 2000: 14).

Even more remarkable was the fact that this indecisiveness extended to religion. With the growth of Hezbollah's regional power in the 2000s, Hani (2013) wanted to know where the Brotherhood stood in terms of Sunni–Shi'a relations:

> I asked three lecturers and received three contrary answers: one claimed that Shi'ites are more dangerous to us than infidels and Jews; the second insisted Sunni–Shi'a differences are minor and should be overlooked; and a third asserted that although differences are substantial, we must work with them for political expediency . . . Brothers were apparently still trying to figure out who their allies and enemies were.

This incident sparked an embarrassing public debate between Brothers in February 2009. Brother Youssef Nada (2009) published an article on the Brotherhood's website asserting that the movement's "fixed position" during his six-decade membership was that Shi'ites represented another jurisprudential school (added to the four Sunni ones), and that Muslims could legitimately adhere to any of the five schools without censure. In other words, differences between Sunnis and Shi'ites were political and historic, not religious. Nine days later, Guidance Bureau member Mahmoud Ghuzlan (2009b) wrote an article on the same official website attacking Nada's claim that this was the Brotherhood's position, and adding that such controversial views should not be published because they cause divisions between Brothers (he recorded that 70 percent opposed Nada's view, 26 percent approved, and 4 percent were neutral – a serious sign of division, in his view). So what then was the Brotherhood's real position? "Our position towards the Shi'ite sect is that we are disinclined to either accept or denounce it, as we prefer not to discuss differences between Muslim sects [in general]." Many were surprised that two veteran Brothers voiced such opposing views on the movement's official page. The General Guide Mahdi 'Akif was pressured to issue a statement, which he finally did in April 2009, after two months of pestering. It was a one-line statement proclaiming that each author represented his personal view and not that of the Guidance Bureau – which remained unexpressed.[24] The truth is, the founder himself preferred to remain noncommittal on this topic. Following a visit by a Shi'ite scholar in the 1940s, future General Guide Telmesani inquired about the gravity of differences between the two sects. Banna advised him not to concern himself with these divisive issues (Telmesani 2008: 313).

But how do seasoned members justify the movement's perceived ambiguity? The first reaction, frequently encountered by outsiders, is to cite the Brotherhood's mélange of pamphlets and proclamations on proposed changes, which they maintain – in the same breath – is perfectly in line with the best models for governance, yet radically different from all of them. Yet if one scratches an inch beneath the surface, it becomes apparent that they are mostly referring to mundane reforms. A case in point is the examples Muhammad Sa'd Tag al-Din (2013) cited to refute allegations that the Brotherhood had no plan to fix the country. He mentioned, for instance, how Brothers helped organize traffic in one of Cairo's most chaotic neighborhoods by drawing up a schedule for microbuses; how others helped systematize bread provision in a poor district; and so on. "Imagine if this sprit of civic engagement spreads across the country?" he asked; "We do not want to produce rigid formulas because each government has different circumstances. We provide an overall framework for civic commitment and cooperation. This model can then be exported to our regional neighbors. Eventually, the whole world would want to benefit from our positive experience." Malik (2013) mentioned how the Brothers' economic plan centers on making Egypt the perfect environment for foreign investment by fighting corruption and establishing the rule of law, so that "finance would flood from the outside world." Meanwhile, Sami (2013) highlighted the Brotherhood's intention to overhaul education through, for instance, introducing computers to schools.

Ahmad Deif (2013) extended this approach to the macro level. An engineer by training, and the Brotherhood's student leader at the American University in Cairo during the 1990s, Deif's two-decade membership exposed him to the movement's national and international operations, and landed him a post at the seven-member steering committee responsible for the implementation of the Renaissance Project (*Mashru' al-Nahda*) – the Brotherhood's political manifesto for the 2012 elections. "The Renaissance Project does not belong to us," Deif explained; "We are merely incubators." The aim was to kick-start national development through pilot projects in small farms, factories, etc. Others should then follow the Brotherhood's lead: "We set the basics not specifics. We want to lay the groundwork for an active civil society, and contribute to the evolution of political ethics." But even the Renaissance Project was not the brainchild of Brotherhood intellectuals. Ibrahim al-Houdeibi (2013), who was intimately involved with the project at its point of inception in 1999, knew it originated with Islamic-leaning thinkers outside the movement. After it had already been six years in the making, the Brotherhood sent emissaries to incorporate elements into their 2005 parliamentary election platform. To beef it up before the 2012 presidential elections,

Deputy General Guide Khairat al-Shatir dispatched envoys to Malaysia, Turkey, Brazil, and Italy to add a few more of their success stories.

To insiders, however, Brothers justify their perceived vagueness in religious terms. The movement could only offer general and seemingly incoherent guidelines not because it lacks intellectuals, but because of the nature of Islam. "Islam does not endorse a specific form of rule," said Sarah Lotfi (2013), repeating what she had learned in group meetings: "There is no fixed model. The Islamic state can be a primitive community or an empire. Islamic societies can be structured in various ways. Whatever achieves justice, effectiveness, and efficiency is Islamic." Since it all depends on the time and place that Islam finds itself in, Islamists need first to know the context in which they will reach power before formulating projects. Qutb added that the problems that would face the rising Islamic state would be unique because of the inventiveness of its enemies. Brothers should not waste time second-guessing their opponents to come up with solutions to the challenges they would throw at them. They should figure out what to do only after they gained power (Qutb [1966] 1980: 189).

Meanwhile, the movement could suffice with ad hoc, tactical positions. As Mikkawi (2013) explained: "Since we do not know when and where we would come to power, we do not concern ourselves with hypothetical scenarios. We follow the spirit of Islamic jurisprudence, which only provides new injunctions when new problems arise." So, for example, when the movement decided to allow Sisters to run for parliament in 2005, it was because it needed the goodwill of domestic opponents and foreign observers: "There were no elaborate discussions on democracy or feminism. We were just being practical." Naturally, when Hani (2013) suggested forming a committee to articulate the Brotherhood model for consultative government (*shura*), as the Islamist version of democracy, he was told that this was a bit premature: "Why should we prepare something now, if we do not know when we will get a chance to implement it?" The experienced cultivator Sanaa' Farghali (2013) recalled how her father, a first-generation Brother, insisted that Islamists did not even know whether they wanted to come to power: "We would be happy to support anyone who applies sharia. Our goal is to achieve human happiness through submitting to the laws of the Creator. We do not want to conquer the world. Once the Islamic model is adopted, it will prove such a success that it will surely spread around the globe." When asked by *Le Monde*, in August 1952, if the Brotherhood wanted to rule Egypt, the second general guide responded: "What concerns us is that the country is governed according to Islamic teach-ings, regardless of who applies them" (Houdeibi 1973: 30). Again, it was Banna who first asserted, in his famous Fifth Congress Address, that Brothers do not seek political power, and would be content with offering counsel to those willing to rule in accordance with Islam ([1949] 1993: 201).

Another frequent justification is that the Brotherhood does not need elaborate theories because it represents Islam, pure and simple. The mission of an Islamic government is to "guard religion first, and conduct worldly government second," as the second guide stated (Houdeibi 1977: 176). And what does Islam say about government? It recommends asking the experts. This is why their plan when coming to power in Egypt, as Radwan (2013) put it, was to employ policy experts in all fields. "But if we will rely on secular professors and technocrats," Hani (2013) asked, "then why do we claim that 'Islam is the Solution?'" A group leader responded with an amusing example: "Cairo suffers from traffic jams. Islam has the solution. Since the Qur'an requires us to consult specialists, then convening a committee of urban planners and traffic officers to resolve the problem is a direct application of Islam." This was no aberration. In his authoritative work *Missionaries Not Judges*, General Guide Houdeibi used this traffic-jam example to demonstrate what the Brotherhood meant by the comprehensiveness of Islam. He cited two Prophetic sayings prohibiting injury between Muslims, adding that experience suggests that allowing motorists to drive as they wish would most probably cause harm to drivers and pedestrians. Hence, Muslims are religiously obliged to organize traffic through laws that safeguard all Muslims (Houdeibi 1977: 105).

However, trusting old-regime experts – to compensate for the lack of internal ones – means that the Brothers would not be able to change much in Egypt. A prime example is the economic policy of the first Islamist president. After the Brotherhood had promised a radical transformation of the country's economic life, Hassan Malik, one of the movement's leading businessmen, concluded after dizzying talks with experts that the old regime's economic program was sound in principle, but undermined by monopolies and embezzlement. The Brotherhood would therefore leave the old policies in place, and turn its attention to fighting corruption (Samir 2013). A more serious challenge, of course, was that these non-Islamist specialists would not want to lend their expertise to the Brothers. This was the situation Sarah Lotfi (2013) found herself in when working with diplomats and international relations scholars to prepare foreign policy memos for President Morsi. To Sarah's surprise, many of these specialists would not fully cooperate with 'Essam al-Haddad, the pathologist whom the president appointed as foreign policy advisor.

A final defense of sticking to generalities is that specifics are divisive. As an umbrella movement for Muslims with different temperaments, devising a concrete ideological program would threaten the movement's unity. If the Brotherhood wants to keep zealots and moderates, puritans and mystics, poor and rich under the same roof, it must eschew detailed debates. In practice, this amounts to allowing every faction to fancy Islamic government as it wishes. Hardline Brothers believe Islamist rule means shutting down theaters, enforcing dress codes, prohibiting alcohol, policing public morality, destroying Sufi shrines, etc. Moderates are convinced it would only lead to minor legal amendments and a greater stress on spirituality. Likewise, the poor hope the Brothers will redistribute wealth and adopt progressive taxation, while the rich rest assured that the movement would only preach social solidarity (Samir 2013). As Mikkawi (2013) asserted, preventing dissent (*fitna*) is the movement's primary goal: "Sometimes up to a third of the members would disagree with this or that decision. No one forces them to toe the line. We are all like independent ships, sailing in the same direction. A strict ideology would deprive the Brotherhood of its greatest asset: flexibility. Islam orders us to preserve our unity above all."[25]

This deliberate embrace of constructive ambiguity as an Islamic virtue explains the Brothers' anti-intellectual attitude. Intellectuals provoke disputes, and disputes invite dissent – as we know only too well from the history of ideological movements.[26] The strength of the Brotherhood lies in the fact that it is just that: a brotherhood, a close-knit society of Brothers and Sisters, who have pledged to stick together for better or for worse. To understand the movement, therefore, one must transcend the individual Brother to examine the society of Brothers as a whole.

2

Building the Brotherhood

One of the most striking things about the Brotherhood is its name. Ideological movements usually carry the name of the new order they strive to impose: so one hears, for example, of liberal, communist, or nationalist movements. The Brotherhood, in contrast, carries the name of an already existing society: the society of the Muslim Brothers. It is as if the movement itself is the ultimate goal. To dispel doubts of organizational narcissism, members are told that the movement is sacred because what it represents is sacred – that is, Islam (Shatla 2013). Without the movement, there can be no return to Islamic rule. In time, however, means and ends become conflated. "We come to believe that Islam is the Brotherhood (*al-Islam howa al-Ikhwan*)," Hani (2013) stated, "that this divine group (*al-jama'a al-rabaniya*) must be preserved against all odds." As Ibrahim al-Houdeibi (2013) succinctly put it: "The organization is the cause of its own being." This unique organizational feature is grounded in a particular interpretation of Islamic social ties, and reinforced by interlocking networks of family, friends, and business partners.

A Brotherhood in God

'The believers are but brothers,' decrees the Qur'an (49: 10). And Prophet Muhammad compared believers to a single body in which, if one organ complained, the rest would attend to it with compassion. The founders of the Muslim Brotherhood drew on these and dozens of comparable religious texts to justify their choice of a name. As mentioned in Hassan al-Banna's memoirs, during the founding meeting, the movement's creators wondered whether they were forming a political club, a religious sect, a social association, or something else. He told them: "We are brothers in the service of Islam. Therefore, we are the Muslim Brothers" ([1948] 1990: 96). 'Brotherhood' (*ukhuwa*), the ninth pillar of Banna's Teachings, refers to "the bonding of hearts and souls with the bond of faith" ([1949] 1993: 313). In explaining this tenet, the cultivation curriculum lists the five characteristics of godly brotherhood: it is a divine blessing; it is a source of emotional energy; it is a bonding of souls; it is the true mark of believers; and it is love in God ("Turuq" 2002: vol. II, 239). Another volume of the curriculum describes brotherhood as the very spirit of faith ("Mabadi'" 2003: vol. III, 207).

And the flipside of godly brotherhood is antipathy to others. 'Loyalty and antipathy' (*al-wala' wal-bara*) is a concept Islamists derive from the Qur'an (9: 23): 'O you who have believed, do not take your fathers or your siblings as allies if they preferred disbelief over belief.' According to the curriculum, a believer must rid his heart of emotional attachment to family and friends if they do not share his beliefs, and substitute them with the primal bond between him and his brothers in Islam ("Turuq" 2002: vol. I, 269).[1] In "Our Call" (*Da'watana*), Banna divided Muslims into four types: those who support Brothers out of belief; those who support Brothers for pragmatic reasons; those who are inclined to become Brothers; and unjust Muslims ([1949] 1993: 12–13). There are no good Muslims outside the Brotherhood and its orbit, and Brothers must rank organizational ties higher than any other, even those of family and friendship. Attachment to your Brothers entails separation from others. According to General Guide Hassan al-Houdeibi, Muslims who do not join the Brotherhood, while not necessarily infidels, are, at the very least, negligent, and a good Muslim should only intermingle with them to urge them to repent (1973: 230). Shatla (2013) described how disorienting it normally is for a young man to learn that his parents – those whom he had considered as a source of wisdom (sometimes even as role models) all his life – turned out to be sinners or simply deluded. One automatically turns to one's new Brotherhood family to fill this emotional gap.

The choice of name, in a sense, elevates Brotherhood membership above most other ideological movements. Without this "Brotherhood of belief," Deputy General Guide Muhammad Habib rightly proclaimed, "the Muslim Brotherhood would have become like any other party" (2012: 122). When you join an ideological organization or even a religious congregation, you commit to a cause and to a community. Not so with the Brotherhood. As an ordinary Muslim, you are in fact tied to other believers in an eternal God-ordained brotherhood. Not being aware of this fact and the ensuing obligations makes you a sinner, or at least gravely negligent. So by becoming a Brother you are not making a new commitment – a commitment you could later rescind – you are merely activating a so far dormant bond you had tacitly accepted when you first embraced Islam. The third general guide, 'Umar al-Telmesani, said that he and his Brothers did not swear allegiance to the movement, "We swore allegiance to God" (2008: 62). By the same token, leaving the Brotherhood amounts to nothing less than reneging on your religious duties: "Here you are renouncing faith not an ideology; you are abandoning God not Hassan al-Banna" (Fayez 2013: 18). Newcomers are scarcely aware of any ideological indoctrination. As far as they are concerned, senior Brothers are tutoring them on the basics of their religion. Naturally, then, defending the movement amounts to defending Islam (Fayez 2013: 29). How could it be otherwise when the founder clearly stated: "We openly declare that every Muslim that does not believe in this approach and work towards fulfilling it, has no share in Islam, and should find another [religious] idea to believe in . . . [This is] the mission God set for us, not the mission we set for ourselves" (Banna [1949] 1993: 101). Little wonder that Brotherhood spokesman Subhi Saleh once proclaimed on television, "I ask God to take my soul [while I am still] a Brother," a slightly altered version of the common prayer for God to take one's soul while one is still a Muslim.[2] When Farghali's (2013) brother was detained, she blamed their father for encouraging him to join the Brotherhood. He responded: "We have no choice. There are only two paths, one leading to heaven, and the other to hellfire."

In the most recent interpretation of the Teachings, Muhammad Sa'ad Tag al-Din held that those who betray their commitment to the Brotherhood might not be completely excommunicated, but must be considered sinners for violating their oath of allegiance (2013: 55–9). In another interpretation of the Teachings, cleric Muhammad al-Ghazali commended the founder for trying to arouse Muslims from their coma (1981: 5). This distinction between conscious and unconscious Muslims is crucial. In "Our Call" (*Da'watana*), Banna maintained that: "The difference between us and our people after we have both accepted faith, in principle, is that their faith is dormant and slumbering in their souls, they neither respect nor follow its injunctions . . . and in their state of obliviousness they might even work against it, whether or not they are aware of it" ([1949] 1993: 15). The Brotherhood, in other words, does not consider itself an ideological movement, or any other type of movement, but an island of awakened Muslims amidst an oblivious community.

The brilliance of this formulation is that it does not appear to be promoting any new ideas; it simply asks Muslims to reexamine their religiosity for a possible discrepancy between what they believe themselves to be (devout Muslims) and what they actually are (violators of Islam). It is a Gramscian strategy *par excellence*. Gramsci held that counterhegemonic movements must push their audience to reflect upon the "contrast between [their] thought and action . . . the [artificial] coexistence of two conceptions of the world, one affirmed by words and the other displayed in effective action" (1971: 326–7). Muslims who want to overcome this dissonance between belief and action have to carry over their religiosity to the public sphere; they have to translate their faith into sociopolitical activism. Becoming conscious of the fact that, as a Muslim, you are already a Brother is the 'passive' aspect of your membership. The 'active' part is to go on and serve Islam with your Brothers. Now, what does Islam want? According to Sami (2013), secular-minded Muslims think Islam is all about praying, fasting, and other acts of worship. But, contrary to this distorted view, Islam could only exist in one grand religious community, an *umma*. As the Qur'an (21: 92) says: 'Indeed this *umma* of yours is one *umma*, and I am your Lord.' But this *umma* is long gone because the caliphate, the political institution that symbolized its unity had collapsed. As a result, 'the duty of the time' (*wajib al-waqt*) – a jurisprudential-sounding term coined by the Brotherhood to refer to the duty that must be prioritized – is to restore the caliphate.

This brings us to one of the Brotherhood's most brilliant recruitment and retention strategies, originally framed by the founder as the 'collective work obligation' (*fardiat al-'amal al-jama'i*). Literally, every Brother has engaged in this logical exercise at some point in his organizational career. And it usually runs like a Socratic dialogue:[3]

- Do you agree that Islam must exist in a united community under the caliphate?
- Yes.
- Does this community presently exist?
- No.
- So would you agree that resurrecting the caliphate is essential to Islam?
- Yes.
- Can you resurrect the caliphate on your own?
- No.

- So would you agree that you are obliged to work with others to achieve this goal?
- Yes.
- Now, regardless of the Brotherhood's faults, do you see a better-equipped Islamist group?
- No.
- So would you agree then that it is your religious duty to join (or stay in) the Brotherhood?
- Yes.

This line of reasoning is couched in Islamic exhortations for collective action, and warnings against individualism. Members are frequently reminded that the most important Islamic rituals are performed collectively: mosque prayers, pilgrimage, and fasting during the holy month of Ramadan (Samir 2013). Qaradawi provided a graphic metaphor using the example of prayer: Muslims are obliged to pray together; they must form straight lines and close the gaps between them; they must toe the line without complaints; they must follow the directions of the prayer leader without discussion; and if the leader commits a mistake during prayer, he should be alerted in a courteous, unobtrusive manner; finally, they must all remain mindful of the fact that God disregards the disorderly line. Prayer therefore supplies, in Qaradawi's view, "a prototype of the organized Islamic group" (1999: 35). Banna had made a similar remark in his memoirs, reminding followers that: "If people saw someone standing out of line, they would not say there is someone not toeing the line, but would say, this line is cricked" ([1948] 1990: 125). In other words, those who disrupt the collective order condemn not only themselves, but the entire group.

Brothers also appeal to the mystic concept of companionship (*suhba*) to further highlight the importance of collective work.[4] Sufism advocates that, for a Muslim to attain the highest level of piety, he must constantly associate himself with the virtuous, with those who radiate spiritual energy. And so the Teachings preach that: "Loving and respecting and praising virtuous people ... brings one close to God" (Banna [1949] 1993: 307). And, indeed, General Guide Telmesani celebrated how "We loved Banna and his successors with all our hearts because they were the ones who opened our eyes and guided us to the light" (2008: 62). The cultivation curriculum lists dozens of supportive verses and Prophetic sayings, such as the one that holds that: 'A man follows the religion of his companion, so beware who you accompany' ("Mabadi'" 2003: vol. III, 205).

Along the same lines, potential drifters are reminded of revelations that forbid Muslims from turning away from the community of believers, such as the Prophet's warning that wolves prey on stray sheep, and that an individual is more likely than a group to be corrupted by the devil. The most critical Prophetic saying here, of course, is the one that asserts: 'Whoever dies without a *bay'a* dies a *jahili* death,' which means that those who are not bound by an oath of allegiance to the leader of the *umma* are like the ignorant pagans who either did not know or refused Islam. Since there is no caliph to swear an oath to, and since the secular rulers of the Islamic world are not claiming any religious titles, Muslims are obliged to pledge loyalty to whoever they believe represents the *umma* (Farghali 2013). This brings members full circle to the penultimate question in the Brotherhood's Socratic ruse: Who is better-equipped than the Brotherhood? As Yasser (2013) explained, as soon as you begin to complain, older Brothers tell you: "Yes, you are absolutely right, the Brotherhood makes terrible mistakes, but who are you going to join: militant Islamists who go around murdering innocent people, or secular Muslims who have no understanding of Islam?" Once a member accepts the collective work obligation, Yasser concluded, "the logic becomes irrefutable." Those who persist in their criticism are presented with an even more disarming argument: "You see Muslims, in general, committing horrendous acts, and you see the Muslim world tailing behind advanced nations, so why not reject Islam as a whole because of the errors and imperfections of Muslims? It is the same with the Brotherhood; we should never doubt our belonging to it, even if members err or if the organization is far from perfect" (Sami 2013).

A State of War

If the Brotherhood is unique among ideological movements in the way it sanctifies its membership, it still goes the extra mile with some of the more typical consolidation tactics. This is why instilling loyalty to the cause (Islam) and love for one's comrades (Muslim Brothers) to 'pull' members together is supplemented by allegations about Islam's enemies to 'push' members away from others. Paranoia, of course, is not alien to ideological groups, and Brothers are no exception. Conspiracy theories, moreover, abound in many parts of the Muslim world – and some are not completely unfounded. Perhaps the difference is that the Brotherhood's version is somewhat broader, and presented to members in a systematic way. The worldwide conspiracy against Islam's faithful brigades includes everyone and stretches across Islam's 14 centuries. In many ways, it is an extension of the immortal battle between good and evil, whose final chapter the Brothers are commencing. So, while Egyptians were merely amused to hear President Morsi's supporters claim he was destined for a lead role in Armageddon, the truth is: millenarianism runs deep in the minds of Brothers.

The first time Brothers are formally introduced to this narrative occurs during the induction course, which regularly features a lecture entitled "The Conspiracy." Here the magnitude and dimensions of the Western–Zionist–Masonic plot are exposed, and Brothers are warned that Islam and its soldiers are in a state of permanent siege and can only survive by sticking together, obeying their leaders, and distrusting everyone else (Radwan 2013). This conspiracy justifies unilateral decisions from the top, since leaders know more than anyone else what is really going on, but cannot share this with ordinary members for security reasons (Mahmoud 2013). More important, resisting it requires unity. Qaradawi, who lividly condemned the global conspiracy against the first Islamist president in 2013, called upon Muslims to unite under a single leadership to fight their enemies: "We cannot resist a collective offensive with individual defenses; chaos cannot counter order; a pebble cannot defy a mountain" (1999: 34).

The general outlines of the global conspiracy against Islam are unpacked in a special section in the cultivation curriculum. The section begins by praising God for deciding to revive the nation once more at the hands of the Brotherhood after Islam had become distorted and Muslims persecuted. Yet, to shoulder this burden, Brothers must recognize the current enemies of Islam: these are "secular Crusaders and Zionists, as well as Muslims devoted to worldly interest, driven by the so-called New World Order." This unholy alliance is led at the moment by the United States, which has invented globalization to corrupt Muslims, who represent the last obstacle to its hegemony. The curriculum then mentions in a footnote that the inhabitants of the United States have all descended from the criminals of Europe and so "their root nature is corrupt" ("Turuq" 2002: vol. I, 441–2).[i]

Globalization corrupts Muslims in numerous ways. There is first the destruction of gender roles and family values through movies and television shows, the fashion and cosmetics industries, and the immoral principles propagated by the United Nations (little wonder

[i]The authors of the curriculum might have heard someone mention how Australia hosted British convicts, and then substituted (probably out of confusion) Australia for America.

that Morsi raised eyebrows by claiming, during his presidency, that UN resolutions on women and children threatened to destroy the world). Other dangerous tools are secular education and media, which do little more than spread lies about the nature and history of Islam; encourage sexual permissiveness in the name of art and freedom of speech; and glorify celebrities and other petty role models. There are also institutional tools, including exploitative multinationals, such as ExxonMobil; the usury-propagating World Bank and International Monetary Fund; and the Internet, which spreads intellectual and moral malice ("Turuq" 2002: vol. I, 442–4). But why go about destroying Islam in such a roundabout manner? According to Tag al-Din, the enemies of Islam lost hope of crushing Muslims militarily, so they turned to neutralizing Islam's inner strength, its "secret power," by reducing it to rituals (2013: 169).

It is crucial for Brothers, however, to understand that this new conspiracy is the latest thrust in the age-old conspiracy against Islam, which included the Crusades and Tartar attacks, modern colonialism, the overthrow of the caliphate, and the implanting of a Zionist entity in the heart of the Muslim world ("Turuq" 2002: vol. I, 447). The curriculum reminds Brothers that they are part of the perennial battle between good and evil: "In every age and in every community, the devil recruits allies . . . and forms them into an army to attack believers using his [twisted] means and tricks," which include mocking and ridiculing; distortion and black propaganda; economic sanctions; and persecution – satanic means used against Muslims in Mecca; as well as civil strife and foreign aggression – satanic means used against Muslims in Medina ("Mabadi'" 2003: vol. III, 225–43).

The modern-day plot, according to Tag al-Din, began in the twelfth century at the hands of a closeted Jew, Johanna of Seville, who invented Orientalism to implement the plans of the Elders of Zion at the hands of future scholars, such as Sir Hamilton Alexander R. Gibb, supported by Christian missionaries, such as another closeted Jew, Samuel Marinus Zwemer. Failing to lure Muslims away from their religion, they enrolled them in secular and Christian schools that pretended to respect Islam, while in reality they were devoted to diluting the influence of religion in the lives of students (Tag al-Din 2013: 170–81). The fatal strike came with the abolishment of the caliphate at the hands of the Turkish Mustafa Kamal. Nowadays, according to the curriculum, Jews fight Muslims through proxies such as the Rotary and Lions clubs, Masonic lodges, and Zionism; and Christians use missionaries and Orientalists to spread lies about Islam. These Islam-hating Judeo-Christians care more for the survival of pandas, whales, llamas, and elephants than they do for the millions of Muslims in Iraq, Afghanistan, Kashmir, Chechnya, and Palestine. This 20-page section of the curriculum concludes with a short exercise requiring members to substantiate the claim that Islam is subject to conspiracy using verses from the Qur'an and examples from the Prophet's life; and then to show how today's conspiracies represent the continuation of this struggle ("Mabadi'" 2003: vol. III, 225–43).

'Ali 'Abd al-Halim Mahmoud, the Islamist cleric who recruited Sanaa' Farghali and her generation (now in their sixties), proposed two reasons for the weakness of the Muslim world. There is the external threat, which is "the alliance of Western countries – the heirs of the Crusaders . . . the alliance of Jews . . . and the alliance of . . . atheist communism and socialism, so they could all cooperate against Islam and Muslims everywhere" (Mahmoud 1994: 7–8). And there is the internal threat, which is "the weakness of Muslim religiosity" due to the seduction of Muslims by "the elements of Western civilization," and the subservience of Muslim rulers to Western powers (Mahmoud 1994: 8–9). In other words, the external and internal threats are both caused by the same enemy: the West and its allies. Even as the United States was pressuring the Egyptian regime to allow Brothers into parliament on the eve of the 2005 elections, Brothers prefaced their 2004 "Initiative on the Principles of Reform" by defining the primary threat to the Muslim world as the American plot to impose Western–Zionist domination ("Mubadarat" 2004).

The only way to reclaim Islam's past glory is to support the Brotherhood – and the West knows it. This is why Qutb spent considerable time exposing the diabolical obsession of today's Crusaders and Zionists with conquering Islam's last stronghold – the Muslim Brothers: "They want to destroy Islamic faith, and the Brothers are its soldiers; they want to wipe out Islamic morality, and the Brothers are its guardians; they want to spread infidelity among Muslims, and the Brothers are the only obstacle" (quoted in Hammuda 1999: 109). And in a more dramatic moment, he claimed: "This stubborn warrior [Islam] is wearing out the international Crusaders and the Zionists! This is the ultimate battle!" (Qutb [1953] 2001: 93). So, whereas a high-profile dissenter once compared the Brotherhood to the Freemasons, in terms of secrecy, rituals, ranks, and symbols (Khirbawi 2012: 26), he seemed to have overlooked one crucial difference: Masons conspired against the world, while Brothers believed that the world conspired against them.

There was hardly a prominent Brother who did not add his own spin. 'Abd al-Qadir 'Uwda, the movement's leading light in the early 1950s, claimed that British Prime Minister Gladstone warned his country's parliament that: "The British empire will gain no foothold in the Islamic world as long as the Qur'an exists" ([1953] 1988: 136). The Brotherhood's second general guide mentioned a secret meeting held in a British military base in 1949, between the British, the Americans, and the Israelis, to conspire against the Brothers, and urge Egypt's monarch to liquidate the movement (Houdeibi 1973: 34). International intrigue continued under President Nasser in the 1950s and 1960s. Americans and Russians sent him urgent appeals to destroy the Brotherhood. Nasser was not a nationalist leader as many Egyptians believe; he was, in Ghazali's description, "a tool in the hand of envious world powers" to finish off Islamism after the failure of Lord Cromer and Britain's other colonial masters ([1954] 1998: 109). The third general guide was sure that "Communists, Crusaders, and Zionists hate nothing more than Hassan al-Banna and the Muslim Brothers" (Telmesani 2008: 75). At the height of the Cold War, in the 1980s, he claimed that Americans and Russians were obsessed with nothing more than destroying Islam, and considered the Brotherhood "their only common enemy" (Telmesani 2008: 308). The result was a most mischievous plan: Soviets invading Afghanistan – with American knowledge and support – to draw in and destroy Islamists. Here and elsewhere, the two world powers pretended to be enemies to kill as many Muslims as possible (Telmesani 2008: 254). Never to be outdone, Qutb similarly dismissed Egypt's successive battles against Israel and other Western powers as "fake wars" meant to create "fake [secular] heroes," like Nasser, to undermine the real heroes of Islam: the Brothers ([1966] 1980: 3557).

Israel certainly received its share of accusations. Deputy General Guide Muhammad Habib exposed how Israeli research centers began in the 1980s a concerted effort to understand the twelfth-century religious environment that produced Saladin in order to prevent its reemergence (2012: 14). Indeed, the Brotherhood had always been Israel's worst nightmare. "We all heard Moshe Dayan, the Israeli Defense Minister, say [in a 1948 press conference in Washington] he would prefer taking on the armies of all Muslim states united rather than face a handful of Muslim Brotherhood battalions," asserted the third general guide with great pride (Telmesani 2008: 37). Another oft-cited – and similarly untraceable – statement has Israeli Premier Golda Meir warning that when the number of Muslims attending dawn prayers equaled those attending Friday prayers, then Israel would be doomed (Tariq 2013). Indeed, Brothers believe that one of the reasons why the West created Israel in the first place was to lure Islamists into Palestine to be liquidated (Sabbagh 2012: 217). Curiously, the Brotherhood is even perceived to be the victim of conspiracies by other Islamist movements, which are either more militant or liberal than the perfectly moderate Brothers (Qaradawi 1999: 234).

Naturally, some Brothers became skeptical about this worldwide conspiracy when they saw Brothers taking over parliament and the presidency through fair elections in 2013. Can the movement let down the drawbridge now, they wondered? Not yet, came the response. It is true that the organization was allowed to seize power, but now there was a counterrevolution brewing beneath the surface. Organizational unity and resolute leadership were as important now as ever; dissent could not be tolerated; and argument over the best way to govern Egypt was a luxury Islamists could not afford (Deif 2013). Of course, the June 30 uprising against the Brothers offered the movement's conspiracy theory a new lease of life. Yet the lengths to which Western governments and media went to defend the Brotherhood's right to rule raised doubts in the minds of many members. If Western capitals had the slightest suspicion that Brothers might threaten their interests in the future, why not welcome Morsi's being overthrown? The response, from the always-prepared group leaders: "God blinded Westerners, forcing them to work against their own good. They are unwitting tools in the hands of the divine" (Shatla 2013).

A Saintly Leadership

With such a besieged mentality, unity becomes the only way to beat the odds. And unity cannot be achieved without a trusted leadership. This is why Brothers are taught always to back their leaders (Radwan 2013). This concept is enshrined in the tenth pillar of the Teachings, which is devoted to Trust (*thiqa*): "Trusting leaders is everything in successful missions." And, by Trust, Banna meant "the soldier's profound confidence in the competence and loyalty of the leader" ([1949] 1993: 313). To start with, Brothers must trust in the leaders' virtuousness. In Islamic doctrine, God subjects the virtuous to trials and tribulations to purify their souls and purge the unholy from their midst. So, whereas members of other ideological movements can hold their leaders accountable, Brotherhood leaders remain beyond reproach, since good as well as bad outcomes reflect the will of the Almighty. As General Guide Mustafa Mashhur put it, in his pertinently titled *Between Leaders and Soldiers*, decisions that appear to have been mistaken should not be blamed on the leaders because they might be God's way of testing members' steadfastness and weeding out the weak and the hesitant. In other words, failure should be regarded as a blessing in disguise (quoted in Abu-Khalil 2012: 28). This explains, for instance, the Brotherhood's unapologetic attitude towards the mistakes that led to Morsi's ousting.

In addition, speaking against such virtuous leaders is a form of backbiting (*ghiba*) and gossip (*namima*), which are religiously prohibited. The Qur'an (58: 9–10) says: 'O you who have believed, when you converse privately, do not converse about sin and aggression and disobedience ... but converse about righteousness and piety.' In the cultivation curriculum, the verse 'O you who have believed, if a disobedient one comes to you with information, investigate, lest you ignorantly harm some' (Qur'an 49: 6) is used to stress the importance of always giving leaders the benefit of the doubt, and assuming the best possible interpretation of their words and deeds ("Madkhal" 1997: 186). When General Guide Mahdi 'Akif (2004–9) was warned that some Guidance Bureau members might have become too cosy with security officers, he kicked his informers out of the office, snapping back: "I do not like people to tell me such things, just as the Prophet used to say, do not speak mischief of my Companions in front of me" (Gallad et al. 2009). Brothers, accordingly, dismiss any critical thoughts or negative feelings against their leaders as "satanic whispers" ('Eid 2013: 33). How could it be otherwise when, as one Brotherhood cleric explained, criticizing the leadership weakens the organization, and weakening the organization makes Islam vulnerable to enemy blows? In other words, by attacking leaders, one undermines Islam itself.[5]

Naturally therefore, leaders are placed on a religious pedestal. Brother Anwar al-Gindy recalled that, when he performed the pilgrimage with Banna, Brothers would get car sick, but the founder would not; their stomachs would twist from hunger, but his would not; they would suffer from walking under the burning sun, but he would remain unaffected (2001: 46). Before Telmesani became general guide, he recorded with pride his faith in Banna: "I saw, heard, and thought with his grace's eyes, ears, and mind, because I had absolute trust in all he said ... I was like a dead corpse in his purifying hands" (2008: 143). When Telmesani himself assumed the top post, he beseeched Brothers to follow their guide in the belief that God directs him to the right path (2008: 112).

This halo is justified by the Brotherhood's inventive claim that the general guide is the "deputy of the currently nonexistent caliph, who in turn is supposed to be representing the Prophet," and, as such, the Brotherhood's supreme leader is the de facto supreme religious leader (*Imam*) of the community of believers, and must be obeyed until the de jure leader (the caliph) returns (Tariq 2013). As a man whose great talent was to synthesize doctrines from a variety of religious and secular sources, Hassan al-Banna's conception of the general guide as the deputy (*na'ib*) of a missing caliph combines the Shi'ite tradition of regarding top jurists as deputies of the Awaited Mahdi (*al-Mahdi al-Muntazar*), and the Sufi concept of the saint (*wali*), who receives instructions and intuitions directly from God. This is why the Teachings instruct that: "The opinion of the Imam and his deputy in the absence of a divine text . . . is to be followed" (Banna [1949] 1993: 306). But then Banna surpassed most other doctrines in his widely quoted description of the rights of leaders: "The leader in the Brotherhood has the same rights as the father in terms of emotional bonds; the professor in terms of scientific respect; the [mystic] sheikh in terms of spiritual nurture; and the [political and military] leader in terms of general policy" ([1949] 1993: 313–14). The relationship between leaders and followers is thus triangulated using these normally unrelated concepts: submission to the moral superiority of the father and the spiritual guide; submission to the knowledge and experience of the teacher; and submission to the bravery and wisdom of the warrior-ruler.[6]

Verses on patience come in quite handy. Since a good Muslim is also a patient one, then those who insist that leaders deliver quick results reveal their own inadequacy. So, for example, Egyptians who voted for Morsi and then turned against him for not making changes fast enough are to be blamed for their impatience. According to Sami (2013), three months before Morsi was overthrown, "once Egyptians get nurtured on the virtues of patience, like us Brothers, they will learn to accept their lot in peace." "Why should we be in a hurry?" asked Ghazali, "Years, decades, and centuries are worthless in the lifetime of messages and nations. What counts is that we remain steadfast on the path" (1999: 7). The curriculum states clearly that Brothers are obliged to perform their assigned duties without aspiring to see the fruit of their work in their lifetime, since Muslims are rewarded for their deeds not by the outcome of those deeds, which is in God's hands ("Turuq" 2002: vol. I, 436). And not understanding what leaders are up to is no excuse. Tag al-Din (2013) asserted that: "A devout leadership with . . . a united and resilient movement is as important as theory and strategy." One could therefore make sense of Brother Hassan al-'Ashmawi's (1985: 82) oxymoronic claim that: "Brothers are revolutionary in their capacity to patiently weather injustice rather than confront it" – a theme later expounded in the much-publicized piece *Intiqam al-Ikhwan al-Muslimeen* (Revenge of the Muslim Brothers), published on the movement's website in April

2008 after dozens of its members had been handed heavy prison sentences. The author begins by threatening that Brothers will avenge themselves against Egypt's unjust rulers – but how?

> [Our] Real revenge is to exert more patience . . . Every young man who heads early [to the mosque] for dawn prayers, and fixes his foot on the frontline, represents a slap on the neck of [every] State Security officer . . . Imagine, my dear Brother, when you raise your hands to begin prayer that you are slapping the face of [every corrupt] judge . . . The revenge of the Muslim Brothers is to embrace their sacred constitution [the Qur'an], their holy book, to recite it and study its meanings and memorize its verses . . . The revenge of the Muslim Brothers is to control themselves, obey their leaders, trust their movement, and endure harm.
>
> ('Abbas 2008)

In his famous Fifth Congress Address, Banna asked "those who want to pick the fruit before it is ripe" to leave the Brotherhood, and then went on to promise: "When I find among you, Muslim Brothers, three hundred battalions equipped spiritually with belief and conviction, intellectually with science and culture, physically with athletics and exercise, at that time if you ask me to overcome sea storms, reach the highest sky, conquer every stubborn and ruthless [ruler], I will." Why 300 battalions? Banna cited the Prophetic saying 'Twelve-thousand [soldiers] will not be defeated for being too few' ([1949] 1993: 191). Some might think that this saying refers to the actual power balance between Muslims and infidels in seventh-century Arabia, but this is beside the point, which is that these 12,000 men must be perfectly equipped religiously, emotionally, mentally, and physically. As Qaradawi explained, Banna requested 12,000 "full believers" – meaning that millions of "half believers" would not do (1999: 81). So, even if the Brotherhood attracts millions of members, leaders could still judge that they are not yet ready for a frontal attack according to Banna's criteria. The leeway this affords leaders became evident during the controversy surrounding the 2012 elections. Young members were itching to seize power following the 2011 uprising. The Guidance Bureau said the movement was not ready and pledged publicly not to seek a majority in parliament or to compete for the presidency. And, accordingly, many members praised their leaders' prudence. A few months later, the Bureau declared it had found in itself the readiness to govern, and mobilized followers to secure control of the legislative and executive branches. Undeterred by this sudden change of heart, Brothers charged ahead without question (Tariq 2013).

In addition to these abstract concepts (virtuousness, patience, etc.), life histories help secure reverence to the leadership. Members are constantly reminded of the terrible sacrifices their leaders had to make. Qutb, the Romantic ideologue who set great store by passionate action, felt that his martyrdom might be his greatest contribution to the cause: it would inflame the feelings of Islamists, discipline their ranks, and provide them with a heroic example of fearless leadership (Yunis 2012: 85). "How could I not trust the virtue of those who spent their prime years behind bars, and suffered humiliation and torture for God's cause?" pondered Mikkawi (2013). This explains why the Brotherhood is keen to familiarize newcomers, especially the young and impressionable ones, with the movement's so-called "prison literature" (*adab al-sujun*). Most of this literature, considering Brothers' scant regard for writing and reading, comes in the form of oral history: "Old Brothers are driven around from one group meeting to another to share stories of pain and loss, their own stories and those of their martyred Brothers. Their presentation is usually so moving that the audience breaks down in tears" (Shatla 2013). The most famous of these roaming presenters is Haj Mabruk al-Henidi, who would tell Brothers how God rewarded him with 55 grandchildren and destroyed his enemies, Nasser and his security cronies ('Eid 2013: 151). There are, however, a number of classic texts. The most widely read – and, not coincidentally, the shortest – is Zeynab al-Ghazali's *Days of My Life* (1999).[7] Zeynab had formed an independent Association of Muslim Women in 1936, but, after offering the oath of allegiance to Banna on the eve of his assassination in 1949, she considered herself part of the Sisterhood. Her claim to fame came later though, when she immersed herself in the desperate attempt to revive the Brotherhood through Qutb's ill-fated 1964 Organization, and landed in prison with dozens of other Sisters. She states in her memoirs that she was shown an order signed by Nasser himself decreeing that she should be tortured twice as hard as men, causing her tormentors to inflict on her as many as 1,000 lashes a day. Zeynab was one of 3 ladies tried in front of a special military tribunal in 1965, along with 40 men, and received a 25-year sentence, though she was released by Sadat in 1971 (Ghazali 1999: 99). Her chilling prison memoirs were further popularized by the regular talks she gave until her death in 2005. Mikkawi, who attended some of these talks, echoed the sentiment among Brothers: "We were so moved when we heard her story, and we began to wonder how could we as young men betray the cause after this old lady had endured so much, and how could we doubt a leadership that counts this saintly figure in its ranks? In all fairness, she taught us manhood" (Mikkawi 2013; Jamal 2013 had a similar experience).

Another living legend is 'Alia al-Houdeibi (2013). Her tribulations spanned two generations, since both her father Hassan and brother Ma'moun were elected general guides (the second and sixth guides, respectively). She recounted how her father, a prominent judge in the late 1940s, longed to retire from the bench and start a lucrative law firm. When the Brothers elected him as leader, after the founder's assassination, he warned his family that if he took on this post they might all starve or get thrown in prison. His wife and children encouraged him to accept. The family's troubles began when the father was first placed under house arrest, months after the 1952 coup. 'Alia recalled how her fiancé had to sneak through the servants' backdoor to meet his future father-in-law. Things took a turn for the worse when the old man received a death sentence in 1954. Although it was commuted to life in prison, and he eventually regained his freedom in 1971, his two-decade tenure as guide (1951–73) was spent mostly behind bars. Meanwhile his wife, son (Ma'moun), and daughter ('Alia) were detained in the mid-1960s. 'Alia was seven months pregnant, and was lucky that the government allowed her to deliver in a hospital – though popular lore in the Brotherhood still has her delivering her newborn in a cold, dark prison cell. Difficulties were not reduced when her brother Ma'moun assumed the top post between 2002 and 2004. He had already spent seven years in prison, and after his release in 1971 the authorities kept harassing him until his last days. While 'Alia herself is considered a role model, she personally feels humbled by the sacrifices of other leaders: "I know they spent most of their lives in prison dreaming about a better future for Islam. I do not feel we have the right to hector them with inquiries about every decision. Not every member is supposed to know everything. It is enough for me to know that we all share the same values." And although her grand-nephew (Ibrahim al-Houdeibi) and her son-in-law ('Essam Sultan) resigned from the Brotherhood with a big bang, she refused even to hear them out during family gatherings: "We never discuss the matter. I do not like to hear anything bad about the Brothers. I know it will only make me upset."

Another member of this heroic generation is Fatima 'Abd al-Hadi. In 1944, before she even turned 30, she was appointed undersecretary of the Muslim Sisterhood, and nine years later she married the revered Brotherhood martyr Youssef al-Hawwash, one of two Brothers executed with Qutb in 1966. Fatima not only knew Banna closely, she also developed strong ties with his family, and was the only non-family-member present at his house while his body was being prepared for burial right after the assassination. She actually helped to carry his corpse down from the house to the police car that was waiting to take him away to the cemetery. Fatima later became a friend and confidante of the family of Banna's successor, Hassan al-Houdeibi, as well as Qutb's family. She got engaged to Hawwash without ever meeting him because he was busy coordinating the Brotherhood's response to the 1952 coup, and only got to spend a little over a year with him in wedlock – during which he was on the run from the police – before he was finally caught. She recalled how, during the few nights they spent together, he would pray all night, and when she complained to her brother, another longtime member of the Brotherhood, he scolded her: "[Your husband's] morals and thoughts elevate him to the sky, while yours keep you stuck on earth. He hangs with the angels, while you live down with humans" ('Abd al-Hadi 2011: 88). Hawwash left her with an infant daughter, Sumaiya, and pregnant with a son, Ahmad, to serve a ten-year sentence. Upon his release, the devout family enjoyed a few months together, before the husband returned to prison in July 1965 to share a cell with Qutb, and to a scaffold in August 1966. Fatima refused to remarry and remained faithful to his memory.

During his long absence, Hawwash had to rely on prison letters to nurture his children. His letter to Sumaiya on her second birthday was quite grim. He sent his daughter a copy of the Qur'an but explained that this was not a birthday gift:

> To be honest with you, my daughter, I do not recognize or accept this celebration [i.e., birthdays] because I find no trace of it in this Qur'an or the Prophet's tradition . . . and everything that is not in this Qur'an and the Prophet's tradition is pagan ignorance: birthdays; Mother's day; the anniversary of the revolution; then the anniversary of the constitution; and spring celebrations. People today have reverted to pagan ignorance . . . I wish you would feel Sumaiya that there is nothing in this world worth celebrating for its own sake, and especially one's birthday . . . only your closeness to God [should be celebrated] . . . Despite all that, I have no scruples in offering you this Qur'an on an occasion worth celebrating and glorifying, that is the holy month of Ramadan in which the Qur'an was first revealed.
>
> ('Abd al-Hadi 2011: 69)

Fatima had another famous Qur'an story, this time revealing the divine grace the family enjoyed. When Hawwash was arrested in 1965, he asked his wife to supply him with a Qur'an. Since they were on a visit to his home village, the only copy available was the one he had sent his son Ahmad from prison a decade earlier. Fatima valued it too much and was reluctant to see it go. Hawwash felt her hesitance and prophesized that, even if he died, God would return the Qur'an to her. Twenty years after his execution, Fatima was visiting her daughter in Saudi Arabia. To her amazement, there was the legendary copy lying on her son-in-law's desk. A stunned Fatima soon learned that, while her son-in-law was praying in the grand mosque of Riyadh, a Brother approached him with her husband's Qur'an. On the morning of his execution, the martyr had entrusted it to one of the Brothers, who immediately fled to Switzerland upon his release. Years later, he heard that a Brother was traveling from Germany to Cairo, and – remembering the martyr's will – took the trouble of traveling there to give him the Qur'an. This latter Brother failed to enter Egypt and ended up in Saudi Arabia where, by mere coincidence, he learned that Hawwash's son-in-law lived in Riyadh and prayed regularly at its grand mosque, and thus finally managed to deliver what had been entrusted to him ('Abd al-Hadi 2011: 73). Brothers retell the story with awe, marveling at God's love of their saintly leaders.

Fatima herself had suffered a horrendous prison experience. She was one of 50 Sisters detained in the summer of 1965, along with the women of the Houdeibi and Qutb families. The imprisoned Sisters included women in their early seventies (such as Hassan al-Houdeibi's wife and sister), young girls in their twenties (such as Houdeibi's daughters and Qutb's sisters), as well as members of the middle generation (like the famous Zeynab al-Ghazali). One of the detainees brought along with her a month-old infant. Another was seven months pregnant, and delivered her son in prison. A third was also pregnant with twins, and died in prison during childbirth. A Sister who was forced to leave her infant behind took charge of breastfeeding the orphans. Fatima herself suffered a hemorrhage after entering prison, and had to have a hysterectomy ('Abd al-Hadi 2011: 77–84). Those who escaped detention did not live in peace either. Fatima's sister, Khairiya, was married to Brother 'Abd al-Latif Mikki, and together they fled to Syria. The husband was tried *in absentia* and lost his Egyptian citizenship. The family was therefore stuck in exile. They were invited to Qatar by Sheikh Qaradawi, who himself was in a voluntary exile. Upon the sheikh's intervention, the Prince of Qatar asked the Egyptian government to reinstate Mikki's citizenship, which they did in 1965. But upon the family's return, the husband was driven straight to prison, where he spent over a year ('Abd al-Hadi 2011: 76).

Another dignified matron is Sanaa' Farghali (2013). Though she was not imprisoned herself, her father, a first-generation Brother and a key member in Banna's militant Special Order, spent long years in prison, and so did many of her family members. She described how her father also relied on prison letters to educate his children – letters she still returns to frequently. She was particularly touched by the fact that her father refused to appeal to Nasser for pardon, as many secular political prisoners did. He taught her, through these letters, that Brothers are bred to accept their fate with dignity. This is why, as she put it, "Even if they make mistakes, my life has taught me that Brothers are noble and trustworthy."

'Abd al-Mon'iem Abu al-Fotouh, who took the lead in merging his Islamic Group with the Brotherhood in the 1970s, confessed that respect for those who lost their best years in prison was a determining factor in his decision to place himself and his comrades under their command. The Brothers were "a legend of endurance and firmness in the face of injustice . . . They were exceptional models of fidelity to an idea, regardless of the pain of detention and torture" (2010: 79). Abu al-Fotouh recognized that there were many ideological and temperamental differences between his puritan group and the politically inclined Brothers, but was confident that their reputation trumped any differences: "An impartial and sincere person could only value the history of those men" (2010: 82). He was personally touched by the romantic affair between Hamida, Qutb's sister, and Kamal al-Sananiri, a Banna confidant. Sananiri's marriage had long captured the imagination of Islamist youth. His first wife had left him when he landed a long prison sentence. Upon learning about his plight from her brother during a prison visit, Hamida Qutb decided to marry him then and there. Hamida had lived to see her brother executed, her sister, Amina, serving a ten-year sentence, and her nephew dying under torture. She was therefore determined to bring happiness to the heart of Brothers. The bride and groom were first united in 1974, a decade after their formal marriage. By that time, Sananiri was 55. And, to the couple's despair, the faithful husband was tortured to death seven years later, during the investigation into Sadat's assassination (Abu al-Fotouh 2010: 76–7). Abu al-Fotouh recalled meeting the soon-to-be-martyred icon:

> When I recall our first meeting, I cannot hold back my tears. It was emotional and moving beyond description . . . In front of me was a man who spent twenty years in prison, and left with a hardened determination to serve Islam . . . His words were like magic. He was the role model I thought I would never find. His presence in my imagination was comparable to the presence of those we read about during the life of the Prophet, those who have been injured and tortured and hurt but endured in order to carry God's message.
>
> (2010: 75)

Of course, Brothers' trust in their leadership is inspired not just by the legacies of those who passed away or into retirement, but by the plight of existing leaders as well. Almost all the senior figures on the Guidance Bureau have been imprisoned, notably the former and current general guides, who both served twenty-year sentences between 1954 and 1974, additional terms in the late 1990s, and again in 2013. Even though contemporaries did not suffer the torture their forebears had to endure back in the 1960s, they still managed to draw the sympathy of Brothers through romanticizing their prison experience. A good example is 'Essam al-'Erian, Guidance Bureau member (since 2009) and deputy head of the Brotherhood's political party. He was detained on five occasions, serving a total jail time of nine years between 1981 and 2011, and was again detained in 2013. Al-'Erian got into the habit of posting some of his prison practices on the Brotherhood's website, recording, for example, how he rose in the small hours of the day to recite the Qur'an, played sports while listening to religious sermons, and spent hours pondering over the great Sufi text *Al-Hikam al-'Ata'iya*. Through displaying their tranquility and inspirational lifestyle, senior Brothers touched the hearts of their young and insecure followers.[8] This is the testament of Malik (2013), a relatively young Brother: "Those elevated to leadership are those most devoted to God. It is their religious devotion that drives them to work harder, and when their Brothers see how hard they work, they entrust them with more responsibilities." Though he never learned the details of the Brotherhood's Renaissance Project, he was confident that those working on it "include the best minds in Egypt, maybe even the world." His father, a forerunner of the Special Order, taught him that details do not matter: "what is important is that we, as soldiers of Islam, value the sacrifice and dedication of our commanders."

Displays of the leaders' righteousness do not only have to draw on their prison experience. Hassan Hatthout, senior leader of the student section during Banna's time, was in fact imprisoned and tortured, but chose to share his sacrifice with Brothers through publishing a love letter he had sent his fiancé before volunteering with Brotherhood battalions in the 1948 Palestine war. Some of the most memorable lines read: "[Religiously] faithful lovers . . . relish in separation if it was for God's sake . . . The love between us flows from God's eternal being . . . Our companionship is for this life and the next . . . Death is our gate to [an everlasting] union . . . O Sister, eternity is never shaken by world affairs . . . Center your life on your relationship with God. Enter His shelter and live under His protection" (2000: 56–9).

Another visible proof of the holiness of the Brotherhood's leaders is that the names of the general guides always reflected the stage in which the Brotherhood found itself – surely, a sign of divine grace. So for example, Banna (the builder) built the organization; al-Houdeibi (the hill climber) raised it above obstacles; al-Telmesani (the seeker) sought the right path for it; Abu al-Nasr (the father of victory) brought it victory; Mashhur (the famous one) made it famous; 'Akif (the engaged) engaged it with society; and Badei' (the splendid) led it to its most splendid era ('Eid 2013: 183–4).

All this, of course, grants leaders almost absolute power over the organization. A close inspection of the Brotherhood's bylaws is quite instructive. The bylaws themselves remained inaccessible to members until 2010. But a textual analysis of the latest version of this fascinating document (last amended in May 2010) reveals how the Guidance Bureau carefully guarded its right to rule. Bureau members are elected if they meet certain conditions (article 7), but the Bureau has the right to appoint additional members regardless of these conditions (article 8). The Bureau is elected for four years (article 9-a), but can continue to serve open-endedly if the circumstances do not allow the election of a new Bureau (article 9-c) – the 2009 Bureau was the first to be elected in 14 years. The Bureau takes decisions collectively, but the General Guide has the right to take unilateral decisions with 4 (out of 16) members, on both urgent and mundane matters (article 11-e). The legislative body, the General *Shura* Council, is composed of 75 members, but can be expanded (by the Bureau) into 90 members (article 12-a), and, although they should be elected according to certain conditions, the Bureau could appoint up to 15 members who do not meet these conditions (article 12-b). The electoral weights of each province in the Council are listed, but the Bureau has the right to adjust them at will (article 13-a). The Council is responsible for legislation, but if the Bureau decides the Council cannot convene, the Bureau has the right to combine the organization's legislative and executive responsibilities (article 32). Notably, the Bureau rarely invites the Council to meet, citing security fears. Also, despite the fact that smaller *shura* councils ought to be elected on the provincial level (article 19) and in turn elect their executive officers (article 25), the Bureau retains the right to suspend the latter (article 30).

But, regardless of the loopholes in the organization's bylaws, the Bureau could simply impose its will. A good example is how, in the 2009 elections, Bureau members wanted to include Sabri 'Arafa, though he lost the local elections in his province (Daqahlia). He was simply allowed to take his seat on both the local and general *shura* councils, and was then elected to the Bureau. Objecting Brothers were told: "Not questioning your Brothers is a sign of faith, and a good Muslim is the one who minds his own business" ("Istiqala" 2012). In the reality-based satire "Sallimli 'ala al-Manhaj!" (Greetings to the Curriculum!), the fictional prefect similarly mocks a Bureau member's opposition to violations of the bylaws: "What bylaws! Did the Companions check the bylaws when the Prophet gave them an order!" The relationship between the Brother and his leaders, the prefect continued, is governed by only three values: "listening, obeying, and trusting." He explained that the Brotherhood had to come up with official bylaws because it operates in a secular Westernized society that is obsessed with laws and regulations. But, in reality, the Brotherhood functions according to one set of laws: Islam. "Bylaws rule men of this world, not [divine] missionaries," the sardonic prefect concluded ("Sallimli" 2010).

To express the Brotherhood's unity behind a single leadership, Mikkawi (2013) compared it to a train: "You could stay on or get off, but you cannot drive it as you wish." The metaphor most commonly used, however, is that of the ship; but not just any ship: Noah's Ark – a metaphor infused with religious connotations. This metaphor is as old as the Brotherhood itself. Sarah Lotfi (2013) remembered how the movement was created at a time of chaos and uncertainty, after the collapse of the caliphate, when there was a need to "bring people together in a society that embodies and preserves Islam." The Brotherhood was therefore principally conceived as a safe ship meant to carry the pious through the storms of dissent. "In a stormy sea," Tag al-Din explained, "if someone jumps off the ship, we are justified to assume he might drown. Perhaps if the weather calms down, we can accept having several ships sailing in parallel towards the same destination. But until then, we must all huddle together onboard" (2013). The metaphor is also used to preach patience. After all, as Qaradawi reminded his readers, it took Noah 950 years to build his ark (1999: 297). Finally, it helps to demystify the Brotherhood's general course:

> In the middle of a mighty flood, the skipper struggles to keep the ship afloat, rather than navigate it towards shore. Noah did not know his final destination. He was ordered to build an ark on sand – which bewildered his faithless contemporaries – and urge believers to get onboard. Those who refused, like Noah's own son, drowned. It was up to God to decide when and where the ark should land. I recall senior Brothers always reciting this verse in our meetings: 'O Son, come aboard with us' – referring to Noah's invitation to his son to join the believers and not rely on worldly means for protection.
>
> (Shatla 2013)[9]

For Shatla, this explains why the Brotherhood is constantly on the defensive, even when it appears to be acting aggressively: "Brothers do not look for ways to sail their ark to a safe destination, but for ways to prevent being overcome by the storm, until God grants them victory through His own mysterious ways." When Shatla asked a senior Brother why the Guidance Bureau decided to compete for the presidency after promising not to, he responded: "If we do not win the presidency, we will end up in jail." In other words, the Brotherhood did not plan to conquer the state to steer Egypt towards a specific end, but largely to "remain afloat," to bide its time until the moment of divine deliverance. The Brotherhood's dramatic fall on June 30 was, to a great extent, the result of this stagnation.

The Social Network

Religious interpretations and metaphors that urge cohesion and obedience help to cement the movement. But people, after all, are the Brotherhood's building blocks. The ideological stress on unity is firmly grounded in dense personal networks. Real friendship (as opposed to simple camaraderie), marriage and kinship ties, as well as business partnerships, strengthen human bonds in ways unknown to any other ideological group. "It is a social rather than an intellectual contract that binds us together," as Shatla put it (2013). Hani described how the Brotherhood's carefully woven web of personal support networks, worship groups, organizational sections, athletics teams, social gatherings, and professional associations envelops each member "three hundred and sixty degrees," all the time and everywhere (Hani 2013). You live in a Brotherhood family, which supplements (and sometimes substitutes) your biological family, and families cluster to create an entire parallel society. "They construct your private and public worlds," Fayez added; "You read Brotherhood literature, written by Brothers on Brothers. You pray in Brotherhood mosques, built and run by Brothers. You marry a Sister nurtured in a family according to Brotherhood guidelines. Even on recreational trips, you meet Brothers, ride buses owned by Brothers, to stay at a place administered by Brothers" (2013: 15).

So if a member loses interest in the ideology, he might still be reluctant to leave. He would immediately be reminded of the fact that: "These are my friends, my wife's friends, my children's playmates, and, in some cases, my parents, in-laws, uncles or cousins, sometimes even my employers or business partners. How could I leave? My life will be devastated, or at least it will never be the same"

(Hani 2013). When Hani resigned, he felt estranged, especially since his wife was a Sister: "I felt like a fish out of water." When Fayez left, his friends turned against him. Even his original recruiter, who had been a friend and teacher for over 20 years, turned away when he saw him coming down the street (2013: 17). Fayez suffered inexorable guilt for 6 years afterwards (2005–11); he felt that he had deserted his Brothers because he was a corrupt person "who did not deserve them." He was also alarmed because he knew that many of those who resigned ended up doubting religion itself in order to relieve themselves of the torment. Frantic, the young Brother implored his old mentors to allow him to sit on family meetings without resuming active membership, but he was turned down. The Brotherhood, they told him, was a package deal, "you take it or leave it" (Fayez quoted in Fakharani 2013). Mahmoud (2013) froze his membership psychologically in 2010, but did not officially leave, so he would not be severed from the community. This largely explains why the Brotherhood has suffered no major dissent in its 85 years (Tammam 2012: 47).

Ahmad al-Bialy (2011), the senior Brother who had become governor under Morsi, had warned in his celebrated article: "Whoever deserts the group will find nothing but estrangement ... His own soul will denounce him, and his family and friends will no longer recognize him ... This is a divine secret." Shatla (2013) tried to provide a less metaphysical interpretation. As a management student, he learned that self-actualization ranks highest on one's hierarchy of needs. The Brotherhood offers members what he described as "a second social chance." In real society, the unskilled end up lonely and unappreciated. But in the society of Brothers, everyone makes friends and acquaintances; everyone gets to be heard and praised, regardless of what they say or do: "You become addicted. If you leave, you go back to being nobody, and you have to survive on your own skills. It is like American college fraternities, but much bigger." He then added with a grin, "When you think of it, it is like a Ponzi scheme. You bank on your social network, even though you have no capital." When the Rab'a al-'Adawiya sit-in was cleared, Shatla noticed that his Brothers were overtaken by fear rather than anger. They panicked because the house that sheltered them collapsed, not just because the idea they upheld was defeated.

This focus on social ties is what makes the Brotherhood unique among ideological movements, political parties, or even religious sects. Sanaa' Farghali (2013) summarized it best: "I did not pay much attention to what the Brothers thought; I observed how they lived. It was their solidarity not their ideas that drew me in." This was crucial for an organization that hosted a variety of Islamist currents, from radicals to reformers, as well as members with different temperaments and interests: idealistic youth seeking change, social introverts searching for company, political activists, philanthropists, public workers, and all the rest. This diversity in goals and dispositions could not be contained, let alone integrated, into a coherent ideological structure. Personal bonds formed the Brotherhood's solid base. And in this parallel community, everyone found what they were looking for.

Like everything else, this was also justified on religious terms. "The society of the Brothers is one where collective virtue overwhelms individual sins," General Guide Telmesani proudly declared; "You never hear a swearword or a curse, but only praise of God, innocent amusement, and unsullied chat" (1981: 39). Sanaa' Farghali (2013) recalled taking strolls with her father down their street where she would see him greet grocers, street vendors, university professors, and lawyers with the same warmth, and refer to them all as his Brothers. Many were attracted by this image of a saintly society. Religious youth could hardly make friends with those they perceived as less religious. They sought those who resembled them in values and behavior. "I stuck with the Brotherhood because I felt comfortable taking my wife and children to their social gatherings," Sameh (2013) confessed. Those still aspiring for piety find it even more necessary to hang out exclusively with Brothers. The more Deif (2013) dwelt in Brotherhood circles, the sharper the contradiction became between the secular lifestyle he was used to and his newfound religiosity; "Seeing how ethical Brothers were was almost a culture shock." Deif was pressed to make an existential choice between his old friends and Islam. Obviously, he chose the latter. And his new Brothers egged him on. Deif's experience was not unusual. In fact, Banna wanted new Brothers to feel the dissonance between their "double, flickering, and contradictory lifestyles," to personally experience the incongruity between Islamic morality and secular decadence, and to resolve this tension once and for all by thrusting themselves into the Brotherhood's arms ([1949] 1993: 141). Very few manage to slip through the net. Unlike Deif, Yasser (2013) refused to discard his old friends, even though most of them were not as religious as he had become. He could not bring himself to follow his prefect's advice to share his personal and professional problems with Brothers he had just met, and continued to confide in his lifelong companions. This is what ultimately helped him to leave when he needed to.

But even those who stay cannot completely detach themselves from their wider society. This is why Brothers and Sisters interact with others using two sets of rules: one for Islamists, and the other for everyone else. Sameh 'Eid described in great detail how they navigate this double existence. In Islamist gatherings, for example, Brothers and Sisters sit separately, but when forced to attend university or professional meetings or even to visit non-Islamist family members, there is no gender segregation. So you might be attending college or employed with a Sister and see other people talk to her directly, but you, as a Brother, should only communicate with her through inter- mediaries, usually a Brother's wife or an old matron. If you knock on a Brother's apartment door, protocol dictates that you take several steps back so that if he is unavailable, his wife can pull the door ajar and whisper inaudibly that you should come back later. But if the porter or grocer comes, the wife would usually open the door all the way and could be heard screaming her lungs out. Brothers also have their own little rituals. For example, Egyptian males greet each other with a kiss on the cheek, but Brothers make it a point to kiss the shoulders. Even the most religious Egyptian would express grati- tude with a simple *shukran* (thank you), while Brothers insist on using the uncommon *jazak Allah khair* (May God reward you with good). Egyptians are not in the habit of taking off their shoes when entering someone's house, but Brothers do – presumably to keep the place pure for prayer. These distinctive rituals help to achieve psy- chological separation, since physical separation is impossible ('Eid 2013: 159–60, 182).

What applies to friends applies even more to families. The Brotherhood had for a long time sought to complement its ideological families with biological ones. This is partly why the Muslim Sisterhood was created. Banna placed a high premium on the role of women in "forming men," and therefore stressed the importance of preserving the chastity of women in order to produce a virtuous community. His first project, back in Isma'ilya in the 1920s, was to institute the School of the Mothers of Believers (*Madrasat Umahat al-Mu'mineen*) for young girls, along with the House of the Repentant (*Beit al-Ta'ibat*) to shelter those who went astray, including prostitutes. Banna established the Muslim Sisterhood in 1933 out of the wives and rela- tives of Brothers, and appointed a female deputy as a link between him and the Sisters. Their oath of allegiance was much shorter and more limited in scope than men's, pledging to "abide by Islamic morals and promote virtue" (Sabbagh 2012: 128–30). The first head of the Sisterhood was an aristocrat, Dame Labiba Ahmad. Ahmad had spearheaded Egypt's first feminist movement with Huda Sha'rawi and Nabawia Musa in 1919, but then broke off with her companions because of their liberal tendencies. After accepting the post, Ahmad penned an article in the Muslim Brotherhood magazine, highlighting her belief that: "The basis of reforming the [Muslim] nation is reforming the family, and the first step in reforming the family is reforming the female, since women are the world's educators, and the woman who rocks the cradle with her left hand, rocks the world with her right hand" (Ahmad 1934). When the Sisterhood moved to Cairo, a 12-member executive committee was formed under Dame Amaal al-'Ashmawi, daughter of the minister of education, and wife of a prominent judge in the state council (Munir Dala, a Brother), and sister of Hassan al-'Ashmawi (another prominent Brother). As another wealthy aristocrat, she owned a spacious house for group meetings (Sabbagh 2012: 135).

Sisterhood activities included recruitment and charity, but one of the most valuable functions was marrying Brothers to Sisters. The cultivation curriculum instructs Brothers to color their homes with an Islamic character: wives must uphold religious customs in dress, tone, nurturing habits; children must be shielded from non-Islamist media and familiarized with sacred history and revelation; Islamic anniversaries must be celebrated and secular ones (including birthdays) shunned ("Madkhal" 1997: 102). To help Brothers meet this goal, they are strongly advised to marry Sisters. This strictly private advice was recently publicized when an insider posted on YouTube a video of Subhi Salih, a movement spokesman, deriding young Brothers who marry women from outside the Sisterhood. Salih scorned those "sissies" (*faluta*) who claim to have found religious partners, who are not Sisters, adding mockingly: "What about those girls we have produced [for you], should we hand them out [to others] for free?" Fallen Brothers who prefer "street girls" to respectable Sisters have not been properly cultivated, Salih concluded. What the Brotherhood wants is for a Brother to marry a Sister to conceive Islamists "by birth," and for all these families to come together in a large Islamist community capable of engulfing the nation.[10] But the Brotherhood has other incentives to press for intermarriage with Sisters. Such wives keep an eye on Brothers, regularly reporting private vices.[11] Also, they represent a means of applying pressure to keep Brothers in the fold. An investigative committee once warned a troublesome Brother that if he did not behave, God would punish him in the hereafter. Then the head of the committee got carried away, turning red and banging his knees: "And we will also punish you right here. Remember that your wife and kids are with us" – meaning that the movement could turn his domestic life upside down ('Eid 2013: 42). In a sense, the Brotherhood is not merely an ideological movement: it is a tribe.

Brothers are generally expected to recruit their parents and siblings. 'Eid, who was married to a Sister, converted his elder and younger brothers, and his sister, and tried – but failed – to persuade his mother to join (2013: 42). And, unless you were married before you joined, not marrying a Sister might cast a heavy shadow over your future in the organization. Mahmoud (2013) said that, before his induction course, his recruiter actually told him and his colleagues that if they were asked whether they were ready to marry a Sister, they must answer in the affirmative or else they would be deselected: "My colleague panicked and said he was planning to marry his cousin. The recruiter seemed distressed, and told him not to mention this to anyone." Some married non-Sisters in secret, but were almost always exposed by other Brothers. Whenever a Brother is ready to tie the knot, he should inform his prefect, who then transfers his request to Sisterhood matrons to select a good match. Senior cultivator 'Abd al-Bar admitted that the process is much more haphazard than it should be: random matches are made and those who refuse are pressured to obey orders ("Taqrir" 2007). One Brother objected to his chosen bride, so his group leader scolded him: "Do you think you are marrying for yourself? You are marrying for God" ('Eid 2013: 162). As one of the founders of the Sisterhood, Fatima 'Abd al-Hadi explained that, although marrying Brothers to Sisters had always been one of the female section's primary tasks, this mission became much more pronounced through the years: "We did not oblige every Brother to marry a Sister, as they do now" (2011: 38–40).

First-generation Brothers and Sisters, as usual, provided a role model. Hassan al-Banna's daughter, Wafaa', was married to his head of student activities, Sai'd Ramadan (the parents of now-prominent European commentator Tariq Ramadan). One of Banna's sisters was married to 'Abd al-Hakim 'Abdin, the Brotherhood's first treasurer, and the other to 'Abd al-Karim Mansur, who was with Banna when he was assassinated. 'Abd al-Rahman al-Banna, the founder's brother and the creator of the Brotherhood's branch in Palestine (later reinvented as Hamas), married in similar fashion. Banna's successor, General Guide Hassan al-Houdeibi, enlisted his three daughters in the Sisterhood, and married off two of them to Brothers, while his son, Ma'moun, became the Brotherhood's sixth general guide. The four siblings of second founder Sayyid Qutb joined the organization (three Sisters and one Brother), and one of them married Brotherhood martyr Kamal al-Sananiri. The first head of the Muslim Sisterhood, Amaal al-'Ashmawi, married Munir Dela, the Brotherhood's undersecretary. She was also the sister of the famous Hassan

al-'Ashmawi, who liaised between the Brotherhood and the Free
Officers, and who, in turn, was married to Sister Qadriya, whose
brother, 'Abd al-Qadir Helmi, was a renowned Brother. Fatima 'Abd
al-Hadi, the Sisterhood's first undersecretary, was married to Youssef
al-Hawwash, one of the three venerated Brotherhood martyrs executed in 1966. Her daughter Sumaiya married Brother Ahmad 'Abd
al-Majeed, who received a death sentence with his father-in-law in
1965, which was commuted to life in prison. Fatima's sister
was married to Salah Shadi, the high-profile Brotherhood representative in the police force, whose two siblings were Sisters. Fatima's
brother, Abu al-Nur, was an active Brother in the student section,
and her two sisters, Khairiya and Thuriya, were married to Brothers.
Finally, Fatima's nephew, Brother Seif al-Islam, married Youssef al-
Qaradawi's daughter. Another founder of the Sisterhood, Fatima
al-Badri, was married to one of the three Brothers executed in 1954.

Organizing the Brotherhood as a cluster of families, with patri-
archs and matriarchs at the head of each cluster, fostered a culture
of deference. Needless to say, family connections opened the door to
nepotism and patronage (Hani 2013). This was especially the case
because family and business frequently intersected. In fact, the cultivation curriculum instructs Brothers to form business partnerships
("Madkhal" 1997: 243).

The Brotherhood was designed to cut across class barriers. Social
solidarity was essential to preserve unity. Members are obliged by
article 10 of the Brotherhood's General Order to provide such solidarity. Upper-class members are encouraged to purify their souls by
helping out those with lesser means, whereas the latter learned to live
contently under the paternalistic care of their social betters. To
balance the potentially divisive drives of the upper and lower eche-
lons, middle-class members, an organizational majority, managed the
whole (Tariq 2013). This brilliant arrangement made everyone happy:
spiritual salvation for the wealthy; immediate relief for the poor; and
political power for the aspiring middle class.

A good example is provided by Sanaa' Farghali (2013). During her
father's extended prison stretches (in 1948, 1954, and 1965–71), his
family's property was placed under state guardianship: "Not a single
carpet could be sold without government approval." But she did not
have to worry because Brothers took care of her schooling, and
eventually all marriage expenses. Ahmad (2013) remembered with
gratitude how the Brotherhood helped to plan and finance his career
shift from engineering to marketing. And Hani (2013) described how
Brothers showered members with financial favors: paying off debts,
furnishing start-up costs, even fixing your car after a bad accident.

These are institutionalized practices. According to the bylaws: "Members of each [Brotherhood] family confront the burdens of life in solidarity, so that if one of them faced setbacks or reversals in his life . . . they are required to cover his expenses and those of his children" (quoted in "Madkhal" 1997: 242). In short, the Brotherhood served as a bank, an insurance company, and a consulting agent. The question is: where did the money come from?[ii]

The short answer is: Brothers donate 10 percent of their monthly income to the movement.[12] Of course, the problem is that no one knows exactly how many Brothers there are. Youssef Nada, one the organization's chief financiers, claims that the Brotherhood receives funds from 100 million members around the world, and calculates that if each member contributed a dollar a month, the Brotherhood could operate with a 100-million dollar budget per month – though Nada admits he has no records to back up his claim (Nada 2012: 61–5; see also Sabbagh 2012: 227). Longtime member Tharwat al-Khirbawi cuts the figure down to half a million fee-paying members (2012: 30). And most Islamist experts endorse this lower estimate (for example, 'Umara 2006: 12; Tammam 2012: 35). When pressed to reveal the real figure, General Guide Mahdi 'Akif swore in a 2009 interview: "I do not know our number inside or outside Egypt. The security services might know better" (Gallad et al. 2009). The current guide said in a 2013 interview with state television that there are no records because of security concerns, but he estimates the number to be about 750,000 members.[13]

A math teacher and seasoned member, Sameh 'Eid, contradicted all the previous estimates. In his calculation, the Brotherhood roughly divides Egypt into 300 districts, each with an average of 60 full members, and 120 juniors, which puts the total at a surprisingly low 54,000 Brothers (2013: 65). If one adds their families and supporters, the Brotherhood's ideological camp would not exceed 200,000. The Brothers' failure to mobilize a sufficiently sizable mass to protect their power in the summer of 2013 might give credence to this considerably reduced estimate. Political scientist Ashraf al-Sharif (2013) used the results of Egypt's first free parliamentary elections in 2012 to calculate the Brotherhood's voting bloc, which includes Brothers, their families, and sympathizers. He argues that the 11 million votes they received during elections to the lower house of parliament – the one that actually legislates – are not a good indicator because

[ii] There have been wild speculations regarding Brotherhood funding. Foreign capital, rich patrons, criminal networks, and other shabby sources frequently come up. This analysis follows the Brotherhood's official line.

Egyptians vote for whoever they think will get things done. A good example is voters in the southern province of Suhag, who in 2005 gave 90 percent of the vote to the ruling party, and in 2011 gave the same percentage to the Brotherhood. However, no one really bothered to participate in the elections to the upper house except Brotherhood supporters, and they ended up garnering 3 million votes.

Away from the numbers game, one could understand Brotherhood funding through examining its financial history. In 1938, Brotherhood treasurer 'Abd al-Hakim 'Abdin obliged each member to invest between a tenth and a fifth of his income in Brotherhood-run companies. The first was the conspicuously labeled Islamic Dealings Company, which began with a capital of 4,000 Egyptian pounds (Banna [1948] 1990: 320). Soon the Brotherhood created a publishing house, mining and weaving factories, as well as land reclamation, trading and advertising companies (Sabbagh 2012: 215). The nationalizations of the mid-1950s, and the socialist laws that followed, restricted private enterprise. But the hundreds of Brothers who settled in the Gulf in the 1960s profited from the oil price hikes of the following decade. Economic liberalization in the mid-1970s allowed Brothers to invest oil remittances back into Egypt's burgeoning consumption bonanza through export–import firms, supermarkets, and money-exchange companies. In the 1980s, Islamists expanded their activities by creating the first generation of Islamic finance companies, which promised astronomical returns (sometimes as high as 30 percent) without usury, to attract the savings of pious Egyptians. Then, after the 1991 Gulf War, thousands returned to Egypt to benefit from the privatization program imposed by the International Monetary Fund (IMF). Brothers now invested in construction, luxury housing, car dealerships, electronics, Islamic schools, media, and tourism (mostly pilgrimage – a multimillion-dollar business). A new breed of Brotherhood businessmen was born (Shatla 2013).

The archetypical example was Khairat al-Shatir. The Islamist tycoon was born to a small landowner and grew up in a humble house in the Nile Delta town of Mansura. Driven by an early political ambition, he joined the socialist Vanguard Organization, and was detained for four months for taking part in the 1968 student protests in Alexandria University, where he studied engineering. Months before graduating, he joined the Islamist student movement, and in 1981 became a Brother. To escape detention, Shatir moved between Saudi Arabia, Jordan, Yemen, and England. He tried his luck in the currency exchange business, but lost a lot of money and returned to Egypt almost broke in 1987. Fortune finally smiled on him when he partnered with Hassan Malik, a wealthy Brother whose family was in the textile business. The new partners launched a computer technology company, Salsabil, which soon expanded into organizing industrial fairs for durable goods. Security closed down the company and detained Shatir briefly for funding Brotherhood activities. It was not all bad though, since his business acumen secured him a seat on the Guidance Bureau, in 1995, where he was put in charge of movement finances. Even after he received a five-year prison sentence for funding the Brotherhood, Shatir continued business as usual, setting up new firms in all fields: pharmaceuticals, tourism, furniture, exported clothes, finance, car dealerships, and information technology. Upon release he was promoted to deputy general guide, and began running his own patronage network within the Brotherhood – one of his first protégés being future President Morsi (Abu-Khalil 2012: 219–29). Al-Shatir received another five-year sentence in 2006. Though he was released following the 2011 revolt, he was not allowed to run for presidency and nominated Morsi instead. Naturally, he was treated as the Brotherhood's mastermind, and as such was one of the first people detained following the June 30 showdown.

Another notable example is Youssef Nada (2012), who joined the Brotherhood in 1960, but spent most of his 52-year membership outside Egypt. Using Brotherhood funds, Nada pioneered modern Islamic finance, and built a business empire in trade, construction, and maritime transportation, with offices in 25 countries in Europe and the Muslim world. This Brotherhood billionaire, christened by George W. Bush, in November 2001, as "terrorism's chief banker," had his accounts frozen by the United Nations between 2001 and 2009, and was tried twice *in absentia* in his home country (in 1966 and 2007) for financing Brotherhood activities. Whereas al-Shatir was considered the movement's finance minister, Nada was officially appointed its foreign commissioner. As such, he negotiated on behalf of the Brotherhood with no less than Khomeini and his successor, Saddam Hussein, the Saud family, the rulers of Qatar and Yemen, and the various Afghani warlords, and liaised with Islamist movements, including the Tunisian al-Nahda. That businessmen, such as Shatir and Nada, could assume such prominent positions speaks volumes on the central role of finance in the life of the organization.

With generous finance, companies providing all types of goods and services, and networks of families and friends, the Brotherhood evolved from an ironclad organization into a largely independent community, living alongside rather than with Egyptians. This parallel existence made it virtually impossible for members to withdraw, even when they disagreed with Brotherhood policies. The reification of the movement also helped to routinize the charisma of its great founders, after the assassination of the first and the execution of the second. Now, the religious halo passed from the founders to the organization itself. But it would be a mistake to focus exclusively on the material organization of the Muslim Brotherhood, and to forget about the binding role of ideology. The truth is that the movement's interpretation of Islam was as important in uniting members as all the other social facts combined.

3

Forging the Ideology

The violent clearing of the Rab'a al-'Adawiya sit-in, on August 14, 2013, was doubtlessly a human tragedy. But, in addition to the death and carnage, it was also an ideological tragedy. The battle to secure Brotherhood power was supposed to be the long-awaited climax in the struggle to restore Islam to its rightful place. That this battle coincided with the holy month of Ramadan, which witnessed most of Islam's early victories, was quite suggestive. Islamists were absolutely convinced – a conviction reinforced every night by their leaders' inspirational speeches – that divine intervention was at hand. They were promised that their deposed president would be miraculously restored to office, and God's empowerment of His soldiers would be complete. They were assured that Archangel Gabriel himself prayed amongst them to support their plight.[1] They heard of sacred visions by holy men and virgin girls celebrating their upcoming victory. And they conjured images of Prophet Muhammad's epic battles against infidels, as well as those of biblical prophets, particularly Moses and David. This was the moment they had always been preparing for: the final trial that would distinguish the faithful from the profane. For about 40 nights, Brothers held vigils, fasting during daytime, and praying from dusk till dawn to make themselves worthy of divine grace. Of course, the rest is history. The only intervention God ordained that hot summer day was that of Egypt's ruthless security forces. The battle was over in a couple of hours, and when the dust settled down it was their enemies who were left standing. Those who saw their sacred campsite laid to waste and their Brothers killed and wounded were utterly traumatized.

This was no historical accident. It had happened before, repeatedly. The ease with which the Brotherhood's halfhearted insurgency in the 1960s was aborted had raised similar questions. After years of hard work, the government simply arrested the entire membership of the 1965 Organization without a hint of resistance. An interviewer asked members of this past generation what their plan was, and they responded that they knew that power was a divine gift (*minna*), so they devoted themselves to God and expected His guidance (Yunis 2012: 313). Sayyid Qutb, the avowed leader of the insurgency, had no experience in clandestine operations, nor bothered to acquire any, since he believed that "the age of miracles has not passed" ([1966] 1980: 1893). Qutb therefore had no practical advice to offer his followers when the government made its move – not unlike the leaders in 2013. In fact, Brothers have always been quite repressible. They operate within the limits decreed by the rulers of the day. They preach in mosques, provide welfare, win elections, and expand their support base. But whenever the government feels like it, they are rounded up without much fuss. Nasser ruled for almost two decades with 40,000 Brothers crammed up in detention camps. And if Sadat had not re-empowered them to undermine the Left, and if Mubarak had not used them as a scarecrow to deter seculars in Egypt and the West from pressuring him to democratize, they might have become permanently consigned to the annals of history. The reason why Brothers caused little more than a ripple in 2013 is that they never prepared themselves for a full-fledged battle, even though they had the capacity to wage one. If it had not been for their militant sympathizers, their bowing out of the political scene would have been even less conspicuous.

The explanation lies in the Brotherhood's unique mindset. "To think clearly is a necessary first step to political regeneration," wrote George Orwell. And indeed, Islamism is based on a clear and simple idea. So simple in fact that it requires no intellectuals or theories: only faith. This idea could be summarized in the Brotherhood's interpretation of the verse: 'If you support God, He will support you' (Qur'an 47: 7). Traditional Muslim scholars understood this verse to mean that if someone undertakes a task with the intention of supporting God, then God endows him with confidence and composure. So if an army wages holy war, for instance, God grants it steadfastness.[i] Islamism is based on a subtle reversal of this standard interpretation. It holds that, if someone becomes pious, God guarantees his victory

---

[i]Check standard exegeses by al-Tabari (d. 923), al-Qurtubi (d. 1273), and Ibn Kathir (d. 1373). Nothing in this interpretation contradicts scientific findings on how missionary zeal enhances worldly performance.

in various worldly endeavors. In other words, if someone perfects his ethics and worship, he becomes eligible for divine intervention on his behalf in politics, economics, and war.

This ideological innovation amounts to no less than an inversion of the conventional understanding of sharia. For 14 centuries, mainstream jurists have believed that the ultimate reward for religiosity was heaven. Otherwise, Muslim rulers and ruled had to muddle through this world relying on the material means of success: building effective political systems, efficient economies, and formidable armies. This is because the world operates according to empirically discoverable laws of causality (*qawanin al-sababiya*), while sharia regulates religious life – even if it sometimes touches on worldly matters. Sharia might decree specific provisions for a handful of criminal offenses, but does not spawn an all-inclusive criminal code; it prohibits certain economic practices, but does not furnish a complete economic philosophy. Implementing sharia, in that sense, is an expression of faith, not a strategy to get ahead in this world. Severing hands is not necessarily better at preventing theft than imprisonment; usury does not cause economic failure; and submitting warfare to ethical guidelines does not bring victory. Indeed, abiding by Islamic law often makes one's life rather difficult – and this is precisely what one is being rewarded for. The recipes for worldly and otherworldly success might sometimes overlap, but never really coincide. This is why the eminent jurist Ibn Taimiya (d. 1328) argued that God bestows victory upon the just state – even if it is infidel – over the unjust one – even if it is Muslim. He understood that justice is the basis of a stable and prosperous polity in this world, regardless of the fate of its rulers on Judgement Day. And when asked whether a strong yet licentious army leader is better than a weak yet pious one, Ahmad Ibn Hanbal (d. 855), one of the fountainheads of Sunni jurisprudence, chose the former, because his strength will enable conquest and his licentiousness will only harm him in the hereafter, while the weak will fail to conquer, and his piety will only benefit him in the hereafter.[ii] Even

---

[ii] The mainstream view is not necessarily the more accurate one. Discussing Islamism's difference from it is meant to highlight Islamism's innovation – not deviation from the right path. This mainstream view could be conjured from various classic texts by the four founders of Sunni jurisprudence, and their most illustrious followers, including Imam al-Haramin al-Juwayni (d. 1085), Abu Hamid al-Ghazali (d. 1111), Al-'Ezz ibn 'Abd al-Sallam (d. 1262), al-Nawawi (d. 1278), al-Qarafi (d. 1285), al-Shatbi (d. 1388), as well as modern jurists, such as Bikhit al-Muti'ie (d. 1935), 'Abdullah al-Seddiq al-Ghumari (d. 1993), and Gad al-Haq 'Ali Gad al-Haq (d. 1966). It is further expounded in interviews with Azhar clerics Khalid (2013), 'Abd al-Bar (2013), and Radwan (2013).

modern-day fundamentalists (*salafis*) subscribe to this view (Khalid 2013).

Brothers turn this traditional conception on its head. Abiding by sharia is no longer just a reflection of religiosity; it is also a way to solicit God's help in advancing in this world. To illustrate using an example from the Brotherhood's jurisprudence, let us consider the case of Friday prayers. A Muslim shopkeeper is obliged to close down for an hour on Friday at noon to attend prayers at the mosque. Traditional scholars urged worshippers to forfeit the income they might incur during this hour for God's sake. Not so for Brothers, who teach their followers that those who shut down during prayers end up making more money than those who do not because their income will be blessed and that of the others cursed (Alfy 2013). So while classical scholars regarded sharia as a religious burden one had to endure, Brothers adopted the unorthodox view that adhering to Islam is the key to success in this world, not just the next.[2] Moreover, they hoped to convince adherents that this was how Muslims had always understood their religion, that their ideology contained no theological innovation (*bid'a*) – a condemned practice in Islam.[3]

Despite this last claim, the Brotherhood commanded 'immanent' rather than 'transcendent' ideological power, to use Michael Mann's vocabulary: it influenced the minds of its own members, but failed to secure universal allegiance for its ideology. And this partly explains why Brothers lost popular backing at such a dazzling speed during Morsi's ill-fated tenure. In his first major speech in parliament, Morsi repeatedly invoked Qur'an verse 9: 76: 'And if only the townsfolk believed and feared [God], We would have poured upon them blessings from heaven and earth.' His audience did not quite understand why their president kept returning to a verse that basically relates Noah's story. Only Brothers deciphered the message: that by obeying God, economic resources would be discovered, political factionalism and social tensions would disappear, and geopolitical rivals would collapse under the weight of their own problems. Apparently, non-Islamist Muslims in Egypt did not all subscribe to the idea that if they waited patiently for Brothers to make good believers out of them, divine blessing would follow. Voters demanded competent leadership with practical solutions. They took the Brotherhood's success in serving local communities as an indicator that they had grand plans for national progress. Brothers indulged them to garner sufficient political clout to implement the cultural transformation necessary to trigger divine support. With single-minded devotion to this concept, they devoted little effort to developing a concrete project that could secure a sustainable majority – thus depriving themselves of a valuable asset in their struggle with old-regime rivals. As soon as it became clear that Brothers had little to offer beyond appeals to patience, mobilizing millions against them was relatively easy. Those who voted for Brothers expected immediate returns. Not many believed in (or cared to examine) the movement's new interpretation of Islam (Alfy 2013).

I refer to this novel interpretation as *religious determinism*. In Hegelian and Marxian thought, when certain historical conditions materialize, change inevitably follows. Islamism maintains, quite similarly, that realizing certain religious conditions prompts historical change – specifically, that producing a godly community triggers a divinely ordained transformation of that community's material situation.[iii] It was certainly hard for an ideology articulated during the 1920s and 1930s not to be tinged by the spirit of the age, with Hegel's world-historical heroes spread by the dozen and Marxism holding sway over minds and kingdoms. But, although determinism was common to both, the secular version proved more adaptable for two reasons. First, Hegel and Marx based their predictions on historical analyses that could later be disputed, while Hassan al-Banna and Sayyid Qutb grounded theirs in a special reading of revelation and sacred history, and accused skeptics of denying divine favor. Second, the preponderance of intellectuals in the field of secular dialectics blunted its determinist edge over time. Islamism, on the other hand, had to do without a Lenin, a Trotsky, a Gramsci, or a Croce, and thus remained stuck in its determinist mold. One must add here that it was hard for Brothers to escape the founders' long shadow, considering that many of the current leaders had been their immediate disciples. It is sometimes easy to forget that Mahdi 'Akif, for example, who joined the Brotherhood when he was only 12 and occupied the position of general guide until 2009, had been nurtured at the hands of Banna himself, and that Muhammad Badei', the current guide, was imprisoned with Qutb.

Religious determinism, of course, is not the term Islamists use to describe their central idea. They present their doctrine in terms of 'comprehensiveness' (*shumuliya*), which is defined in the Fifth Congress Address: "We believe that the rules and teachings of Islam are comprehensive in organizing people's affairs in this life and the next, and that those who believe that these teachings only cover

---

[iii] This is not to be confused with *fatalism*, which implies passive acceptance of one's fate. Religious determinism, in contrast, requires considerable action, but the action is directed towards producing a godly community to prompt historical change, rather than acting on the world directly.

worship and spiritual matters are mistaken. Islam is belief and worship; homeland and citizenship; religion and state; spirituality and practice; revelation and sword" (Banna [1949] 1993: 181).[4] This new creed of comprehensiveness was immediately projected onto the organization itself, described by Banna in the same address as "a puritan movement; a Sunni congregation; a mystic truth; a political association; an athletic team; a scientific and cultural league; an economic corporation; and a social doctrine" ([1949] 1993: 185). And the founder was duly applauded for transcending those Muslim reformers who limited their efforts to one aspect of reform rather than calling for total change in the nation's mind and spirit (Mahmoud 1994: 12–13). Or, as Brotherhood cleric Youssef al-Qaradawi remarked, whereas secular intellectuals sufficed with stimulating the mind, Banna and his followers were spiritual healers, political and economic visionaries, social reformers, and first-rate athletes (1999: 84).

Less hagiographic accounts, such as Richard Mitchell's study of the origins of the Muslim Brotherhood, made clear that this comprehensive Islamic order was conceived "without much specification as to what [it] meant in terms of government theory and practice" (Mitchell 1993: 40). The cultivation curriculum was quite general: "Whenever true Muslims are found, with true faith in their hearts, the Islamic order emerges automatically" ("Madkhal" 1997: 272). Banna preached that comprehensiveness required Islam to become the "public spirit that spreads its hegemony over rulers and ruled alike"; conceived Brothers as this "new spirit that will run through the heart of this nation"; and – in an unfailing Hegelian move – made the state the true repository of public virtue ([1949] 1993: 113, 152, 170). His successor, General Guide Hassan al-Houdeibi, was similarly noncommittal. When pressed to identify what the Brotherhood stood for, he repeated the need for Islam to dominate the affairs of state and society (1997: 21). In his words, the Brotherhood merely signifies the "resurrection of Islam, pure and absolute" (1973: 192). This was a faithful echo of the founder's oft-quoted advice. In a letter addressed to Brotherhood branch leaders, on September 8, 1945, he wrote: "If [people] complain that you are vague, tell them . . . O People! We are Islam" (Banna [1949] 1993: 252).

Yet, despite all this talk of comprehensiveness, Islamism appeared to many outsiders as an ideology of 'negation.' Islamists were defined by what they were against (liberalism, capitalism, socialism, etc.) not by what they practically stood for. Islamists argue, on their part, that their main preoccupation is to revive Islam itself. And the only way they can defend the urgency of this mission in countries teeming with millions of practicing Muslims is by insisting that Islam must be implemented either fully or not at all. Insiders, however, understand that if they succeed in their hoped-for spiritual regeneration, if Muslims become 'knights in the morning, and saints at night,' God will conquer the earth on their behalf. Brothers do not need to concern themselves with how to change the world, but to focus on changing themselves, as in the Qur'an (13: 11): 'Indeed, God will not change a people's condition until they change themselves.' Stated best by Deputy General Guide Muhammad Habib, Brothers consider themselves "a veil for divine power" (2012: 123). He recalls the night of August 20, 1979, when General Guide 'Umar al-Telmesani was invited to a live debate with President Sadat, and solicited the advice of senior Brothers, only to be told not to worry because: "God will speak [through you]" (Habib 2012: 147). Telmesani himself spread this logic among young members: if they devoted themselves to God, He must come to their aid (1981: 77). This is the crux of the Brotherhood's well-rehearsed maxim: 'God mends deficiencies, not negligence' (*Allah yajbur al-qusur lal-taqsir*). As the third general guide explained: "If after exerting our utmost effort we fail to accomplish our objective, and if God knows – and He is the all-knowing – that we have not spared any effort, He would intervene" (Telmesani 2008: 305). In the mind of someone like Sami (2013), a countryside Brother with a humble education, this translates as follows: "If I perform the manageable duties, God will take care of the difficult ones." But in the summer of 2013, God did not intervene – at least not on the Brotherhood's side.

Tragically, Brothers thought this was the year of their divine empowerment (*tamkin*), since they controlled the state for the first time. The blow was therefore much harder this time around. Recall how hard-hit Leftists were in 1989 when they realized that socialism had failed to spread as they had expected. And recall that their frustration was based on the fact that their historical calculations proved inaccurate. Now imagine how they would have felt if they had more than material analyses to support their expectations; imagine if they had the certainty of faith. This was the case with Islamists, who rested their hopes on a carefully construed theological version of history.

Theological History

What use is history for those blessed with revelation? In the case of Muslim Brothers, history was essential to demonstrate that whatever they claimed about the future had in fact occurred before. History had the power to stamp their predictions with the certitude of reality. Marxists and liberals, for instance, could assure their audience that the future should turn out the way they predicted because the past and present point in that direction. However, they could not claim that this promised future had ever been realized before. Islamists, on the other hand, present their followers with a stronger guarantee: that religious determinism not only has worked before, but is the only 'law' Muslims could deduce from their history. Islamism's historical law is an altered version of Ibn Khaldun's thesis that states rise and fall as their founders drift from vigor to laxity. For Islamists, holy men inherit the earth as a reward for their piety, and are doomed to lose it to another godly community when they turn away from their divine provider, become vain and sinful, and believe they could master the world on their own, using material means.

Revelation is used to reinforce this message. Two examples from the cultivation curriculum include Qur'an 24: 55: 'God has promised those who have believed among you and done righteous deeds that He will surely grant them succession upon the earth just as He granted it to those before them'; and Qur'an 5: 54: 'O you who have believed, whoever of you should revert from his religion, God will bring forth [in their place] a people He loves and who love Him [back]' ("Madkhal" 1997: 241). But revelation is only used to buffet Islamist historical logic. As Banna stated: "it is from the pages of history that we derive [the] certainty that [if Muslims] cultivate spiritual strength and moral righteousness, the material instruments of power will hail to them from all directions" ([1949] 1993: 50). This is why, in outlining the Islamist conceptualization of power, in the Fifth Congress Address, he stressed that the "first category of power is the power of belief and conviction, followed by the power of unity and affiliation, then the power of arms and weapons" ([1949] 1993: 199).

As one might expect, Islamist history draws heavily on the texts relaying the life of the Prophet and his Companions. At first, the experience of this founding generation was treated only as a source of inspiration. So, for example, Banna would quip that this or that Brother reminded him of Abu Bakr's mercy, 'Umar's uprightness, Uthman's generosity, or 'Ali's judiciousness. He would also name Brotherhood institutions after Prophetic landmarks, such as the Hara' Institute for Youth, after the cave the Prophet worshipped in, and the Khandaq Club, after the glorious Battle of the Trench ([1948] 1990: 125). He would justify his various positions by drawing on the historical experience of the Prophet, for example when he decided to nominate himself for parliament in 1942 to imitate the Prophet's preaching Islam in the infidels' assemblies, then excused his deal with the liberal prime minister to withdraw his nomination by referring to the Prophet's armistice with infidels, *Sulh al-Hudaibiya* (Sabbagh 2012: 88). Banna's goal was to endow his Brothers with the Companions' belief that they were destined to guide humanity to God's path, and that He would therefore "direct them, provide for them, support them, and grant them victory if people forsake them" ([1949] 1993: 137).

Though this metaphysical view of history was not to be shared with materialist skeptics who might riddle it with unnecessary complications, Banna could scarcely resist invoking it when addressing non-Islamists. For example, in his circular to the rulers of the Muslim world, entitled "Nahwa al-Nur" (Towards the Light), he urged them to return to the Islamic path because history had vouched for its success. Banna added that world leadership was in the hands of the East before passing to Western hands with the rise of Greece and Rome, and returned to the East with the prophets of monotheism and the spread of Islam, before being snatched once more by the modern West: "This was the law (*sunna*) of God that does not alter ... and it is now time for a strong Eastern hand, shadowed by the banner of God" to reach out and assume its due leadership of the world ([1949] 1993: 69–70).

With the second founder, however, began attempts at conscious modeling. Qutb famously started his "Signposts" by condemning the entire world for reverting back to pre-Islamic pagan ignorance, *jahili-yyah* ([1966] 1982: 8). In his view, "History has come full circle to the day this religion was first revealed to humanity," and Islam, therefore, had to be reintroduced to the world right from the start (Qutb [1966] 1980: 1256). Qaradawi endorsed this exciting view: "The nation needed a new message to renew the Prophet's message, and new companions to bear the burden shouldered by the first Companions" (1999: 11). Qutb and Zeynab al-Ghazali therefore refashioned the cultivation process to mirror that of the Companions. Prophet Muhammad spent 13 years in Mecca nurturing his Companions, spiritually and morally, before moving to Medina to establish the Islamic state that would vanquish his enemies. Qutb and Ghazali therefore put together a 13-year cultivation program, after which they could contend for political power (Ghazali 1999: 5, 45). Though this specific timeframe was later discontinued, its spirit was institutionalized. The most recent version of the prefects' training manual clearly states: "Studying the life of the Prophet and the emergence of the [embryonic] Muslim community provides the primary support and essential reference point for figuring out how to execute [our mission]" ("Madkhal" 1997: 88). And the curriculum itself describes cultivation as "a process performed by our ancestors [the Companions] in their everyday life" ("Turuq" 2002: vol. II, 133).

One must not underestimate the huge psychological effect this has had on Brothers. For any practicing Muslim, the founding years of Islam are the golden age he or she grows fond of at home, school, and mosque. Through hearing stories and evocative sermons, Muslims not only learn to venerate this heroic epoch, but also long for it with all their hearts. Joining the Brotherhood offers the closest possible parallel; it takes one back in time through constantly invoking images of the past and striving to relive it. Brothers feel themselves walking through the old streets of Mecca, and dreaming of the day when they would finally establish the ideal community of Medina. But of course – and here is the catch – imposing Islamic rule requires Brothers to become as ready as the Companions were. Cultivation should continue until a blessed lot comes to being. Only the 'generation of anticipated victory' (*jil al-nasr al-manshud*), in Qaradawi's terms, could lead the metaphorical flight from Mecca to Medina (1999: 65).

This helps resolve the endemic debate among students of Islamism over the Brotherhood's position towards violence. Those who denounce the Brotherhood as a terrorist organization point to its violence-laden rhetoric. Those who portray it as a moderate political movement highlight how little violence it has actually committed. The contradiction between rhetoric and action vanishes when one understands the Brotherhood's Mecca–Medina divide. When overpowered, Brothers like to believe they are still in Mecca, when *jihad* was shunned and the only concern was to breed pious Muslims. Like the Prophet and his Companions, they should not be prematurely provoked to battle. At no point, however, do Brothers forget that they are preparing themselves spiritually and physically to conquer the world. Mecca could only be a preparation for Medina.[iv] And the influence of this imaginary division could be detected in post-2013

[iv] Again, the Brotherhood's view of *jihad* is notably different from the traditional one. For mainstream jurists, Mecca and Medina are historical episodes, not replicable models. The claim that Islam could be somehow 're-launched' is quite alien. Once the message of Islam had spread, only a legitimate Muslim ruler (not a political group) could proclaim *jihad* against a non-Muslim *state* (not impious Muslims or individual infidels). Historically, this meant that only the caliph, or dynastic rulers under his nominal rule, could declare *jihad*. The collapse of the caliphate ruled out this condition, since modern rulers, whether dictators or democrats, do not meet the criteria for a legitimate Muslim Imam, who traditionally combined secular and religious functions (Khalid 2013).

Brotherhood debates about whether they might have mistakenly thought they were in Medina because they officially controlled the state, while they were still in fact in Mecca because they still needed more spiritual preparation (Alfy 2013).

Some hope that once they reestablish the glory of Islam in one country, Egypt or elsewhere, "The whole world will stand witness. They will be amazed. It will be beyond their imagination. And they will certainly want to copy our model to replicate our success" (Malik 2013). But Qutb left no doubt regarding the Brotherhood's intentions: "It is naïve to assume that emancipating humanity could be achieved through preaching ... Islam must remove all obstacles by force" ([1966] 1982: 51). Brothers commonly argue that Qutb was radicalized by his prison experience, yet Banna's writings were no less infused with notions of holy struggle. *Jihad* was an important part of his vision for mobilizing youth, bequeathing them a martial spirit, and foiling the global conspiracy against Islam. When devising membership ranks, he reserved the highest one for the 'warrior Brother' (*al-akh al-mujahid*). Banna then went on to form the Brotherhood's first militia, the armed volunteers that came to be known as the Special Order (*al-Tanzim al-Khas*). The militia participated in the 1948 Palestine War, and targeted British camps along the Suez Canal. When the Brotherhood was dissolved in 1948 by an increasingly suspicious Egyptian establishment, the Special Order turned to urban violence, assassinating politicians and judges, and blowing up public buildings. Banna famously disowned these individual acts of violence carried out by overzealous youth, who were "neither Brothers nor Muslims." His successor, Hassan al-Houdeibi, also denied that the Brotherhood attempted to assassinate President Nasser in 1954, although Brother Mahmoud 'Abd al-Latif was caught with a smoking gun.[v]

Curiously, Houdeibi himself, who publicly admonished some of Qutb's excesses, confessed to Zeynab al-Ghazali that when he first read "Signposts" in prison, he became ecstatic and believed that "Qutb is the message's only hope" (Ghazali 1999: 43, 48). The reason for the general guide's optimism might be because Qutb had reintroduced the Special Order in a more systematic way. Since the Brotherhood was too large to provide martial cultivation to all its members, an elite group must be cultivated. Unlike the Special Order, it should not be separated from the main body, but should instead

[v] Whether senior Brothers order specific acts of violence could never be fairly ascertained, but the imagery of holy war and the coming conquests can lead some Brothers to get carried away.

cut through all organizational levels and be represented in every section. The 1965 Organization was the first crude attempt to found this "privileged martial class of Janissaries" (Yunis 2012: 202).

Envisioning the Brotherhood as the reincarnated first Muslim generation offered practical guidelines. In fact, sacred history became the bread-and-butter of movement doctrinaires. Here are a few examples. When the Brotherhood decided to contest the 2005 parliamentary elections with full force, members received a crash course on select verses from the seventh and eighth chapters of the Qur'an (al-Anfal and al-Tawba), which highlight how Muslims won their early battles through dedicating time and money to the cause (Hani 2013). The elections were then presented as a form of *jihad*, and those who did not fully participate were compared to those who had abandoned the Prophet during the bitterly fought Battle of Tabuk ('Eid 2013: 35). Participation in Mubarak's corrupt system was justified by reference to Qur'an's twelfth chapter (Youssef), which mentions how Prophet Joseph accepted a cabinet post under the infidel Pharaoh (Mikkawi 2013). When some complained of the absence of a clear economic agenda, they were reminded of the reign of the Fifth Rightly Guided Caliph, 'Umar ibn 'Abd al-'Aziz, whose virtue all but obliterated poverty, to the point where charity was no longer needed (Malik 2013). When a few Sisters questioned the leadership's decision to nominate the uncharismatic Morsi for the presidency in 2012, the Qur'anic reprimand of Israelites for rejecting Saul's divinely decreed kingship was evoked (Farghali 2013). And when members became frustrated with the movement's post-2011 appeasement of old-regime forces, they were reminded of how Prophet Muhammad forgave his enemies after occupying Mecca (Sami 2013).

Of course, delicate decisions required more profound justifications. Young Brothers indignant with their leaders for abandoning revolutionaries to their fate during the brutal Mohamed Mahmoud Battle in November 2011, in return for a foothold in the new parliament, were placated with a quite novel interpretation of the story of Prophet Moses. Like the Brothers, Moses had a comprehensive reform plan. Alas, his plan had to be shelved for an entire decade because of his hot-bloodedness. For when Moses saw his kinsman being attacked by an Egyptian, he rallied to his aid, killing the aggressor, and then having to flee to escape punishment. The Guidance Bureau heeded the lesson. They would not be dragged into a battle to defend a few hundred revolutionaries at the cost of delaying their grand plan to save millions of Muslims (Tariq 2013).

Successful employment of the founding history of Islam encouraged Brothers to try their hand at more elaborate narratives. If their claims about history were to be convincingly elevated to general laws, the evidence must stretch beyond a single generation. But who could play the role of historian, considering the Brotherhood has none. In the 1940s, Egyptian men of letters, such as Ahmad Amin and Taha Hussein, ventured bold revisionist histories, but their histories offered no clear lessons. Qutb tried to remedy their failure by hiring four Egyptian historians to help him rewrite Islamic history to emphasize the relationship between spiritual struggle and worldly success. But those he found were tainted by the West's secular approach to history (Yunis 2012: 180). A better solution was to ignore properly trained historians and assign the task to trusted Islamists. As Mikkawi (2013) explained, Islamists were unhampered by Western historical traditions, and focused their work on reinforcing the general laws already derived from revelation. By the 1990s, an emerging coterie of Islamist historians had neatly divided Islamic history into a few cycles. And soon these cycles were reduced to a handful of major ones. The best-sellers, expectedly, were the action-packed Ayyubid defeat of the Crusades in the twelfth century, and the Mamluk defeat of the Tartars in the following century. The more thoughtful among Brothers would spare a few extra days to master the eight-centuries-long Muslim reign in Andalusia, or the slightly briefer six centuries of Ottoman rule. Muhammad Sa'ad Tag al-Din, who joined this new wave of Brotherhood historians, surveyed Islamic history from revelation to the collapse of the caliphate to trace how periods of material weakness coincided with those of moral degeneration (2013: 133). He explained how an engineer like himself could take on such a daunting scholarly task as follows: "If one specializes in a single science, say engineering, one develops the capacity to grasp the underlying logic of all other sciences [including history], since all sciences unite at the summit" (Tag al-Din 2013).

Yet, without doubt, the most prolific of this new breed of historians was Raghib al-Sirgani, a urologist by training, who devoted little over a decade to interpreting 14 centuries of Islamic history, from the birth of the Prophet to the 2011 Arab revolts and everything in between – mostly in his spare time, since he also practiced medicine and taught urology at Cairo University. His work was first posted on his website (islamstory.com) in the form of audio lectures (an average of 12 hours per historical cycle), subsequently transcribed into over 50 volumes (all downloadable from his website). Sirgani also penned dozens of historically inspired political pamphlets; appeared regularly on Islamist television channels; and became a frequent guest in Brotherhood battalion trainings and camps. As one might suspect, such a fast-track research project by a part-time amateur could at best provide historical snapshots. So, despite casual references to politics and society, the overwhelming focus is on the Muslim community's oscillation between virtue and decadence. The lesson – unsurprisingly – is that the virtuous conquer, and the corrupt falter. A case-in-point is the 'tragedy of Zeriab,' which Sirgani recounted in a 1-hour lecture. This debauched folksinger led astray the otherwise somber and godly community of eleventh-century Córdoba, leading to their defeat in battle. In contrast, the saintly Almoravid brotherhood isolated themselves from their decadent North African society, and led an austere life modeled after the first Muslim generation. They were rewarded with successive conquests in Africa, crowned by a resounding victory against the Franks of Andalusia. Unfortunately, once the second generation of Almoravids became morally corrupted, their dynasty crumbled, even though their armies were still intact.[5] Military effectiveness, in other words, is not a function of size or arms; it simply hangs on the moral character of the community. Brotherhood historians teach Brothers what they already know: a pious leadership that enhances its subjects' religious commitment brings them victory.

Sirgani was also fairly imaginative in providing parallels between the Brotherhood's behavior and that of the Prophet and his Companions. When young Brothers complained that their leaders failed to punish the corrupt politicians and officers of the old regime after 2011, Sirgani won them over by an elaborate analogy. Here the Islamist historian recalled the crisis that followed the murder of the third Caliph 'Uthman at the hands of thugs run by the Islam-hating Jew Ibn Saba'.[vi] Muslims divided over whether the fourth Caliph 'Ali should punish the perpetrators first or stabilize the polity. The dispute led to two horrendous battles, in which dozens of Companions were slayed. Sirgani argued that Egypt faced the same situation in 2011, when thugs, probably run by Jewish conspirators as well, were causing havoc to divide Muslims. The Brotherhood chose to follow in Ali's footsteps and postpone any action against Egypt's old-regime criminals until they consolidated power. And young Brothers should take heed from the past and not spark another civil war.[6]

History was again invoked, in December 2012, when civil activists surrounded the presidential palace to protest against the Brotherhood's new constitution. An internal pamphlet comparing the old and new Battle of the Parties on 11 points circulated among Brothers. It equated the alliance between the Jews of Medina and the infidels of

---

[vi] The conventional view is that the caliph was killed by rebels from Egypt and Iraq over a political dispute.

Mecca to the emerging alliance between the secular activists in Egypt and Western powers, and pointed out that in both cases Muslims were placed under siege, in Medina and the presidential palace; in both cases they sought a peaceful settlement, the Prophet negotiating with infidel tribes and President Morsi with secular leaders; and in both cases God rewarded His servants with victory. The comparison naturally ends by charting the future course: just as Muslims punished the traitors of Medina (Jews of the Bani Quriza tribe), they should act decisively against modern-day traitors.[7]

Sirgani's website also featured the work of other Islamist historians. One such historian is 'Abd al-Halim 'Uwis, a graduate of Cairo's Teachers' College, like Banna and Qutb. 'Uwis was mentored by the Brotherhood's cleric Muhammad al-Ghazali; joined Qaradawi's International Union of Muslim Scholars; and secured a position as professor of Islamic culture at Riyadh's Ibn Saud Islamic University. When he died in 2011, an impressive Guidance Bureau delegation adorned his funeral at his hometown of Mahala. Indeed, the cultivation curriculum features many of 'Uwis' historical insights, such as the one in which he lists 40 reasons for the fall of Andalusia – mostly things like "following infidel customs, traditions, and laws . . . indulging in entertainment, singing, luxuries . . . committing sins openly" ("Mabadi'" 2003: vol. III, 232–3).

Reviewing his copious oeuvre is instructive. 'Uwis contributed a 30-volume interpretation of the Qur'an for youth; a 13-volume encyclopedia on contemporary Islamic jurisprudence, which covered everything from proper worship to health care, gender issues, economics, and criminal justice; and another 7-volume encyclopedia on Islamic administration. 'Uwis then went on to publish 57 books on all aspects of Islamic history. If this does not convey the breadth of his reach, it is enough to mention that in a single volume – and not a very long one for that matter – he determined the causes of the rise and fall of 30 Muslim polities. A year before he passed away, in 2010, he published his *Falsafat al-Tarikh* (Philosophy of History), a short book with an ambitious subtitle, "Towards an Islamic Interpretation of the Cosmic Laws and the Social Rules."

'Uwis began this book with epistemology, stating that the history of Prophet Muhammad and his Companions has been handed down to Muslims from such authentic sources and in such minute detail that they must take it for granted. In other words, this sacred history "could no longer be considered a matter of historical interpretation, but rather historical beliefs, endowed with the certainty of religious beliefs" ('Uwis 2010: 20). In contrast, he went on, pagan, Jewish, and Christian histories have been distorted to reinforce their false values ('Uwis 2010: 91). 'Uwis then turned to theory, noting regretfully that, although the Qur'an provided Muslims with a comprehensive framework for interpreting history, traditional scholars remained blind to it until the twentieth century when Islamists came along. What is this framework? In a nutshell, there is a causal relationship between the spread of sin and the fall of nations. And sin itself results from the "intellectual perversity" of adopting foreign ideas and values. This leads to the mental and psychological defeat of individuals, and ultimately the nation's downfall. The conclusion: "It is deviant morality that is the path for civilizational collapse rather than material or technical weakness" ('Uwis 2010: 151–60).

What the great historian Ibn Khaldun missed, according to 'Uwis, is that socioeconomic and political factors count less than religious ones in Muslim history (2010: 123). This is because Muslim history revolves around the battle between good and evil, while secular histories are consumed in class or national conflicts ('Uwis 2010: 203). This last bit distinguishes Islamism from other religious or intellectual schools. Unlike puritan preachers who invoke revelation to warn their congregations against the Lord's wrath, Islamists claim to have arrived at this law inductively through empirical study. But, unlike secular historians and their general patterns, the Islamist historical law is theologically qualified by the fact that it only applies to Muslims. It is a special law that God has devised for Muslims alone, and has revealed to them through their own history. As Sirgani elaborated time and time again in his work: divine wisdom decreed that non-Muslims could succeed through material means, but Muslims cannot do without religion lest they turn away from their creator. This is a sign of divine mercy, Sirgani explained, because if Muslims thrive without Islam they might abandon it and become too attached to material means. To keep them perpetually attached to Him, God made victory in this world contingent on religiosity, not material means. Therefore, general historical patterns do not apply to Muslims; and those of Islamic history do not apply to anyone else. This brilliant tweak is essential to justify to Islamists why Western nations were so powerful in every aspect despite their immorality (Tariq 2013). By the same token, it explains why the Muslim world has so many resources, yet remains underdeveloped. "It must be divine punishment," Malik (2013) conceded.

A classic case study is the Muslim defeat in the Battle of Uhud, Islam's second great battle against the infidels of Mecca. Before the battle, Prophet Muhammad stationed a squadron of archers on a hill and asked them not to leave their post under any circumstances until he personally called them down. The battle first ended with a Muslim victory, but as soon as the enemy fled, the archers rushed down to secure their share of the loot. The Muslims' back was thus exposed, allowing the army of Mecca to outflank and defeat them. The question is: why were the Muslims defeated? Traditional Muslim scholars and historians provided a straightforward answer: because of the tactical mistake of the archers. Islamists had a different interpretation. The tactical mistake could have been easily salvaged if God wished it to be. The enemies might not have noticed the Muslim vulnerability, for instance. But God decided to punish Muslims for disobeying His Prophet. In other words, the cause of defeat was metaphysical not material (Khalid 2013).

The cultivation curriculum is designed to hammer home this specific theme. It makes clear that victory is "a divine reward in which material causes are suspended and miracles and wonders appear," and that this is meant to strengthen the bond between "the heart of the believer and divine grace." The pious should therefore "detach themselves from victory, from its means and ends" and accept that it is merely the outcome of God's absolute will. However, Muslims should not remain idle, but rather should redirect their energy towards spiritual elevation, since there is a causal link between "military battle and purifying souls" ("Turuq" 2002: vol. I, 117–19). The curriculum quotes the second general guide's advice: "Your primary battlefield is yourself. If you conquer it, you could conquer anything else" ("Turuq" 2002: vol. I, 453). And, of course, the curriculum could not have failed to add that some of the most dangerous sins are "doubts, objections, and protests" against the leadership ("Turuq" 2002: vol. I, 139). Likewise, accepting material theories of causality leads to defeat because secular historians see only the "apparent causes and superficial circumstances" and are deprived of witnessing God's handiwork. Those who are taught by God Himself have no need for professional historians ("Turuq" 2002: vol. I, 141).[8] Of course, the Battle of Hunayn represents the paradigmatic case study. Here a strong and well-armed Muslim army fled the battlefield upon encountering a much more inferior army. The curriculum introduces Qur'an 9: 25, which discusses: 'the day of Hunayn when your great numbers pleased you, but it did not avail you in the least . . . then you turned back, fleeing.' And the conclusion is: "reliance must be on God not on numbers and weapons," since victory belongs to the faithful ("Turuq" 2002: vol. I, 274).

None of this was new. The contribution of the movement's historians was limited to providing hard evidence for long-held Islamist beliefs. Ghazali had famously declared a few decades back: "I do not hold the Tartars responsible for destroying the caliphate in Baghdad.

The caliphate collapsed under the weight of palaces steeped in sin . . . I do not hold the Crusaders responsible for abolishing our rule in Andalusia. It was the effeminate and sumptuous [Muslims] who pulled down the Islamic banner from those green valleys" (1981: 11). The Brotherhood cleric even exonerated modern Western colonialism from its devastation of the Islamic world by laying the responsibility at the doorstep of Muslims who have abandoned their religion and were deservedly abandoned by God (Ghazali 1981: 17).[vii] The law was even more precisely stated in General Guide Hassan al-Houdeibi's assertion: "In mathematics, one plus one equals two. Not so with God" (1973: 100). He remarked in a June 1953 lecture commemorating Islam's first military victory that the Prophet's greatest worry before the Battle of Badr was that his soldiers would rely on their numbers and weapons, and forget that they could only be victorious if they did not sin while their enemies did. The general guide thus advised: "fight your passions and desires before you fight your enemies" (Houdeibi 1973: 117, 126). And he used a short story to elaborate. A Brother once attempted to blow up a British munitions depot on the Suez Canal, but it was heavily guarded and surrounded by barbed wire, so he fled. That night he pondered his failure, and blamed his past sins. He repented wholeheartedly, performed the ritual wash, prayed for forgiveness, and returned to the British camp the following night. And lo and behold, he found the wires torn and the guards staring blankly at him without seeing him – as if blinded by God. He accomplished his mission and returned safely home (Houdeibi 1973: 130–1). Houdeibi concluded dramatically, "We are like the shepherd who was asked why he was not guarding his sheep [from the wolf], and replied: 'I have mended my relation with God, and so God mended the relation between my sheep and the wolf'" (1973: 265).[9] Another senior leader, Muhammad al-Behiri, mentioned how a spiritually equipped Brother blew up a train full of British soldiers and emerged unscathed ('Eid 2013: 72). A Brother based in al-Azhar stuck the same chord with an article published on the Brotherhood's Freedom and Justice Party (FJP) website. According to Sheikh Muhammad 'Abdullah al-Khateeb, the Zionists panicked when they first confronted the martyrdom-seeking Brotherhood militia in 1948. Whenever they heard their distinctive hymn – 'Rise Scent of Paradise, Rise' – the Jews would simply drop their weapons

---

[vii] One should mention that Ghazali lamented in his final years: "I have [finally] learned that our [Islamist] understanding of Islamic history is superficial, and that of the history of humanity is a little over nil" (quoted in Qaradawi 2000: 255).

and flee. Banna foresaw this, Khateeb continued, and assured those Brothers who had no weapons to travel to Palestine without fear, since they could collect the weapons that Zionists would leave behind.[10]

Of course, members with some familiarity with history as an academic discipline realized something was amiss. Sarah Lotfi (2013), who trained as a political scientist, found it a little odd that Islamist histories glossed over the socioeconomic, political, and geopolitical contexts of the events they studied. She nevertheless preferred them to secular histories that overlook the role of spiritual and metaphysical forces. Tariq (2013), who was taught to dismiss material interpretations of history, decided to learn more about the conventional Islamic view. Browsing through Islamic websites, he stumbled upon an unlikely mentor: a Saudi cleric by the name of Hatim ibn 'Arif al-'Awni, who took Islamists to task for investing too much in divine intervention. 'Awni highlighted the fact that, despite the presence of the most pious Muslim generation in seventh-century Mecca, God postponed war until a proper city-state was established in Medina because war, like anything else in life, required material power. Furthermore, as 'Awni argued, securing material power in the modern world requires experts in politics, economics, and war, not enthusiastic Muslims with amateurish interest in those fields. His conclusion was harsh: snubbing material power in anticipation of some sort of miracle amounts to heresy.

But Tariq's critical approach was fairly uncommon. When a group of Brothers attended a lesson by a non-Islamist professional historian on the causes of Saladin's defeat of the third Crusade, they were torn between their sympathy for this well-meaning historian, and their tendency to humor outsiders to conceal their peculiar views on history. After much discussion, they decided that the best way to enlighten this deluded historian, without subjecting themselves to scrutiny, was to present him with a gift-wrapped book on the true causes of Saladin's victory. The 500-page tome dwelled, in a painfully repetitive prose, on the great warrior's piety: how he led his court in prayer; how he humbled himself to religious scholars; how he chose his generals and ministers from among the most devout; how he filled his time with supplication; and how his worship became particularly intense before battle (Alfy 2013).

One can hardly overstate how this distinctive mindset has influenced Brothers' everyday practices. On a trivial level, they would frequently hear about the Brother who was asked to stay home by his prefect, but then disobeyed him, and as a result ended up in a car accident; or the one who married against the leadership's wishes and suffered an ugly divorce; as well as other numerous examples of what they call 'sin's bad omen' (*shu'm al-ma'siya*) ('Eid 2013: 188). More substantially, however, Islamism's unique historical law has shaped their political understanding. As Hani (2013) pointed out:

> For years, we were told that the reason why victory has been withheld for so long was because of the irreverence of a handful of members, who are either negligent in their worship or not entirely obedient to the leaders. Each of us was repeatedly warned that he might be delaying victory because he was not striving hard enough on the path of piety: he was missing dawn prayers, or not fasting two days a week, or not performing enough complementary acts of worship. We therefore constantly interrogated ourselves.

In fact, an anxious Hani once queried Sirgani on this question, and the Islamist historian responded unflinchingly that, according to his historical calculations, the Brotherhood's empowerment was overdue, and that it must be the moral deficiencies of Brothers that were holding it back. Ibrahim al-Houdeibi (2013) further elaborated:

> During battalion trainings, coordinators would administer questionnaires recording how many times we performed prayers at the mosque, and how often we did this or that act of devotion . . . When our performance was found lacking, we would be castigated for allowing Muslims to suffer in Palestine and elsewhere because we were too lazy to worship. Even a minor slip-up in organizational activities, such as putting together a freshmen's reception at college, would be immediately blamed on the organizer's lax moral standards. My old prefect recently wrote on his Facebook page: 'no misgiving occurs without a sin, and none is lifted without repentance'. I asked him: what about prophets and saints, who suffered through no fault of their own. He never responded.

This attitude shifts responsibility from leaders to followers. Movement failures become occasions for self-flagellation among members. It also extends leaders' considerable latitude in adopting policies they previously condemned. During a Friday sermon in a Brotherhood mosque in California, Mubarak's brokerage of a ceasefire agreement between Hamas and Israel in January 2009 was passionately denounced. How could Egypt abandon the Palestinians in Gaza to the Israeli war machine and then add insult to injury by forcing them to make peace with the aggressor? But when Morsi mediated a very similar truce under very similar circumstances three years later, the same California-based cleric warned those who dared compare the two positions that

Mubarak never intended to fight the Israelis and was therefore a traitor, but the Brothers were equipping the nation spiritually for *jihad* – even if this took decades – and were therefore heroes. Sensing that his congregation was not completely convinced, the cleric drew a trump card from history. Citing some obscure narration, he claimed that during the seventh-century Islamic conquest of Persia, 100,000 Muslims rode their horses over water to pursue their enemy across the river – a 'saintly miracle' (*karama*) they earned through piety. The Brotherhood was preparing a nation that would deserve such miracles in battle. Faced with a still skeptical audience, the cleric concluded defiantly: "If you reject this story, it is because the materialist ideas of this foreign society you inhabit [America] have corrupted your faith."[11]

In a lecture delivered two months after the 2011 popular uprising, Sirgani shared with a huge crowd how the revolt demonstrated Islamism's special historical law.[12] Although Islamists did not trigger the revolt, they should not hesitate to grab power because the overthrowing of Mubarak was their divine reward. In fact, the revolt vindicated the Brotherhood's unique law in the face of increasing in-house criticism. During the last decade of Mubarak's rule, young, urban Brothers pressed their leaders for a more concrete confrontational strategy, since spiritual struggle seemed insufficient. Their leaders counseled patience. Then came the January 25 revolt, when a bunch of well-intentioned civil activists, supported by millions of desperate citizens, forced Mubarak to hand authority to the supreme military command, which, in turn, decided to transfer power to an elected authority, which turned out to be the Brotherhood – divine intervention indeed (Jamal 2013).

This is why Malik's (2013) main concern during the Brothers' remarkably short tenure in power was that they might become too preoccupied with politics and economics and forget about worship: "My only fear is that they start banking on their worldly skills and turn their back to the mosque. Internal and external enemies cannot overthrow them unless they begin to believe they can do without divine blessing." His sentiment, notably, echoed that of first-generation Brother Hassaan Hatthout, whose concern was that the Brotherhood might become so successful politically that it abandoned its role in "transforming Egypt's entire population into a faithful nation . . . [endowed with] morals and spiritual depth." Once this was achieved, coming to power and "all the rest should be easy" (2000: 112–14). Little has changed since the 1950s, when Hassan al-'Ashmawi, the Brother charged with liaising with the Free Officers, attributed the movement's crushing political defeat to its neglect of the sacred mission to rescue Muslims "immersed in amusement and frivolity, and preoccupied with desires, pleasure, and egotism" (1985: 13). Malik, Hatthout, and 'Ashmawi testify to the effectiveness of the cultivation curriculum, which warns that those who press the Brotherhood to shift from producing pious Muslims to material strategies are pushing it away from divine empowerment ("Turuq" 2002: vol. I, 497).

With such a mindset, any setback, including the defeat of Islamist rule in 2013, is presented as a divine test of the Brothers' religious steadfastness. Brotherhood cleric Fawzy al-Sai'd proclaimed on stage at Rab'a al-'Adawiya that: "Whoever doubts Morsi's return [to power], doubts the existence of God Himself."[13] Some solemnly swore in front of thousands of protesters that General Sisi was the Anti-Christ.[14] Those implored by friends and family to leave the sit-in before disaster struck heard these verses recited night after night: '[Remember] when the hypocrites and those whose hearts are diseased said, "Their religion has deluded them." But whoever relies on God, then indeed God is mighty and wise' (Qur'an 8: 49).

Two weeks after Morsi's ousting, Sirgani noted on his website that, whenever Brothers feel confused, they ought to return to the Prophet's life to judge their current situation: "Are we in [the Battle of] the Trench, so we must persist until God prevails, or are we in [the Battle of] Uhud, so we must withdraw ... and treat our hearts' sickness before trying again."[15] A month later, he seemed to have made up his mind, alerting besieged Brothers at Rab'a that they were in the same position as Moses and the Israelites who were chased to the sea by Pharaoh and his soldiers and thought they were doomed before God parted the sea to save them and drown their enemies. Brothers only needed to keep the faith, as Moses did (Tariq 2013). Shortly afterwards, Khadija, the daughter of leader Khairat al-Shatir, proclaimed in front of her father's prison cell that "God will part the sea" for the believers and destroy the new Pharaoh.[16]

Tag al-Din (as Tariq 2013 reports) offered a more elaborate comparison. The fight over Brotherhood rule in the summer of 2013 replicated the one between Saul and Goliath, which ended with the defeat of the tyrant and the establishment of the Kingdom of David. Morsi here is cast as Saul, who was crowned by God despite his people's reluctance. Saul knew he was destined to fight an epic battle against Goliath, and those who have become attached to his corrupt ways – an allusion to Egyptians longing for the return of the old regime. To test his soldiers, Saul ordered them not to drink from a river they came across despite their thirst, just as Morsi asked his followers not to accept the coup despite their weakness. The few who passed the test and crossed the river, or camped in Rab'a in the present-day story, are the true believers. Saul's faithful soldiers were rewarded with a miraculous victory – a single slingshot from a lonely shepherd by the name of David knocked down the enemy – and Morsi's followers should expect no less. So when Shatla (2013) tried to reason with his longtime friend – and key minister under Morsi – that Brothers must accept tactical defeat, he barked back: "Are you going to drink from the river?" In Tag al-Din's narrative, however, a final test remains. When the armies lined up, the Israelites complained, as in Qur'an 2: 249, 'We have no power today to face Goliath and his soldiers.' Only those who had absolute trust in God's support responded: 'How often has a small faction defeated a larger one with God's permission?' These faithful few would soon discover that it only takes a slingshot from a poor shepherd like David to destroy a mighty army and build God's kingdom (Tariq 2013). Brothers expected this slingshot when their enemies struck on August 14, but to no avail.

One must wonder, however, to what extent this special historical law could be used to justify movement blunders. And the answer lies in Mikkawi's (2013) sanguine disposition: "Time is open-ended. Victory is inevitable. God promised we would eventually prevail." "God does not support us because of who we are," Sami (2013) explained, "but He supports us because we are the custodians of His religion. We work for Him alone and He guarantees our triumph, even if only at the very end of time, at the Day of Judgement." Prophetic narratives foretell that a Rightly Guided Caliphate will materialize before the Final Days, and, with enviable optimism, Sana' Farghali (2013), already in her sixties, hopes to see it through. The only source of frustration for Malik (2013) is that not all Muslims are as stoical. With his head bowed, he recited the verse (Qur'an 12: 21): 'And God will prevail in His domain, but most people do not know.'

The Power of Dreams

Sacred history is complemented by history made sacred. Brothers recorded their own past in hagiographic accounts, memoirs, and well-rehearsed anecdotes. The function of these records was to demonstrate Islamism's unique historical law in action, to show how God had in fact bent the rules for His pious servants. Brothers learn, for example, that, before Banna succumbed to his wounds, in February 1949, he implored God to devastate the realm of the king who ordered his assassination. And verily so: the 1952 coup overthrew the Egyptian monarchy. They are also told that when Nasser ratified the execution of Qutb, in August 1966, the second founder cursed him on his way to the scaffold. And in less than a year, Nasser's state was spectacularly defeated in war. Similarly, Sadat was assassinated days after he detained General Guide Telmesani, in September 1981 (Alfy 2013). And in September 2011, General Guide Muhammad Badei' declared in a visit to Upper Egypt that the 2011 revolt was "a blessing from God and not the product of any individual, group, or political party effort. All due is to God."[17]

But many of these divine favors occur on the individual rather than the national level. The cultivation curriculum recounts how Banna was once invited to Cairo University (or the Muslim Youth Association, in another version) to refute the secular views of Taha Hussein, one of Egypt's literary giants in the 1940s. Once he took the podium, it was as if God held the book in front of him and allowed him to flip through its pages. This miraculous feat drove Hussein – who was hiding backstage – to meet him secretly afterwards and confess that he was so overwhelmed by Banna's critique that he was willing to revise his views ("Mabadi'" 2003: vol. III, 261; Sabbagh 2012: 84). Zeynab al-Ghazali recalled that, on her first night in prison, she was dressed in white and locked in a cell full of rabid dogs for 3 hours. She closed her eyes and began to pray. Claws and teeth tore into her flesh and she felt herself soaked in blood. When she was finally released from this horrendous ordeal, she opened her eyes and there was nothing. Her clothes were shining white and there was not a single scratch on her body (Ghazali 1999: 56–7). On another occasion, her captors sent a giant man to rape her. She bit him after yelling: "In the name of God!" The monster instantly fell dead at her feet. Next, her captors took her to a small room and released dozens of rats through the window. She recited a short prayer and the rats marched back out of the window in single file (Ghazali 1999: 118–20).[viii] Deputy General Guide Muhammad Habib experienced a less dramatic, though equally mystical, episode. Habib ran for the 1987 parliament in Egypt's southern province of Asyut. On the night of the vote, he saw in his dreams a prominent Islamic scholar running towards him, crying 'God is great!' He woke up and told Brotherhood campaigners not to worry and to leave it all to God. And, sure enough, he won – but not before witnessing an incident that under-

---

[viii] The rest of Ghazali's memoir contains instances of torture that did affect her. In a sense, her story combines saintly protection with mortal heroism and endurance.

lined the supernatural element in his electoral victory. When Habib was on his way to the polling station, he found himself driving behind an anti-Islamist professor, also on his way to vote. A few hours later, a mutual acquaintance told Habib that this professor recounted the most bizarre story to him. Although he intended to vote against the Brotherhood, when he saw Habib in the rearview mirror, his body began to shiver to the point where he could no longer control the steering wheel. So he parked the car and walked to the voting booth, almost hypnotized. And to his shock, the pen ticked the box next to Habib's name against his wish (2012: 209).

These small miracles are prevalent enough in the personal histories of Brothers, but much less so than dreams – the last form of communication between heaven and earth, according to one Prophetic narration. Dreams, as a sign of blessed knowledge, are sanctioned in Banna's Teachings: "true belief and correct worship and struggle generate a God-instilled light in the hearts of the chosen ones," and these "inspirations, thoughts, revelations, and omens" could be considered a form of divine knowledge ([1949] 1993: 305).[18] Picking up on this note, the cultivation curriculum instructs prefects to dissect with Brothers the various types of dreams and train them on how to interpret them and ascertain their legitimacy ("Madkhal" 1997: 36; "Turuq" 2002: vol. II, 148). The founder added in his memoirs that a "good omen is the believer's blessing in this world" ([1948] 1990: 13), and recounted one of his personal visions:

> [During adolescence] I saw myself in the village graveyard. An enormous grave shook hard before it burst open, releasing a flame that reached the sky before assuming the shape of a giant. He [the giant] told those gathered around that God had allowed them to commit all [the sins] that He had prohibited, that they were now free to do as they wish. I alone stood up to him and yelled: "Liar!" before turning to warn the crowd: "O People this is cursed Satan coming to tempt you ... do not listen to him."
>
> (Banna [1948] 1990: 26)

This and other visions confirmed the founder's sense of mission. Banna also mentioned other members' dreams, such as the 70-year-old Brother who dreamt he was guarding the movement's camp in Asyut during the summer of 1939 with a sword in his hand (to mimic first-generation Muslims) and found himself suddenly shouting 'All praise be to God!' until he saw a bolt of light between the camp and the sky above ([1948] 1990: 341). A man informed Banna's wife, in a dream, of the day of her son's death weeks before; and the same man reappeared to warn her of her daughter's death – and this time

Banna borrowed money to prepare for the funeral days before the daughter even got sick (Hatthout 2000: 22–3). In fact, Banna learned of his own assassination the night before in a dream and told his family (Sabbagh 2012: 222).

Zeynab al-Ghazali saw the Prophet four times during her time in prison, and he reassured her in the first dream: "You are on the right path Zeynab, you are on the right path" (Ghazali 1999: 60). On another occasion, her tormentors tried to starve her to death, but when she fell asleep, she saw angels dressed in black silk and white pearls bringing her meat and fruit on trays of gold and silver. She ate with pleasure, and when she woke up she felt full – in fact, she still found the taste of food in her mouth (Ghazali 1999: 115). Youssef Hawwash, the martyr of 1966, also saw the Prophet regularly during his decade-long imprisonment. While his cellmate, Sayyid Qutb, was writing his voluminous interpretation of the Qur'an, Hawash helped interpret the chapter on Prophet Joseph, since the Israelite prophet visited him frequently. Jesus was there too, keeping Hawwash's spirits high by foretelling that his and Qutb's jailer (President Nasser) was going to be humiliated in war. Days before his death, Hawwash saw himself standing at the end of a long line headed by Prophet Muhammad and his Companions. He asked the Prophet whether the Brotherhood had altered his religion, to which the Prophet replied: "No, you remained faithful, faithful, faithful." And, after his execution, he visited his wife in a dream in the form of a giant angel flying over green fields ('Abd al-Hadi 2011: 88–9).

Holy visions circulated widely during Morsi's presidency, and even more so after he was overthrown. The aging Brotherhood cleric Jamal 'Abd al-Hadi recited the most intriguing one, in which Prophet Muhammad and President Morsi stood side-by-side to greet a Muslim congregation. Upon hearing the call to prayer, the Prophet stepped back and invited the Islamist president to lead prayers. This indicated passing the mantle of leadership from the Prophet to the Brotherhood.[19] And, during the Rab'a sit-in, sacred visions were recounted night after night on stage. In one of them, according to the Brotherhood's chief propagandist Safwat Hegazi, a virgin girl saw the general commander who ousted Morsi drowning in blood and screaming that the Brotherhood would return to power only if followers sacrificed more blood. Another dream recounted on stage in Rab'a is of a cleric who saw the Prophet lying down next to him, and then vacating his place so Morsi could sleep in the same spot.[20] Growing up with these inspiring stories fuels the desire of each member to one day resemble these blessed figures. And this is precisely what the Brotherhood promises: to transform average Muslims into quasi-saints.

The Art of Producing Men

Religious determinism has dictated the Brotherhood's line of business, which is to produce the godly community that will bend the laws of nature to its favor. This solves the paradox of why an ideological movement with the size and experience of the Brotherhood has no concrete program for political, socioeconomic, and geopolitical transformation. Sympathizers give Brothers the benefit of the doubt and blame their lack of a clear platform on years of underground existence. Detractors champion the much less favorable claim that Brothers are affecting ambiguity to hide their secret agenda for change, just like Ayatollah Khomeini did in Iran. The real explanation lies somewhere in-between. The movement neither has tangible plans, nor is entirely clueless about its long-term designs. The Brotherhood is simply a womb. Its mission is to produce the men and women who will bring about change. There is no need for a plan. The mere existence of this exceptionally devout community guarantees success in every field. As the second general guide famously proclaimed: "Establish Islam in your hearts, [and] it will be established on your land" (Houdeibi 1977: 66). The fifth guide, Hamid Abu al-Nasr, similarly declared that "building men is much more difficult than building institutions" (Sabbagh 2012: 241). There is no need to speculate on what an ideal Islamic state would look like. "Whenever true Muslims are found," Qutb wrote, "the Islamic order emerges automatically" ([1966] 1980: 3165). As Rida (2013) explained, in a slightly defensive tone, the Brotherhood never claimed to have a program for change. Its aim has always been to create the embryonic community that will eventually generate the desired Islamic order:

> Brothers and Sisters perfect their religious behavior; they intermarry; families multiply; and the community of believers eventually engulfs the entire nation. You see it unfold before your eyes. You actually live in this godly society, whose members model themselves after the Companions, constantly support each other, and forgive flaws and transgressions. You believe this experience can be generalized. Our platform is quite straightforward: when we all become virtuous, then everything will be all right. Muslims will be happy to return to their religion; women will voluntarily accept the role assigned to them; people will become kind and charitable; non-Muslims will admire and respect the Islamic model; and secular intellectuals will testify to the fairness of Islam.

The Brothers' primary concern, therefore, is to deepen their piety and spread it to others. "They wish to refashion society in their image;

this is their plan," concluded Mahmoud (2013) after a quarter of a century in the Brotherhood's orbit. As Banna dictated in the Fifth Congress Address: "The goal of the Brotherhood is to create a new generation of believers that will adopt the true teachings of Islam and stamp (*tasbugh*) the nation with a comprehensive Islamic flavor, and [our] means to accomplish this is . . . cultivating missionaries to pose as role models" ([1949] 1993: 198). And, on the eve of the Second World War, all that Banna had to offer Egypt's embattled prime minister, 'Ali Mahir, was just this: men. In his October 1939 letter to the premier, Banna advised: "choosing the men to entrust with formulating and implementing reform measures is more important than the content of the reforms themselves." The founder then proposed charging Brothers with these government reforms, "not because they are currently unemployed . . . but because those 'reactionaries' [as Brothers were derogatively described] who have strengthened their relationship with God have been guaranteed divine support" ([1948] 1990: 354–5). No wonder that the third general guide used to say: "Banna did not write books, he crafted men" (Telmesani 2008: 82). And little had changed by 2012, when the Brotherhood spent its year in power packing the bureaucracy with its members, rather than formulating specific plans for how to move forward. For, as 'Essam al-'Erian (2006), deputy head of the Brotherhood's political party, put it: "Islamism is a living movement that cannot be fossilized into a theory."

This meant – as Tag al-Din summarized perfectly – that when you perform the oath of allegiance to join the Brotherhood, you basically pledge to become a certain type of person rather than to accomplish any specific mission (2013: 89). Brothers are expected to act as "human models," living embodiments of Islamism (Tag al-Din 2013: 29). Or, as Farghali (2013) put it: Brothers should be "Islam walking on the earth." But the end goal, as the more strategic Habib realized, is to spread out and propagate this model (2012: 35). This is not to be achieved through proselytizing, but rather, as the founder indicated, through intermingling with people so that they want to imitate Brothers (Banna [1948] 1990: 183). We do not preach ideas, said Mikkawi (2013): "We put on an attractive lifestyle for all to see." This is how we measure success, added Malik (2013): "We observe the person before and after coming into contact with Brothers. We expect a visible change in the way he deals with his wife, children, parents, neighbors, colleagues." More systematically minded members like to use modern vocabulary. The Brotherhood, according to Ahmad Deif (2013), is a "human collectivity of reformers" concerned with providing the right environment for citizens to lead progress. Sarah

Lotfi (2013), the political scientist, described Brothers as the "solid moral base" for an Islamic civil society: "We implant morality, and morality prompts action." Shatla (2013) added playfully: "We do not interact with society, we infect it. We do not persuade, we contaminate. We are like good viruses carefully prepared in incubators, then set off to find new hosts."

History again provides the chief inspiration. The Prophet succeeded because he produced Companions. These holy men and women were "the energy source he unleashed" into the world ('Uwis 2010: 95). Islamist historian 'Abd al-Halim 'Uwis wrote that civilizational regeneration relies on human beings and materials. The history of the Islamic civilization proved that once you have an individual taken with an idea, the rest automatically follows. People are the raw materials of civilization. If you produce the right men, you can change history (2010: 147, 224). 'Uwis then got carried away with his own metaphor, describing the need to impregnate the womb of civilization and then insulate the embryo from external influences so that it would preserve its parents' genes. He compared this allegorical womb to the prison, isolated oasis, and cave that prophets Joseph, Moses, and Muhammad spent time in, respectively, before emerging with the divine message (2010: 173–9). The engineer Tag al-Din preferred a mechanical metaphor. The Brotherhood is like "a workshop for recycling and manufacturing human products." It inputs the inferior materials that have been corrupted over the years to produce a superior metal. The Teachings, in this comparison, are the "manufacturing standards" used to measure output and correct deviations (2013: 76). Tag al-Din provided another image, this time an architectural one, inspired by the fact that al-Banna translates as 'the builder' and his Teachings were divided into 'pillars'. Individual Brothers in this metaphor are bricks; recruitment is like choosing the best raw materials; cultivation makes them equal in size and shape; trials and tribulations are like the oven that hardens them; and brotherly love is the cement that holds them together (2013: 85–7, 99). The modestly educated Sami (2013) agreed. Material changes are easy. The real challenge is how to build the human being who will lead change.

The dissident Khirbawi described the process in a much less positive light: members are treated as mindless objects stacked on shelves and operated according to the movement's instruction manual (2012: 125). Jamal (2013), who attended a four-day training course for prefects in 2004, discovered that the overriding theme was sharing best practices in molding newcomers into similar units. Ahmad (2013), one of thousands on the receiving end of this process, compared the work of prefects to Chinese acupuncturists: "They are masters of psychology. They know which nerves to press to transform very different individuals into standard molds." Longtime member Sameh 'Eid compared the Brothers to the Mamluks, the slave-warriors bred by insecure caliphs to serve as their praetorian guard. The Brotherhood is simply a modern "Mamluk organization" (2013: 172). Shafiq (2013), who refused to join, rejected the Brotherhood's insistence on "suppressing deviations and refashioning individuals into human objects resembling one another in dress code, body language, tone of voice, vocabulary, and temperament."

To the extent that the Brotherhood has a plan, it is the seven-step design set out in Banna's "Ela al-Shabab" (To the Youth): creating the Muslim individual, whose thinking, emotions, and values exemplify Islam; then the Muslim family that lives according to Islam; then the Muslim society, composed of numerous Muslim families; then the Muslim government that reflects the perfect Muslim society and revives Islamic glory; then uniting all Muslim governments in one organization (a modern caliphate); then reconquering the lost lands of Islam (Andalusia, the Balkans, Southern Italy, and the Mediterranean isles); and finally assuming 'tutorship of the world' (*ustaziat al-'alam*) ([1949] 1993: 99–101).[21] The remarkable continuity in the Brotherhood's platform is evident in the fact that, when the Guidance Bureau was pressured to produce a new vision for the twenty-first century, it reproduced Banna's seven stages – almost verbatim – in its 2004 reform initiative ("Mubadarat" 2004). Focusing on rebuilding the Muslim individual, as the road to world conquest, was appealing in its simplicity and practicality, Sameh (2013) thought: "Political regeneration from below gave us a lot to work with. Just by reforming your personal behavior you were already contributing to this global scheme."[22] It is like trickle-down economics, only in the opposite direction: trickle-up morality.

And just as neo-liberals would invoke the success of a small-town entrepreneur to demonstrate how global capitalism works, Islamists were good at using individual examples to make grand claims – a strategy that ignored economies of scale: what happens when small-scale, local experiments are projected onto a national or international level. So while Brothers speak very eloquently about micro-level changes, and their hoped-for ripple effects, they are less convincing on macro-level issues. In the summer of 1936, the Brotherhood's founder dispatched a circular to the rulers, ministers, and parliamentarians of the Muslim world, proposing 50 urgent reforms in government. His practical suggestions were fairly mundane. He urged politicians to avoid partisanship; he implored governments to improve the lives of citizens and encourage agriculture, industry, and mining; and he called for closer ties between Muslim countries. What he really focused on was religious advice, such as "Propagating the Islamic spirit in government agencies so that citizens feel obliged to abide by Islamic teachings . . . Monitoring the private behavior of employees, and discarding the separation between the personal and the professional . . . Ending the working day early enough to facilitate worship [long night-time prayers] and going to bed early [to attend dawn prayers at the mosque] . . . Adjusting the work schedule to fit prayer times." In terms of social policy, Banna advocated fighting indecency, prostitution, and gambling; imposing gender segregation, and strict censorship of television, cinema, songs, and novels; organizing summer vacations according to Islamic principles; and resisting the foreign customs embraced by the social elite. In economics, he proposed centralizing alms collection and prohibiting usury (Banna [1948] 1990: 298–302). Plainly, Banna had little more to offer than any commonplace religious tutor. His successor, Houdeibi, was much more candid about how little practical advice Brothers had to offer: "We have no problem with the existing order, except with regards to some laws and procedures that are not in accordance with sharia" (1997: 53). The Brotherhood's chief legal scholar, 'Abd al-Qadir 'Uwda, confessed that once these sharia laws are in place, "it does not matter whether rulers are conservative or progressive, republican or monarchical" ([1953] 1988: 42). The liberal-minded Nada diluted the Brotherhood's platform even further. Islam, in his view, preaches justice and equality, and whatever regime guarantees these values is acceptable (2012: 129).

Then in 2007, after two years of criticism of a Brotherhood that had secured one-fifth of parliament but balked from proposing substantive bills (even for show), the Guidance Bureau delegated one of its own, Mahmoud Ghuzlan (2007), to unpack the Brotherhood's slogan 'Islam is the Solution' for those who accused the movement of intellectual bankruptcy. The result was a three-page article posted on the Brotherhood's website. Ghuzlan started by explaining that Islam had introduced general principles that cover all walks of life, and that Muslims had adopted them all through their history, until the onslaught of Western secularization. It was therefore the Brotherhood's goal to revive these religious principles before attempting – sometime in the future – "to translate [them] into programs, laws, and solutions." What Ghuzlan admitted, in so many words, is that Brothers have yet to articulate a specific project, but they are dedicated to propagating Islamic principles. And what are these principles? Ghuzlan furnished his curious readers with a relatively long list: freedom of belief and expression; consultative democracy; the people's right to elect their leaders and hold them accountable; equality before the law; the right to life, property, dignity, work, and welfare; fighting poverty and corruption; and upholding the rights of women and minorities. How these principles differ from those advocated by every decent (and not-so-decent) politician was not made clear.

That same year, Mahmoud (2013) was invited to participate in drafting the Brotherhood's first party program. 'Essam al-'Erian chaired the opening sessions, then handed it down to future President Morsi. However, the formality of the sessions, and the dismissing of any critical debate, left Mahmoud quite disillusioned. One incident stuck in his head: he had proposed, along with other young members, to state unambiguously that the Brotherhood supported the right of non-Muslims to assume the presidency. The elders responded, without much enthusiasm, that this was not possible because one of the president's primary vocations would be to invite foreign dignitaries to convert to Islam. Feeling patronized, Mahmoud objected, so he was politely asked not to attend the remaining meetings. To his surprise, a political program was announced only three weeks after the process had begun. He later learned that General Guide Mahdi 'Akif was challenged during a newspaper interview to present a program fit for a real political party, and so he prompted Brothers to quickly furnish him with such a document for public relations purposes.

Even reform-minded Brothers recoil from venturing too far into details. For example, 'Erian (2006) insisted that Brothers are merely trying to revive religion because it is a formative element of any national culture – nothing more. Abu al-Fotouh (2006) wondered what was wrong with expecting Egyptians to learn more about their religion, and then reflect what they have learned in parliament. But what if members of parliament decided to ignore these lessons and follow their whims? Should they be reined in through some form of clerical oversight? Abu al-Fotouh refused to entertain the possibility. Pious Egyptians would surely want to be ruled according to Islam, and would enshrine this in their constitution.

To get a clearer picture of the Brotherhood's ideology in action, let us skip generalities and consider one specific macro-level issue: Islamism's economic policy. In the Islamist worldview, Brotherhood-affiliated historian and judge Tariq al-Bishri wrote, "the economic order does not shape society, it is, on the contrary, shaped by social morality" (2008: 66). This seems to be the overriding theme in Banna's "al-Nizam al-Eqtisadi" (Economic Order). The founder's laundry list of economic prescriptions includes: prohibiting sinful activities (usury, gambling, etc.); promoting social solidarity to reduce income gaps; restricting luxuries; and upholding private property as long as it does not hurt the public interest.[23] He also offered a few random suggestions, such as developing independent lines of credit instead of investing in foreign bonds, encouraging industry (including home-based manufacturing), agricultural reform, and progressive taxation ([1949] 1993: 268–79). This same eclectic approach characterized the Brotherhood's 2004 platform ("Mubadarat" 2004). None of the Brotherhood's economic proposals was particularly Islamic, and none could be identified as particularly conservative or progressive. Some Brothers tried to get creative. In the late 1970s, the third general guide suspected that moving from agriculture to industry might all have been a big mistake. But how could Egypt rectify this when it had already lost much of its arable land? Telmesani looked around for rich soil, and did not have to go too far: the Sudan seemed to offer plenty. So his solution was forced migration of Egyptians to farm lands in the Sudan, followed by economic unity between the two great neighbors. Meanwhile, Egypt could rely on the largesse of foreign investors. Western businessmen, according to the general guide, are always "chasing after the dollar, the sterling, and the franc," so why not open up our markets to them (Telmesani 2008: 290–2)? Apart from these curious forays, the Brotherhood preferred to play it safe by copying-and-pasting whatever the Egyptian government seemed to be doing at the time. During the monarchy, Brothers appealed to the paternalism of aristocracy; during the socialist epoch, the focus shifted to social equality; and when the Egyptian economy was liberalized, Islam's respect for private property and enterprise was duly highlighted (Tammam 2012: 68).

When challenged by secular political activists, Brothers tend to improvise. Hani attended a 2005 seminar at the press syndicate where 'Essam al-'Erian, then head of the Brotherhood's political committee, was pressured to outline the movement's economic philosophy. The veteran Brother responded that he and his colleagues were currently studying the economic sections of other parties' manifestos to see how they could be combined in the most effective way. "Not only did he admit that the movement had nothing original to contribute," recalled a dumbfounded Hani (2013), "but it also became clear as he went on that he never even bothered to leaf through these party programs."

What about the Brotherhood's businessmen? Yasser (2013), a financier by profession, tried to correct some of the "utter nonsense" his Brothers repeated, but was regularly put down: "I was amazed at how they considered their businessmen – who are really little more

than glorified merchants – great economic thinkers. As an expert, I
was quite sure they understood neither business nor economics."
Walid (2013), one of Egypt's top bankers in Islamic finance, dealt
frequently with Brothers after they came to power. He also believed
their vaunted economic experts had a wholesale trade mentality. They
were no more than "skilled commodity movers," as he put it. But
what he found particularly striking was their poor grasp of Islamic
finance – supposedly their strong point. The Brothers he met on
panels designed to discuss ways of reconfiguring Egypt's post-revolt
economy had to resort to Islamist bankers from abroad. And even
those were market-oriented technicians, with limited economic
imagination.

Sociologist Joel Benin captured the frustration of Egypt's fairly
organized textile workers in the 1940s with the "didactic and abstract
character" of the Brotherhood's views on labor-management relations. Working-class Brothers mostly emphasized the need to maintain "brotherly relations" between union members (Benin 1988:
218). Benin compared the Brotherhood's hope for a just economy
regulated by Islamic principles to what E. P. Thompson described as
the "moral economy" among the eighteenth-century English crowd
(1988: 219). Charles Tripp's *Islam and Moral Economy* picks up on
this theme. The Islamist aspiration for a moral economy, Tripp
thought, was not based on empirical studies, but rather on an "ideal-
ized picture of the past." Their "self-consciously moralizing positions" owe little to their understanding of how the modern economy
works.[24] The bottom line is: Islamists believe they could render
Muslims impervious to material attractions through moral training
(2006: 6–7).

> The intention is to build up the inner bastion of resistance to a world
> driven mad by the pursuit of profit, the gratification of material desires
> and the alienating effect of a market-driven commodification of human
> qualities. Re-connection with the self, imagined as a repository of
> identifiably Muslim virtues, and through the self to a specific under-
> standing of God's command, becomes the principal undertaking.
>
> (Tripp 2006: 200)

This supports the conclusion of political Islam scholar Olivier Roy
that the whole idea of an Islamic economy is a late twentieth-century
invention. Islamic law and morality set forth several concepts with a
clear "economic impact," but they were never meant to provide a
coherent economic philosophy. In line with their understanding of
Islam's comprehensiveness, Brothers tried to counteract that by presenting a "functional ensemble that would offer a middle ground

between the two systems of the twentieth century, Marxism and capitalism" (Roy 1994: 132–3). They were not terribly successful. Their macro-economic concepts were at best rhetorical, and all their hope still rested on individual virtue (Roy 1994: 35). Ahmad Deif (2013), a senior member on the steering committee of the Brotherhood's much-flaunted Renaissance Project, laid out the movement's economic plan during its tenure in power:

> Our underlying philosophy is to produce a new kind of individual, an individual confident in divine favor. In economics we hope to create new kind of businessmen, one less concerned with profit, expansion, and consumption, than with developing society, creating jobs, encouraging a knowledge-based economy, and so on. We want selfless businessmen who understand that Islam obliges them to appropriate resources to benefit others.

Inverting Sharia

Religious determinism, the theological history that sustains it, and the project of producing a godly community it inspires, all amount to an inversion of the traditional understanding of sharia. Instead of just abiding by sharia as a religious duty, one also hoped its application would bring success in the temporal world. The second general guide, Hassan al-Houdeibi, published an article in 1947 rejecting the introduction of positive laws to the civil code, even if they did not contradict sharia. In his view, sharia must be adopted exclusively because "this is the source of its blessing and the secret of its power" (1973: 16). 'Abd al-Qadir 'Uwda, the Brotherhood's foremost legal scholar in the 1950s, claimed that, by adhering to sharia, Muslims destroyed the Persian and Roman empires, defeated the Crusaders and Tartars, and became "masters of the world and leaders of humanity for more than a thousand years" ([1953] 1988: 49). He therefore believed that the goal of law in Muslim society was not to regulate behavior, but to bless the collective spirit of the nation ('Uwda [1953] 1988: 38). And, according to the third general guide, the enemies of Islam finally figured out this well-hidden secret, and thus concentrated their nineteenth-century imperialist onslaught on sidelining sharia – a curse that Muslims must undo (Telmesani 2008: 54–5). Not surprisingly, Deputy General Guide Muhammad Habib disliked fundamentalists (*salafis*) because they only called for applying sharia for its own sake (as in Saudi Arabia or Afghanistan), unlike Brothers who approached its application as a means of reclaiming Islam's past glory (2012: 107).

What inspired this unconventional view? Political scientist 'Emad Shahin (2013) concluded, after years of studying Islamism, that the collapse of the caliphate, the highest symbol of Muslim unity, forced Hassan al-Banna and his generation to treat sharia as a substitute. The modernizing Ottoman caliphs' disregard for sharia was blamed for their tragic downfall, and upholding it was perceived as the only way for Muslims to regain power. From this reconceptualization of sharia arose the need to seize power – in order to control law and policymaking – as well as civil society – in order to control culture and education. This was another paradigm shift. Islamic scholars had traditionally acted as pressure groups, urging rulers and ruled to uphold sharia. There were corrupt sycophants who spent their day in court, and scholars of impeccable integrity. There were those active in public life, and those insulated in closed scholastic communities. But none of them attempted to capture political power and oversee the implementation of sharia from above (Khalid 2013). Eschewing this centuries-long division of labor, Brothers wanted their comprehensive organization to administer Islam comprehensively – on the political, legal, military, socioeconomic, and cultural fields. In short, the Brotherhood was making an unusually inauthentic bid in the name of authenticity (Zubaida 2005; Hallaq 2013).

Expectedly, this new outlook alienated traditional scholars. Banna anticipated their hostility, warning his followers that "religious people and clerics will express surprise towards your understanding of Islam" ([1949] 1993: 169). Brothers should not be deterred, as the cultivation curriculum instructs, because Banna's doctrine is derived from "evident truths available to all those who care to see" ("Madkhal" 1997: 35). Traditional jurists, of course, argue that these evident truths are based on unusual interpretations of revelation, to which the Brothers respond by insisting that anyone has the right to deal directly with the texts, and not have to rely on past Islamic sciences (Houdeibi 1977: 221).[ix]

Curiously, Brothers not only invert sharia wholesale, they also invert a few of its specific injunctions. Radwan (2013), an Azhar scholar and longtime Brother, was frequently torn between his religious training and membership duties – and never as much as when it came to the rule of 'necessity permits that which is otherwise prohibited' (*al-darurat tubih al-mahzurat*). The application of this rule

[ix] Ironically, Islamism's epistemological attitude towards religion overlapped considerably with secularists – their archenemies: both advocated the right to ignore the sciences of jurisprudence and exegesis and interpret texts directly. Instead of treating inherited knowledge as building blocks to be carefully scrutinized and built on, they regarded it as simply outdated.

was usually straightforward. The most typical illustration – commonly cited in jurisprudential works – is allowing desert-stranded Muslims to drink alcohol to save their lives. Brothers extended this rule, granting themselves the right to commit prohibitions to secure the organization. And they justify this jurisprudential move as follows: since the Brotherhood represents Islam, then its defeat is no less than the defeat of Islam, and surely anything goes when the fate of Islam itself is at stake. In a sense, this logic conflates two distinct principles: Islam's law of necessity, and Machiavelli's ends-justify-means principle. As the clerically trained Khalid (2013) explained, the Islamic injunction is limited to averting immediate danger to the life or health of the individual when no other option is available. The law should be used neither to achieve gains, nor to preempt danger. In short, necessity is measured in the narrowest sense (in jurisprudential jargon, *al-darura tuqadar bei qadriha*). Islam does not condone making a virtue of necessity. Not so for Machiavelli, who permits immoral actions to secure moral ends.[25] This is precisely what Brothers do. Though, in a Machiavellian twist of the first order, Brothers ground their actions in Islamic jurisprudence and curse the immorality of the Florentine theorist.

In the name of necessity, therefore, Brothers allow themselves considerable latitude. Before coming to power, the movement had the right to do whatever was necessary not only to protect itself, but also to hasten its success. Nepotism was condoned to cultivate personal bonds and prevent the infiltration of security agents. Embezzlement went unpunished because scandals could tarnish the movement's reputation. Autocracy was excused by the need for swift action. Hani (2013) tolerated much of this without complaint, but for him the 2005 parliamentary election was the straw that broke the camel's back: "We acted no different from the corrupt ruling party: offering bribes, making false promises, taking advantage of the people's illiteracy and ignorance. These violations, we were told, were permissible because we did not seek personal gains, only to promote Islam." The Brotherhood's questionable handling of the transitional period after the 2011 uprising was another dark episode, prompting the resignation of many longtime members. But it was all presented as the last necessary step towards seizing power ('Abd al-Bar 2013). Yet little changed after the Brotherhood actually came to power. Usurious IMF loans were accepted in order to boost the economy, lest the Brotherhood lost votes. Prohibiting the sale of alcohol was shelved to appease Western governments. Sharia penalties (*hudud*) were ignored so as not to offend global human rights organizations. When censured for compromising their religious ideals, Brothers claimed it was all done in the name of practical necessity; that a good Muslim must learn to navigate the "no man's land between religion and reality" (Houdeibi 2013).

The Brotherhood's most frequent violation, however, had always been disinformation. In the words of a particularly harsh dissident, Brothers "lie as often as they breathe" (Khirbawi 2012: 269). Again, it is all religiously sanctioned. Prophet Muhammad once said that 'war is deception'. Since Brothers are involved in a perpetual war against the enemies of Islam, then deception is the order of the day. For example, Brothers could be disingenuous when dismissing critiques, even if they were true, because critics most likely hated Islam. They could also lie to get ahead in the world, since the personal success of Muslims strengthens Islam as a whole. Brothers could even lie to each other. Leaders must lie to followers to hide their flaws, lest these followers lose faith in them, and so in the organization, and perhaps Islam itself. And followers often lie to leaders about the most trivial things (why they showed up late to a meeting or failed to turn up somewhere) so they will not become marginalized and miss their chance to serve Islam ("Taqrir" 2007). Indeed, never has lying for the sake of Islam been more systematic.

That being said, only an unfair critic could accuse Islamists of deliberate malice. The truth of the matter is: Islamism, like any other ideology, owes more to the conditions in which it was conceived than its luminaries would like to believe. An ideology developed at such a low ebb in Islamic history – with the caliphate collapsing irreversibly, and Muslim lands being carved up between frighteningly superior powers – is expected to seek hope in divine deliverance and to do whatever it takes to survive. And origins cast a long shadow over a movement's development. This is why it is necessary to consider the foundation and development of the Muslim Brotherhood.

4

The Slow Rise and Rapid Fall
from Power

Unconventional times call for unconventional measures. The unorthodoxy of Islamism is the product of a nineteenth-century intellectual crisis that has yet to be resolved. In the Christian world, the relationship between religion and the state has been determined by theological breakthroughs, political compromises, and, above all, war. In the Muslim world, it has been simply skipped over after a few shy attempts. In place of a historic settlement, Muslims were left with a black hole that continues to consume every attempt at serious reform. Basically speaking, what believers find in their books today still contradicts their temporal existence; neither has been adjusted to fit the other. By highlighting these clear and present contradictions, Islamists continue to draw the sympathy of practicing Muslims. This is why exploring the history of these unresolved tensions is the key to understanding Islamism's peculiar origins.

From its earliest days, Islamic scholarship crystalized into a discipline akin to nineteenth-century academia. Communities of researchers pored over various branches of knowledge (theology, jurisprudence, linguistics, etc.) in learning centers across the Muslim world. Students were free to choose their tutors in this fairly decentralized setting. Once they mastered a particular subject, they would receive the tutor's endorsement (*ijaza*) to write and lecture on it. Scientific worth was determined by peer review, rather than official position. More importantly, Islamic scholars (*'ulama*) jealously guarded their autonomy, just as modern universities strive to. One way of doing so was by refraining from outright interference in politics – a position facilitated by their recognition that in Islam, religion does not direct politics, even if they sometimes overlap. It is true that some *'ulama* attached themselves to policymakers – just like modern-day academics – but the overwhelming majority shunned official posts and inhabited the realm of civil society without losing any of their scholastic clout. Rulers who sought religious legitimacy would submit to Islamic injunctions, at least superficially, to avoid being criticized by influential *'ulama*. And those who sufficed with the legitimacy of the sword did very well without religious blessing. Either way, the *'ulama* appreciated the limits of their power and seldom attempted to administer rulers, who, in turn, were judicious enough to let them be. Hence, one of the key differences between Christian and Islamic histories is the absence of an institutional relationship between the royal court and a centralized ecclesiastical hierarchy. Doubtless, the relative weight of religious and political authority shifted from one epoch to the next, with the *'ulama*'s influence reaching its zenith under the Ayyubid and Mamluk dynasties in Egypt and the Levant between the thirteenth and fourteenth centuries.[1] But, in general, Muslim scholars and rulers coexisted in separate (though intersecting) spheres. They sometimes negotiated, sometimes clashed, but mostly worked around each other with minimum friction.[2]

This all began to change with the rise of Ottoman power in the sixteenth century. As the first non-Arab caliphs, and as new converts, Ottomans could hardly feel comfortable with Islamic scholarship developing autonomously in Arab lands. Hence, Ottomans began to centralize religious authority, with a state-appointed grand jurist presiding over official representatives of each of the four Sunni schools (Ziadeh 2013: 38). Soon, the scramble for offices replaced peer recognition, leading to a significant deterioration in the discipline as a whole.[3] Also, the swelling of the Ottoman mandarin-like bureaucracy drew many ambitious young men away from religious sciences to positive law and administration. Scribes were becoming just as estimable as scholars, and certainly more generously rewarded. These cumulative changes reoriented religious authority from an independent social force to a mediator between rulers and subjects, which in turn meant that their political utility had increased just as much as their social prestige had depreciated.

The *'ulama*'s downward spiral experienced a brief reversal in the late eighteenth century when the Mamluks succeeded in reasserting their dominance for a few odd years. And in fact, scholars played a key role during the Napoleonic conquest (1798–1800), and the subsequent crowning of the Albanian adventurer Muhammad 'Ali

(r. 1805–49).[i] Little did they suspect that this latter step had effectively placed them on the road to oblivion, for Muhammad 'Ali's
modernizing zeal was uncompromising. The new ruler of Egypt and
the Levant, by most accounts, harbored no ill feeling towards Islam.
His aim was to preside over a modern state. And the first step in any
such modernization project was to rein in corporate bodies, such as
the *'ulama*. Across the Mediterranean, parallel reforms were being
applied at the heart of the caliphate under Mahmoud II (r. 1808–39)
of Constantinople.[4] Feeling threatened as never before, the *'ulama*
naturally panicked, and adopted for the first time a fierce (almost
fanatical) attitude against change. In their minds, modernization was
nothing more than an elaborate ruse to destroy Islam – a poison
whose only antidote was unflinching defense of tradition. This
obstructive role was quite uncharacteristic of Muslim jurists who
never previously allowed the sacred origins of Islamic law to reduce
their "flexibility in fashioning formulations in line with the con-
straints of their contemporary societies and the contingencies of
power" (Zubaida 2005: 3).[ii]

Yet, by the nineteenth century, the *'ulama* had not only modernizing rulers to contend with, but also a rising intellectual elite bent
on flogging their reluctant societies into the new age. This progressive
group originated in the bureaucracy. By the late eighteenth century,
Ottoman scribes had come to see themselves as political theorists in
their own right – even though their theories really boiled down to
one simple suggestion: imitate the West.[5] In Egypt, this secular elite
could be traced to the students 'Ali dispatched to Europe during the
early nineteenth century so they could learn to administer his bureaucracy and vocational schools.[6] Unlike the modernizing caliphs of
Constantinople, Muhammad 'Ali had little appreciation for Western
law and social sciences. His aim was to copy European advances in
applied sciences without adopting their secular philosophy. But, in a
curious twist of fate, the Azhar scholar he assigned to guard the faith
of the first delegation of students became the chief apostle of the
Western way of life. Rifa'a al-Tahtawi's 1831 account of his Parisian

---

[i] Curiously, the *'ulama* were quite influential on both sides of the fence: some
(such as 'Umar Makram) led popular revolts against the French, while others
(such as Sayyid al-Bakri) facilitated colonial administration.

[ii] Unlike their Christian counterparts, Muslim *'ulama* never challenged
natural science discoveries in geography, geology, physics, chemistry, etc.
Hence, they were never before seen as an obstacle to scientific progress. This
began to change during the nineteenth century as a result of their profound
sense of insecurity.

journey captured the imagination of his countrymen, and, upon his return, he created a school for teaching foreign languages and translation. Another enchanted Egyptian, 'Ali Mubarak, moved from religious to secular education, and instituted the Teachers' College to rival al-Azhar in producing schoolteachers – eventually producing the two founders of the Muslim Brotherhood. Muhammad 'Ali's attempt at limited borrowing therefore unleashed an irreversible avalanche.[iii] Eventually, Azhar scholars themselves would succumb to Western sciences, with Grand Imams holding doctoral degrees in philosophy from the Sorbonne.[iv]

Sadly for Muslim modernizers, reorganizing military and administrative affairs along European lines averted neither Ottoman defeat on the shores of Greece in 1827, nor the Egyptian–Levantine defeat at the gates of Constantinople in 1840. Their heirs – considerably weakened and increasingly in awe of Western power – replaced selective learning with wholesale imitation. Hence, the reign of Tanzimat (1839–76) in Turkey and Khedive Isma'il's Europeanization of Egypt (r. 1863–79) witnessed the total embrace of all things Western: language, art, music, architecture, down to costumes and cuisine. As Ibn Khaldun so adeptly explained, the weak, blinded by their desire to emulate the strong, rarely stop at adopting those elements of strength they lack; instead, their inferiority urges them to mimic the habits and lifestyle of their conquerors. And, as Algerian sociologist Malik bin Nabi predicted, the weakening of Islamic culture rendered Muslims 'susceptible to colonization'. Before the nineteenth century ended, most Muslim provinces came under Western domination.

Henceforth, a new breed of colonized and culturally insecure intellectuals placed their hope in a long-due Arab Renaissance, rallying to their Parisian-styled salons dozens of novelists, poets, journalists, translators, and social reformers, to propagate the principles of the French Revolution: individual liberty, nationalism, and scientific thinking. And, with history on their side, they managed to displace the *'ulama* as cultural leaders. At the same time, secular education proliferated at the hands of Christian missionaries, and a modern university was established in Cairo in 1908, followed by an American

[iii] Western cultural hegemony provoked a similar reaction outside the Muslim world. Dynasties as diverse as Manchu China, Tokugawa Japan, and Romanov Russia sought to strengthen themselves by learning from their adversaries, and, to their dismay, ended up borrowing more than they had originally intended.
[iv] The first was Mustafa 'Abd al-Raziq (1945–7), and the most recent is the current Imam, Ahmad al-Tayieb.

one in 1919.[7] The Egyptian and Levantine social elite shepherded their children through Western education at home and abroad. Religious schools, by contrast, attracted the poorer, less ambitious types.[8] What unfolded was a subtle process – brilliantly captured by Mitchell (1988) – to produce new forms of personhood. Hourani depicted the widening schism between secular and religious spheres as follows:

> Behind the division of institutions there lay a division of "spirits" . . . the two systems of education had produced two different educated classes in Egypt, each with a spirit of its own. One was the traditional Islamic spirit, resisting all change, the other, the spirit of the younger generation, accepting all change and all the ideas of modern Europe . . . This meant not only the absence of a common basis shared by the two groups; it meant also the danger that the moral bases of society would be destroyed by the restless spirit of individual reason, always questioning, always doubting.
>
> (1962: 138)

Gradually, secular Muslim intellectuals, "both inspired and created by their counterparts in the evolving modern societies of Western Europe and North America," relegated Islamic scholars to the cultural periphery (Esposito and Voll 2001: 12–14). And the *'ulama* responded with an obstinacy fit for those on the threshold of becoming entirely irrelevant. But this proved to be self-defeating, because it justified their collective dismissal as a fossilized lot. Liberals now dominated the intellectual arena, with nationalists and communists trailing behind. In other words, the right, left, and center of the cultural spectrum were effectively Westernized.[9] In 1919, it was liberals who led Egypt's first national uprising and drafted its first modern constitution, as the *'ulama* were sinking deeper into the cultural background.

But right before the curtain fell on traditional Islamic scholarship, one Azhar scholar attempted a last-minute gambit to save his peers from eclipse. Muhammad 'Abduh (d. 1905) scarcely doubted that the modernizing elite were good Muslims with a sufficient understanding of Islam to guard against sacrilegious views. His great fear was that the increasing attraction of secular education, coupled with waning enthusiasm for Islamic sciences, would ultimately produce a religiously ignorant generation that would unwittingly trample over Islam in its wild pursuit of modernization. Religious scholarship must catch up with modernity or risk total oblivion. 'Abduh recognized that by the late nineteenth century it was no longer realistic to dissuade Muslims from embracing modernity; the only hope was to convince these fervent modernizers that Islam was not an obstacle. In his mind, the only way to bridge the gulf between old and new was to show that the changes taking place "were not only permitted by Islam, but were indeed its necessary implications if it was rightly understood" (Hourani 1962: 139). 'Abduh's reform campaign, however, was destined to fail. Not only had the intellectual field become too polarized for reconciliation, but also a proper revision and updating of Islamic sciences required decades. His lifework was inevitably flawed, and his eclectic innovations discredited Islamic reformism for years to come.[10]

'Abduh's unsuccessful campaign, however, triggered two opposing trends that materialized in the 1920s. First, secular luminaries – convinced that the *'ulama* had no intention of compromising – took it upon themselves to liberate Islam from the clutches of tradition by a critical evaluation of Islamic history and thought.[11] Alarmed *'ulama* upped the ante with accusations of heresy, and sometimes outright excommunication. But the more they resisted, the more the educated urbanites came to see religious scholarship as hopelessly reactionary. Soon, the frustrated elite dismissed jurists altogether as blind copiers of past knowledge, and argued that Islam obliges Muslims to rely on individual reason. Worse still, their twentieth-century descendants grew up with a highbrow disdain for religious reactionaries who fed on the naiveté of the pious (Abu al-Magd 2006). Those who inherited 'Abduh's project on the secular front thus reinvented themselves as new Muslim reformers. Combining rigorous knowledge of Western philosophy with a casual understanding of traditional Islamic sciences, they began hammering down centuries of jurisprudence to the applause of their equally frustrated audience. A few even attached themselves to Western universities and set about reexamining tradition in a more systematic way using the modern sciences of philology, discourse analysis, and anthropology. Though their works were inaccessible beyond the academy halls, their conclusions served to undermine further the legitimacy of tradition in the minds of educated Muslims.[12] Instead of seriously addressing some of the (not necessarily irresolvable) discrepancies between the traditional understanding of Islam and modernity, secular intellectuals hoped these discrepancies would simply vanish under the weight of their progressive onslaught. In reality, time only served to exacerbate these hastily suppressed differences.

The second result of 'Abduh's failure was that it left his religious students increasingly anxious about the emboldened seculars. There was no time to reconcile *al-wafid wa al-mawruth* (new and inherited values) in a methodical fashion (Bishri 2007). This was especially the case with 'Abduh's closest follower, the Levantine cleric Rashid Rida. With the abolishment of the caliphate in 1924 – an unprecedented and previously unthinkable calamity – Rida became convinced that it was too late to synthesize tradition and progress. He prayed for a savior to put secular dissidents in their place and reestablish the caliphate,[v] and shared his thoughts with a bright young student who visited him frequently. His name was Hassan al-Banna.

On the Shoulders of Primary Schoolteachers

The Marx and Engels of Islamism were born in the same year (1906) in similarly small villages far from the capital, attended the same college (Teachers' College), and started their careers as primary schoolteachers. Yet their journey to Islamism could not have been more different: the first consumed since childhood with religious zeal, and the second growing up as a Westernized secular, flirting occasionally with atheism. Hassan al-Banna was born in al-Mahmoudiya in the Nile Delta province of Behira to a watchmaker with an amateur interest in religious scholarship. He memorized the Qur'an as a child, joined a mystic sect (al-Tariqa al-Hasafiya), and founded a Society of Fine Ethics when he was only seven, later transformed into the Association for Prohibiting Sin during his adolescence. Although both groups did little more than mail anonymous complaints to the parents, husbands, and employers of wrongdoers, they indicated Banna's early enthusiasm for combating sin in an organized fashion. They also demonstrated how this enthusiasm was tempered less by the patience of a scholar than by the eagerness of an activist. This is why he preferred the Teachers' College to the long and arduous path of religious learning at al-Azhar (Banna [1948] 1990: 17).

Sayyid Qutb, on the other hand, was born to a smallholding family on the outskirts of Asyut in Upper Egypt. Repulsed at a young age by local clerics who failed to "simplify religion for the public," Qutb snubbed Azhar and embarked on the path of secular education (1999: 40). Qutb graduated to become a primary schoolteacher in 1933, and assumed a few bureaucratic posts at the Ministry of Education between 1940 and 1952. Unlike the vigorous-looking and socially engaging Banna, Qutb was plagued by poor health, always appearing pale and heavy-eyed, and leading the life of a chronically depressed introvert in the then-desolate district of Helwan, outside the capital.

[v] Rida actually hoped the Wahhabi al-Saud family would claim the caliphate and bring order to the nation.

He found solace not in religion, but in literature and sensual poetry, and was quickly drawn to a circle of European-inspired intellectuals, patronized by the towering liberal novelist 'Abbas Mahmoud al-'Aqqad. An extremist by nature, Qutb embraced atheism, joined a radical liberal party (*al-Sa'di*), and penned provocative articles advocating things as shocking as nude beaches (Moussalli 1992: 23; Yunis 2012: 69).[13] Interestingly, an enraged young Brother showed the latter article to Banna to ask for his permission to punish the author, but the founder did not want to waste time on a "juvenile halfwit thirsting for attention . . . [and] absurdly fascinated by the Western civilization" (Hammuda 1999: 66). It was this very civilization, however, that managed to turn Qutb around. His disenchantment began with a mission to America (1948–50) to study modern education techniques.[14] His "America allati Ra'ayt" (The America I Saw), published in three installments in the weekly *al-Risala* in December 1951, was a ringing indictment of all things Western. Qutb described America as the "greatest lie the world has known," and Americans as unethical, racist, materialist, lustful, and violent (Yunis 2012: 182). And, partly because Americans were visibly ecstatic about Banna's 1949 assassination, as he claimed, Qutb suspected that Islamism might be the last garrison against Western penetration (Moussalli 1992: 30). Proclaiming himself born again in 1951, Qutb commemorated his rebirth with the famous polemic, *Ma'rakat al-Islam wal-Ra'smaliya* (The Battle between Islam and Capitalism), and began contributing regularly to the Muslim Brothers' *al-Da'wa* newspaper.[15] Two years later, he joined the Brotherhood.

But besides their varying career trajectories, Islamism's two founders operated in very different political contexts. Banna commenced his work under the liberal monarchy of the 1920s. His first missionary forays to mosques and cafés were carried out openly in Egypt's most European city, al-Isma'iliya, which was named after Egypt's most Westernizing ruler, Isma'il, and which hosted the multinational administration of the Suez Canal. Banna even ran for parliament twice, though he was persuaded to step down in 1942 and lost in 1944. Not only that, Banna enjoyed the luxury of sending letters of advice and reproach to ministers and monarchs. Qutb, in contrast, converted to Islamism on the eve of the 1952 coup and the authoritarian regime it produced. He spent most of his time behind bars, and had to resort to underground agitation. Eventually, both were executed – so it did not seem to have mattered much to them personally – but their strategies were colored by their distinctive epochs.[16] Banna could reasonably aspire to re-Islamize through sermons, writings, and educational initiatives, while Qutb had to place his hope on a secret vanguard. Yet both targeted state power. Nor was Banna immune to the temptation of seizing power through a frontal attack. He did, after all, promise Brothers, in his oft-quoted Fifth Congress Address, to lead them against their tyrannical rulers once they had 12,000 soldiers equipped spiritually and physically for battle. 'Essam al-'Erian (2006), head of the Brotherhood's political section, excused this newfound obsession with state power as one of the contingencies of modernity. Once the caliphate was replaced by modern statehood, Islamists could no longer afford to ignore political power as conventional 'ulama had done, even if this required a major revision of Islamic jurisprudence.

In other words, the Muslim Brotherhood was a unique response to an unsettling epoch, epitomized by the sudden collapse of the caliphate. For 14 centuries, the caliphate – the symbol of unity between religious and temporal powers in Islam – had vacillated between glory and frailty without a hint that it might one day be abolished. When the blow fell, no religious justification had been prepared. Banna clearly appreciated the gravity of the situation. When liberal Prime Minister Mustafa al-Nahhas praised Mustafa Kemal, vanquisher of the caliphate, in an interview with the Anatolia Press Agency, on June 14, 1936, the founder of Islamism warned him in a letter that Egypt was facing "the most dangerous juncture in its entire existence" (Banna [1948] 1990: 293). Driven by this exceptional development, Banna felt justified to flout tradition, and pioneer a new strand of jurisprudence. And, not surprisingly, he found sympathizers among zealous Azhar students, such as Ghazali and Qaradawi, who derided their tutors for being satisfied with pleas for some Muslim ruler to pick up the mantle of the caliphate, before returning to their petty scientific squabbles. In fact, Banna publicly scolded a leading cleric, Youssef al-Digwi, for being insufficiently concerned with the secular onslaught ([1948] 1990: 69).

Henceforth, Banna and his Brothers were perceived as Islam's saviors in the most literal sense. According to an authentic Prophetic narration, God furnishes Muslims with a religious reviver (*mujadid*) every century. In most cases, the reviver was defined by scholarly consensus.[17] For Muhammad al-Ghazali, the founder of the Brotherhood was unquestionably the reviver of the twentieth century. Indeed, Ghazali described his mentor as the most illustrious interpreter of the Qur'an, the most skillful spiritual healer, the most faithful fundamentalist, and the greatest Muslim historian: "God has combined in him the talents he had divided between many [of His subjects]" (1981: 6). Qaradawi was a bit more inventive, contending that this reviver need not be a single man, and that the term could refer to an entire movement. In today's complicated world, he concluded, the Muslim Brothers collectively assume this hallowed role (1999: 37). Another notable addition was Tag al-Din's claim that, although the reviver normally limited his efforts to religious affairs, the fall of the caliphate decreed that the new century's reviver must reform religion and politics together (2013: 22–7). Even Qutb's most radical ideas, such as the blanket excommunication of non-Islamists, were sanctioned by the feeling that all was lost, and that it was up to a new group of Prophetic Companions to resurrect Islam from the ruins. In contrast to the reserved *'ulama*, with their obscure jargon, it was invigorating for scores of frustrated Muslims to hear a prominent Brother like 'Uwda boldly comparing Western-inspired laws to pagan idols, and judges applying them to priests in their temple, and then calling on Muslims to trample upon these "bastard children" ([1953] 1988: 12–14).

That being said, the unorthodoxy of the experiment by these lay Muslim activists alienated those properly versed in Islamic sciences. And the fact that the Brotherhood could not secure Muslims' universal allegiance made it vulnerable to repression by regimes backed by traditional *'ulama*. Brothers remained 'organic' intellectuals, *à la* Gramsci, organizing and educating followers and deriving legitimacy from cultural activism. The *'ulama*, however, cast themselves as Foucauldian 'specific' intellectuals, resting on solid academic credentials. In the end, as Foucault rightly predicted, activists received only partial and conditional support from the wider population, while accredited experts had a better chance of securing public deference. This is crucial to understanding how pious Egyptians could turn against Brothers in 2013 without feeling that they had turned against religion as such.

The Great Ordeal

The repression of the Muslim Brotherhood did not begin in 2013, but six-and-a-half decades before. Egypt's last monarch first dissolved the organization in December 1948 after documents found in a Jeep exposed its militant wing, the Special Order. Brothers claimed that this was a Western conspiracy to punish their formidable show of force against Zionists in Palestine and British soldiers in Egypt. The Special Order, they insisted, was not directed against Egyptians. But their claim became less convincing when the movement's banning triggered a violent campaign, including the assassination of the prime minister who issued the order (Mahmoud Fahmi al-Nuqrashi), and the judge who presided over the case (Ahmad al-Khazindar), and the blowing up of the court building that held the Jeep's documents. And just as Brothers did in 2013, Banna declared that these were individual acts of violence by rogue elements. The regime responded by killing Banna, and the Brotherhood responded by supporting the 1952 coup.[18]

As far as Brothers were concerned, the Free Officers were carrying out the movement's orders. Back in 1941, Banna had charged Major Mahmoud Labib with recruiting army officers. On his deathbed, in December 1951, Labib entrusted Colonel Nasser with the secret list of recruits. Taking their cue from their dead comrade, the Brothers subsequently empowered Nasser to run the Brotherhood's army branch (Hammuda 1985: 33–7). On the eve of the coup, Nasser liaised with Brother Hassan al-'Ashmawi, and waited for the green light from General Guide Hassan al-Houdeibi ('Ashmawi 1985). Nasser then lifted the ban on the movement in 1953, and hired Qutb as cultural advisor. But the coup leader had a different story. Nasser admitted that a few of his men had joined the Brothers because he wanted to secure the support of all opposition groups, but he owed them no allegiance. Naturally, he refused to consult with the Guidance Bureau when forming his cabinet. Angry Brothers set out to undermine him by backing General Muhammad Naguib (the coup's nominal leader), encouraging army mutinies and popular riots, and inciting the British against the young colonel.[19] In response, Nasser dissolved the group once more, in January 1954, and detained the general guide and dozens of Brothers. After a short-lived rapprochement, during which Brothers were released in return for supporting Nasser, the Guidance Bureau decided that the ambitious colonel had no intention of sharing power, and decided to escalate resistance. On October 26, 1954, Mahmoud 'Abd al-Latif, a member of the Brotherhood's Special Order, fired nine shots at Nasser during a speech in Alexandria. They all missed. Although 'Abd al-Latif was caught red-handed and confessed, the Brothers swore that these were harmless sound shots fired by a Nasser crony, and that their man was simply in the wrong place at the wrong time. Nonetheless, a furious Nasser authorized a brutal anti-Brotherhood crackdown: over 20,000 members were detained (including General Guide Hassan al-Houdeibi and Qutb), two senior members were executed (one of them the firebrand judge 'Uwda), and ten received long prison sentences (including the future second, third, and fourth general guides).

Learning the hard way that they could not rely on the sympathy of the masses, Qutb devised a new strategy with the blessing of

General Guide Houdeibi.[vi] Its manifesto, *Ma'alim fei al-Tariq* (Signposts), circulated among imprisoned Brothers, and was smuggled outside prison, in 1963, by the general guide's son, Isma'il (Yunis 2012: 305). What the Brotherhood needed, according to his new strategy, was a hardened *'isba mu'mina* (vanguard of believers) to impose Islam on a reluctant world – a new generation of Prophetic Companions. Like members of the Special Order, they would adopt a secretive and militant outlook, but instead of remaining secluded organizationally from mainstream Brothers, they would proliferate their ideas throughout the Brotherhood.[20] Islamist matron Zeynab al-Ghazali received instructions from Qutb through his sister Hamida, and together with Brothers Youssef Hawwash and 'Abd al-Fattah 'Abduh Ismai'l, they attempted to restructure the organization along those lines. By 1964, over 200 members were onboard, and Qutb planned to lead them personally after his release in February 1965 (Yunis 2012: 305).

Expectedly, such an operation could not have gone unnoticed in Nasser's security state. Another major crackdown raised the number of Brotherhood detainees to 40,000, and added 3 new names to the execution list: Qutb, Hawwash, and Ismai'l. Again, the Brotherhood insisted that Qutb did nothing more than make a few minor alterations to the cultivation process; that his extremist views were caused by torture; and that Nasser's diabolical government had only released him on health grounds in 1965 to be able to nail him down the following year on a more serious charge. Be that as it may, those detained in the mid-sixties, the so-called '1965 Organization,' continued down the path set by Qutb. And, four decades later, they secured a majority in the Guidance Bureau.

Learning to Live with Authoritarianism

What Brothers described as the great ordeal (*al-mihna*) of the 1950s and 1960s might have been a terminal one, had Nasser's successors not found some use for them. One might never again have heard of the Brotherhood, had Sadat not decided to employ them against his leftist opponents, and if Mubarak had not decided to showcase them as the alarming alternative that awaited Egypt, should he be deposed

---

[vi] The general guide later retracted his approval of some of Qutb's conclusions, in his 1977 tract *Du'a la Quda* (Missionaries Not Judges). Yet Qutb's writings have remained the main stock of every cultivation curriculum, and the bread-and-butter of cultivators on all levels.

– an accurate claim, as events revealed. On their part, Brothers decided to combine the doctrines of Banna and Qutb to adapt to their new environment: they would capitalize on the space made available to them by rulers to garner popular support, while continuing to nurture their pious vanguard to take power when chance allowed (as it did in 2011). They would also use the Banna–Qutb divide to convey a sense of division to outsiders. This served two purposes: first, in urging rulers, activists, and foreigners to concede to the doves, lest the hawks take over; and second, in dismissing any militant ideas or practices leaked to the press as the work of rogue Qutbists.

The immediate challenge facing the Brotherhood in the 1970s, however, was how to absorb the fundamentalist (*salafi*) youth that had been active in universities under the rubric of a new organization: the Islamic Group (*al-Jama'a al-Islamiya*). Unversed in Islamism, these students grew up under the influence of Wahhabi thought, which infiltrated Egypt after the oil boom through mosques, cheap Islamic books and cassettes, and tens of thousands of Egyptian expatriates. Islamic Group activists had no elaborate theories about the comprehensiveness of Islam or the laws of history; they simply wanted to put pressure on rulers – as fundamentalists had done throughout Islamic history – to implement a few legal injunctions: prohibiting alcohol, outlawing usury, segregating genders, etc. They mostly acted as secular pressure groups. They also dealt openly with society and felt no obligation to conceal their beliefs from outsiders until they were religiously prepared to handle the truth. In short: they were not Muslim Brothers. Yet Brothers realized that if they did not coopt them, they would have to compete with them (as they did with their progeny in 2013).

The person targeted for the merger negotiations was 'Abd al-Mon'iem Abu al-Fotouh, the most prominent member of the Islamic Group, and a future presidential candidate. If he could be turned around, thousands of the group's members would probably follow. Abu al-Fotouh and his generation were in high school when the devastating military defeat of 1967 shattered their belief in Nasser's nationalist socialist project. Their mistrust of Nasser naturally made them suspicious of his accusations against the Muslim Brothers. "The image I had of the Brotherhood was turned upside down," Abu al-Fotouh remembered; "They suddenly became a model for sacrifice" (2010: 25). He and his comrades began to attend sermons by Ghazali and Qaradawi, but there was no other way to learn more about Brothers since they were in prison. So Abu al-Fotouh and his generation turned to the next best thing: the *salafism* that was regularly preached in mosques. After joining Cairo University's medical school in 1971, Abu al-Fotouh and his pious colleagues were incensed by the dominance of secular groups – the heirs of nineteenth-century intellectuals, radicalized during the Nasser years: "I recall that when I read their [wall] magazines, and the attacks they leveled against Islam, I would feel sad and cry. I used to wonder: could this be an Egyptian university? This drove me and other religious students from humble backgrounds to . . . clash with Communists and leftists" (2010: 29). Once they set their mind to it, Islamic activists attracted thousands of supporters, and soon controlled the student unions of major universities, starting with a landslide victory in Abu al-Fotouh's medical school in 1973 – with Abu al-Fotouh himself elected leader of Cairo University's Student Union, and achieving national fame after exchanging words with President Sadat in February 1977. The Islamic Group used their newly won prerogative to enforce gender segregation in study halls, Qur'an recitation before lectures, and art censorship. They also invited preachers (like Ghazali and Qaradawi) to campus, and organized Islamist summer camps. Their popularity and tough-mindedness rendered them even more valuable to the Brotherhood.

The man who took it upon himself to bring these energetic students under the guidance of the Brotherhood was the third general guide, 'Umar al-Telmesani, who had just emerged, in 1971, from a 17-year prison sentence. This soft-spoken man immediately enchanted Abu al-Fotouh, convincing him that the generation gap between Islamic Group activists (all in their early twenties) and Brothers (mostly in their late fifties) was a divinely ordained plan to combine the energy of the young with the prudence of the elders. In 1975, Abu al-Fotouh and a select group of associates attended Brotherhood family meetings and liked what they saw. By 1980, a merger was successfully concluded, with around 40,000 activists joining the Brotherhood.[vii] As agreed, Islamic Group cadres were appointed in the Brotherhood's governing bodies, and after a decade of restructuring, the two organizations became finally synchronized. At the same time, the Brotherhood decided to complement its domestic expansion with an international one, charging Mustafa Mashhur and Mahdi 'Akif (the future fifth and seventh guides, respectively) with creating the International Organization (al-Tanzim al-Dawli). By 1989, the Brotherhood had assumed its final form, domestically and internationally (Madi 2005: 185–91; Abu al-Fotouh 2010: 91, 128).

[vii] Many of those who rejected the merger turned to militancy under the rubric of the (now militant) Islamic Group and its sister organization, the Islamic Jihad. Others, including the founders of the 2011 fundamentalist al-Nur party, continued down the path of civic activism.

Two years after this structural overhaul, the Brotherhood experienced a similarly significant shift in organizational culture – a shift crucial to smoothing relations between the fundamentalist youth and Brotherhood veterans. Hundreds of Brothers had settled in Saudi Arabia in the 1960s to escape Nasser's prisons, and many more headed there after their release in the 1970s to compensate themselves financially for the time they served in prison. Saudi authorities welcomed them as long as they did not meddle in the kingdom's politics. But the Brotherhood's sympathy for Saddam Hussein made their life there quite precarious, and most of them returned home after the 1991 Gulf War. Years of exposure to Wahhabi dogma meant they had a lot in common with the *salafi* youth. Senior Brothers thus welcomed back the returnees with open arms, even though many of them preferred to serve the movement in the buzzing new field of Islamic media: satellite channels and websites. A case in point is Safwat Hegazi, a Saudi-educated Brother who resettled in Cairo in 1998 to host shows on the prime *salafi* channel, al-Nas, before becoming a major sponsor of Morsi's presidential campaign and the chief propagandist of the 2013 sit-ins. Another prominent example is Hazem Salah Abu Isma'il, the Brotherhood's candidate for parliament in 2005, and presidential candidate in 2012, also a regular on al-Nas, and the undesignated leader of most Wahhabi-oriented Brothers. This inter-fertilization of fundamentalist youth (now referred to as the seventies generation), Wahhabi-influenced Brothers, and embedded Qutbists produced a bloc of "Brotherhood Puritans" (Tammam 2012: 119). But although this new alliance seemed to manage fairly well, trouble was simmering under the surface.

The heart of the problem was that the seventies generation was committed to civic activism. In their experience, the number of seats won in an election was the only tangible measure of success. To reconcile their strategy with the Brotherhood's metaphysical doctrines, they had initially agreed on a division of labor, whereby activism would be used to propagate the message, broaden the recruitment pool, and draw public and international support, while old-time cultivators devoted themselves to producing their godly community through in-house indoctrination. In line with this arrangement, General Guide Telmesani approved – in a landmark decision – the Brotherhood's participation in parliamentary elections, to use this political pulpit to spread God's word (2008: 243). And the activist clique delivered as promised. In an electoral alliance with the liberal al-Wafd in 1984, the Brothers became part of the largest opposition bloc in parliament, with 15 percent of the vote (58 seats). In 1987, Brothers took over two small parties, the socialist al-'Amal and the liberal al-Ahrar, and won 17 percent of the vote (60 seats). Brothers joined other opposition forces in boycotting the 1995 election to protest against the eschewing of judicial oversight. And, in 2000, they ran as independents, capturing 17 seats, which was more than the total number won by other opposition parties. Then came the remarkable victory of 2005, which increased their share to almost 20 percent of the vote (88 seats). A similarly impressive electoral record was achieved in professional syndicates and student unions. In less than a decade, 21 syndicates, including roughly 2.5 million professionals, fell under their control. The signal success was in the Medical Syndicate in 1986, followed by the Engineering, Pharmacist, and other syndicates. They even managed to secure 75 percent of the vote at the ultra-secular Lawyers' Syndicate in 1992. At the same time, Brothers dominated student unions in public universities throughout the 1980s and 1990s, and in 2000 extended their influence to the American University in Cairo, historically a secular bastion (Kandil 2011).

Tensions within the Brotherhood arose because the activist branch seemed to be getting ahead of the organization. For one thing, electoral successes provoked harsh government responses. In 1995, security forces raided Salsabil, the software company of Brotherhood magnates Khairat al-Shatir and Hassan Malik, and retrieved documents implicating the Brotherhood in anti-regime plots – a case reminiscent of the 1948 Jeep case. Senior Brothers faced military trials, and over 1,000 of their foot soldiers were detained. This was followed by another backlash in 2007, which also ended with military tribunals and widespread arrests. Another problem was that activists now hoped that just as they had brought Brothers into legislative and civic councils, they could one day have them voted into executive office. This essentially required outperforming the ruling party in delivering goods to voters, as in any other democratic transition. But the Brotherhood's ideology was about guiding Muslims, not serving them – as one dissident put it: for Brothers, "Islam is the solution, and Muslims are the problem" (Khirbawi 2012: 166). Utilitarian-minded voters should be humored as a stepping-stone to power, nothing more (Samir 2013). More problematic for the Guidance Bureau, though, was that the leaders of the activist wing were now hailed in the media and amongst the organization's urban youth as 'reformers' and encouraged to wrest power away from the old guard. According to the 1980 deal, seasoned Brothers were supposed to manage the organization, while civic activists basically ran a public relations campaign. Veterans never intended to become backseat drivers, nor were they willing to tolerate talk of hawks and doves within the Brotherhood. And so they decided – and eventually managed – to put the self-proclaimed reformers in their place.

In 1996, the Guidance Bureau withdrew its previous approval for the formation of a political party. When Abu al-'Ela Madi and 'Essam Sultan, the seventies-generation couple who had spent years on the project, decided to go ahead anyway and form al-Wasat party, they were accused of embezzlement and fired. Others were isolated from positions of influence within the movement, and young Brothers were asked to dismiss their statements as propaganda designed to win popular and foreign approval. When Abu al-Fotouh, in particular, persisted in his critiques of the organization, members were warned that he had been recruited by the Americans, and was only kept in the Guidance Bureau so that senior Brothers could keep him in check (Abu-Khalil 2012: 17–20). Also, the activists' most stunning electoral victory, in 2005, was undercut by the general guide's confession that the security apparatus had actually engineered it from start to finish.[21]

The seventies generation fought back, presenting themselves as the true inheritors of the moderate Banna, and their rivals as shadowy products of the Special Order and Qutbism. Their call fell on sympathetic ears in Cairo and Alexandria. Young, educated urbanites believed that the 2005 parliamentary victory provided the Brotherhood with a popular mandate to lead democratic change. But they were disappointed both during and after the elections. Wahba (2013) was assigned to the campaign of Hazem Salah Abu Ismai'l, the controversial lawyer-turned-preacher. He was startled by how Brothers ran the campaign just as the ruling party did: buying off voters through empty promises or hard cash. The only difference, in his view, was that secular politicians promised their voters 'salvation' during their tenure in parliament, while Brothers extended the promise to the hereafter as well. More surprising was the fact that nothing distinguished the movement's political and socioeconomic platform from secular ones. Learning that the Guidance Bureau had no moral qualms about riding into parliament on the back of America's post-9/11 'democratic crusade' and Mubarak's security acolytes further undermined the senior leadership (Mikkawi 2013). Tariq (2013), nonetheless, remained optimistic, convincing himself that perhaps the Guidance Bureau was keeping its trump card up its sleeve until it secured victory at the ballot box. But after managing to form the largest opposition bloc since 1952, the Brotherhood's members of parliament simply sat on their hands. Not a single memorable proposal, let alone legislation, came from their quarter. Inaction in parliament was made worse by their perceived mediocrity in the media after the elections. And respect for the leadership hit an all-time low when Guidance Bureau members publicly endorsed the accession of Gamal Mubarak, the president's discredited son, in return for a larger role in political life. Still hoping that the leaders had some sort of a secret plan, Tariq asked one of the Bureau's strongmen, during a private gathering at his in-laws, about how they intended to resist the planned succession. The senior Brother shrugged and replied back in all seriousness: "God knows." Shatla (2013) summarized the frustrations of his young comrades best: "We suddenly felt that Brothers were incapable of learning and developing. And, in our estimation, they were held back by two factors: first, they inhabited a parallel self-sufficient universe; and second, they could never test the validity of their ideas through open debate because they insisted on hiding their beliefs when addressing outsiders." Hubris reached its zenith when senior members began mumbling about how Islam was actually "indebted to the Brothers for keeping it alive."

Despite their intricate indoctrination, in 2005 some of the educated city youth found the discrepancy between the Brotherhood's ballot box victory and the poverty of its performance quite appalling. The fact that the Brotherhood failed to secure a single seat in the 2010 parliament proved beyond doubt that the previous electoral victory was yet another regime maneuver in its endless game with Washington. The looming succession crisis added urgency to their critique. Mubarak was preparing to pass the mantle to his son in September 2011, and the Brothers' sheepish attitude could only have encouraged the old tyrant. Critics became vocal. 'Abd al-Mon'iem Mahmoud, Ahmad Samir, Ibrahim al-Houdeibi, Sameh 'Eid, and others shared their concerns with the wider public through blogs and op-eds, but failed to win over mainstream Brothers, let alone the leadership. So, instead, they considered complementing their social media activism by joining disgruntled youth from other political parties in united front movements, such as the April 6 Youth Movement, and the We Are All Khalid Said Facebook page, to prepare for a popular uprising sometime before the anticipated succession in 2011.

Meanwhile, the Brotherhood's conservative leadership began to set its house in order. When the movement experimented with drafting a political party manifesto, in 2007, conservatives, led by Mahmoud 'Ezzat and Rashad al-Bayumi, flexed their muscles, discarding suggestions to support the election of women and non-Muslims to the presidency – a symbolic gesture (since neither was ever likely to win) that underlined the influence of hardliners. This was followed by a major reshuffle in leadership through the contentious elections of the Guidance Bureau in 2009. The wavering Guide Mahdi 'Akif was convinced to step down; his deputy and aspiring successor Muhammad Habib was sidelined for his misplaced sympathies; Abu al-Fotouh was ousted; 'Essam al-'Erian, the other high-profile activist, was effectively tamed by a seat on the Bureau; provincial hardliners (including Morsi) were added; strongman Khairat al-Shatir kept his seat, even though he was in prison; and the ultra-conservative Muhammad Badi'e, who had actually been imprisoned with Qutb, became the new general guide (Tammam 2012: 27–8).

The reformist youth and their mentors watched as their dream of changing the organization from within was being crushed. Most hung around until 2011, when they threw themselves into the throes of the popular revolt that overthrew Mubarak, and then resigned. But just as they had failed to unite their ranks inside the Brotherhood, they also dispersed themselves in five different political parties, weakening Abu al-Fotouh's hand during the presidential elections in 2012. Hardcore Brothers had always been better at discipline and organization. And now they hoped that their eight-and-a-half-decade crusade was finally about to pay off.

Endgame: Divine Empowerment and its Discontents

The January 25, 2011 uprising caught the Brotherhood unprepared. It was the work of young secular activists, and Brothers initially preferred to stay out of it. But some of their disgruntled youth ignored the order and participated anyway. After three days of rallies, the Guidance Bureau realized this was much bigger than expected, and directed Brothers to join the Day of Rage, on January 28. Hoping to use the revolt to extract concessions from the regime, Muhammad Morsi and Sa'ad al-Katatni (future president, and speaker of parliament and head of the Brotherhood's Justice and Freedom Party, respectively) were dispatched, on February 1, to negotiate with 'Umar Suleiman, Egypt's intelligence chief. They offered to help (or, at least, try) to deflate the uprising in return for a larger share of the political pie. Refusing to have their arms twisted, regime loyalists hired thugs to clear Tahrir Square, the revolt's epicenter. The Battle of the Camel, on February 2, sabotaged the secret talks, as protesters were now determined to press on. And the army eventually seized the opportunity to oust Mubarak on February 11.[22]

The Brotherhood now faced a much graver challenge than that of its 2005 parliamentary victory. The revolt had redistributed power within the country's ruling 'power triangle': the tension-ridden partnership between the military, security, and political institutions. The security forces lost their overriding dominance of the ruling bloc, and were now forced to share power with the once-marginalized military. Only the political slot was open for negotiation. Mubarak's ruling party was in its death throes, and the civil activists who collectively led the revolt were in a state of utter chaos. The Brotherhood was the only organized political force poised to benefit from the upheaval. But how far did it want to push the revolutionary process? The General Bureau made a fateful decision during those early days in the transition period and stuck with it until they were overthrown from power two years later: that is, to focus its efforts on replacing the ruling party at the pinnacle of Egypt's authoritarian regime rather than spearheading revolutionary change. This was their chance to seize sufficient power to implement their religious transformation program from above through education, culture, the media, etc. And this goal, of course, determined their strategy: to convince the all-powerful coercive institutions that if they were kind enough to take on the Brotherhood as a new partner, it would not rock the boat. Appeasement, therefore, became the order of the day.

Brothers dutifully avoided any hint of challenging the autonomy and privileges of the armed forces (economic or otherwise), and made sure they stayed on the right side of the Supreme Council of the Armed Forces (SCAF) all along – even when Morsi was elected president in the summer of 2012. In his first (and only) reshuffle of the general command, on August 14, Morsi carefully avoided anything that might offend military sensibilities. The aging Defense Minister Hussein Tantawi and his Chief of Staff Sami 'Anan were decorated with medals and appointed presidential advisors. Other high-ranking officers were even better rewarded: the outgoing navy commander was charged with administering the Suez Canal; the air defense commander was named head of the army's industrial complex; and SCAF strongman Muhammad al-'Asar became assistant defense minister. The president then chose their replacements from a list of senior commanders. Director of Military Intelligence 'Abd al-Fattah al-Sisi, long groomed by the outgoing defense minister as his successor, was handed the defense portfolio. The Commander of the Third Field Army Sedqi Sobhi was promoted to chief of staff. And on the night these measures were announced, Morsi promised, in a highly indicative speech, to respect the military's autonomy.

Brotherhood courting of the security apparatus, however, dwarfed its deference to the military. And thanks to the movement's support, Egypt's security establishment emerged unscathed from the post-revolt turmoil. Indeed, Brothers encouraged repression throughout the transitional period, blaming protesters on each occasion for

taking the law into their own hands, and repeating security allegations that revolutionary activists were either hired guns or the unwitting pawns of foreign plots to destabilize Egypt. In parliament, they
spared no opportunity to praise Egypt's gallant law enforcers and
shield them from any inquiries. And in one of his first televised interviews as president, Morsi announced that the Interior Ministry had
been rehabilitated and was performing the most patriotic of duties.
The president not only buried a fact-finding commission report detail-
ing security abuses during the 18-day uprising,[23] but audaciously
congratulated police officers for their valuable contribution to the
uprising itself, calling them partners in Egypt's "second crossing" –
the first being the much-celebrated crossing of the Suez Canal on the
first day of the October 1973 war. Needless to say, security violations
continued during Morsi's short tenure, and, soon enough, hotheaded
Islamist supporters augmented official coercion.

Why did the Brotherhood adopt this position? The most straightforward answer is that Brothers had no stomach for taking on the
country's formidable custodians of violence, even though uniting the
revolutionary camp under their command might have provided them
with a fighting chance. Moral entitlement is another good reason.
Brothers had earned the right to rule after eight-and-a-half decades
of spiritual purification and sociopolitical toil. Most of the movement
leaders lost their best years behind prison bars before Egypt's young
revolutionaries were born. Moreover, Brothers were religiously
obliged, as the true representatives of Islam, to protect the faithful
against secular activists and their delusions, not to unite with these
seculars to reform the political system. These were all good reasons
for appeasing the forces of coercion and sacrificing revolutionaries at
the altar. And there is a kernel of truth in each of them. But the
Brotherhood's attitude largely stemmed out of its unique ideology.
Brothers aspired to regulate public morality, foil global conspiracies
against Islam, and eventually secure worldwide hegemony. Yet they
had neither an army nor a security force, and counted instead on
divine support to boost their ranks. Now, the pious vanguard fell
upon a large army and an experienced security force that was not of
their making, but could be – with God's grace – converted to their
cause. And so what many might dismiss as excessive pragmatism,
even cowardice, was in fact a perfect application of what they saw
as the Prophetic strategy of turning enemies into allies. This is why
family meetings during the transitional period presented one example
after the other of obstinate infidels who tortured and battled early
Muslims before transferring their energies to Islam's service. Prefects
stressed the example of 'Umar, who used to torture his servant for

converting, then went on to become the second Rightly Guided Caliph; and Khaled ibn al-Walid and 'Amr ibn al-'As, who defeated Muslims in major battles, then became two of Islam's greatest generals (Alfy 2013). Surely, the same could be expected of officers who repressed Brothers for decades.

As it turned out, deferring to the military and security was not enough to consolidate power. The army, in particular, needed to relieve itself of the burden of everyday governance in order to focus on rebuilding its combat capacities and pursuing means of projecting regional power. Brothers were thus expected to stabilize the political arena, but they failed to deliver because of their ineptitude at political bargaining – a skill they never bothered to develop. It was clear that none of the three political contenders (Islamists, old-regime loyalists, and civil activists) was strong enough to rule alone. Alliances were necessary to break this balance of weakness. But, instead of siding with either old-regime or revolutionary forces, Brothers tried to play them off against each other to buy time. Old-regime politicians suspected that, despite their sugar-coated promises, Brothers were not willing to share the spoils of Egypt's patronage state. And civil activists resented the Brotherhood's attempt to hijack the revolt without any serious intention to see it through. Unfortunately, Islamists failed to appreciate that their ham-fisted tactics would inevitably drive their political rivals into a tactical alliance against them, and that such an alliance was bound to force military officers to revise their stance. Hence, the stage was set for another major showdown on June 30, 2013.

Apart from the Brotherhood's barefaced support for military and security transgressions, civil activists were most vexed by the Brotherhood's attempt to dominate the Constituent Assembly charged with drafting a new constitution. A constitutional declaration, in March 2011, tasked parliament with appointing a 100-member Constituent Assembly. A heated public debate produced a gentlemanly agreement that this future-shaping body must be sociopolitically inclusive. But in March 2012, the Brotherhood-led majority controlled 65 seats, and allocated only 6 seats to women and 5 seats to Copts. A quarter of the members (including representatives from Azhar and the Coptic Church) refused to participate, and the deadlock was broken when the State Administrative Court dissolved the Assembly because it was illegal for members of parliament to elect themselves. After intense negotiations failed to convince the Brotherhood to stop trying to control the constitution-writing body, Islamists went ahead and formed a new assembly, in June 2012, with only 30 percent non-Islamists, most of whom again walked out. A few days later, SCAF issued a constitutional declaration assuring Egyptians that it would appoint a new assembly if this one failed to achieve consensus. Steaming ahead regardless, the Guidance Bureau directed Morsi to issue a constitutional declaration, on November 20, that protected their cherished assembly from dissolution, and placed the president above the law.

Immediately afterwards, the Brotherhood flogged the assembly to approve the new constitution in a marathon 16-hour session, on November 30, and pass it through a popular referendum in 15 days. Massive protests erupted, and thousands camped outside the presidential palace only to be cleared off, on December 6, by a band of armed Brothers. Very few probably had a chance to read, let alone comprehend, the 230 articles of the hastily conceived document. Less than a third of registered voters bothered to show up for the referendum, and only 63 percent granted their approval. Brothers were undeterred by the slimness of this popular mandate since their job was to guide Egyptians to the right path rather than hammer out a national consensus. As Brothers seemed incapable of compromise, civil activists now resolved to undermine Brotherhood rule, even if it meant receiving help from their old regime enemies. A two-pronged attack ensued, with revolutionary agitation on the street and in the media, combined with bureaucratic and judicial sabotage of any attempt at orderly government (leading, among other things, to energy shortages and blackouts).

That being said, the Brotherhood's opponents could not have fielded enough protesters to legitimize a military intervention, had the common folk abstained. It was the Brotherhood's incompetence at government and the fact that they had no concrete plan to offer that drove millions into the streets on June 30. And it was the Brotherhood's decision to turn a political clash into a full-fledged religious war, through an inflammatory rhetoric made convincing by dispersed acts of violence, that guaranteed the public's blanket endorsement for their brutal repression. Brothers had not fully appreciated how practical their countrymen were, even if they were practicing Muslims; or that, despite their verbal enthusiasm for Islam, they voted for Brothers mainly because they thought that their success as service providers in professional syndicates, student unions, and local communities, could be replicated on a national level. But the movement was evidently unprepared to rule. Not only did it lack a tangible alternative to the existing system, but also it had no cadres to run the state (Radwan 2013). When the Higher Election Commission prevented the Brotherhood from using its signature campaign slogan 'Islam is the Solution' because of its religious connotations, Brothers

came up with an even vaguer slogan: 'We bring good to Egypt.'
Disillusioned with the Brothers, Egyptians preferred risking back-
tracking into functioning secular autocracy to the certainty of sliding
into what they saw as incompetent religious rule.

So perhaps the Brotherhood's cardinal mistake was its underesti-
mation of the masses – or, more accurately, its overestimation of its
ability to direct them using religion. It was not terribly flattering, for
instance, to hear Brotherhood spokesmen brag during parliamentary
elections that, if Islamists nominated a dead dog, the people would
still vote for it (Alfy 2013). This was only true in the minds of
Brothers. Opinion polls and voting patterns during the transitional
period showed a different reality. For example, 57% of voters were
still undecided on the eve of the country's first free parliamentary
elections, and the Brotherhood had the support of only 31% of the
decided ones. When it came down to it, only 55% of registered voters
turned out, and 44% gave their vote to the Islamic alliance, which
included the Brotherhood's newly established political arm (the
Freedom and Justice Party) and a few smaller parties, while 25%
preferred *salafis*, a totally untested political quantity. More signifi-
cantly, over 70% of voters believed that the country's major challenges were economic, and only 17% cited religion as their major
concern.[24] More revealing still was the fact that, in the first round of
the presidential elections, the Brotherhood received no more than
24.8% of the vote, with the old-regime candidate (General Ahmad
Shafiq) in hot pursuit with 23.6%, followed by Islamism's ideological
nemesis (the national socialist Hamdeen Sabahi) at 20.7%. And in
the second round, with only one candidate to defeat, Morsi barely
captured 51% of the vote.[25] Evidently, Egyptians were much less
supportive of Islamism than Brothers liked to believe. Worse was to
follow. Six months into Morsi's presidency, 52% of Egyptians still
placed their trust in the military, versus 28% in the presidency.[26] And
in 12 months, Morsi's approval rating plummeted from 79% to
32%.[27] This downward spiral continued even after Morsi's tenure
came to an end. A poll released by the Pew Research Center, in May
2014, revealed that the percentage of Egyptians who had a generally
favorable view of the Brotherhood slumped from 63% in early 2013
to 38% a few months after his ouster, and that, during the same
period, those who believed that religious parties should be allowed
to participate in government dropped from 47% to 31%, and those
who insisted that Egyptian law should be strictly based on the Qur'an
also dropped from 62% to 48%.[28]

Dismissing the possibility that pious Egyptians could ever defy
Islam's chief representatives was the last nail in the Brotherhood's

political coffin. As stubborn and scornful of his people as Mubarak was, the old dictator was wise enough to grasp that concessions were necessary to deprive his challengers of popular support. And, sure enough, in each of the three speeches he delivered during the 2011 revolt, Mubarak relinquished significant ground: dismissing the cabinet; cashiering the entire leadership of the ruling party; dissolving the infamous Policy Committee; forming a legal commission to purge the constitution of unpopular clauses; and pledging that neither he nor his son would run in the upcoming presidential election, which was only 9 months away. Morsi, in 2013, in contrast, would not yield, not even offering to reshuffle the cabinet or reinforce his legitimacy via popular referendum. When warned of the gathering rebellion, he put down his opponents as a handful of old-regime scoundrels, and delivered an incredible 3-hour-long speech (156 minutes, to be exact), on June 26, ridiculing some of these imaginary foes by name. After being shown helicopter-recorded footage of the millions who demonstrated against him on June 30, he still held that this "Photoshop revolution" drew no more than 160,000 people. Morsi then went on to deliver his second (and, as it turned out, last) record-breaking speech on July 2, when he waved his fist belligerently and repeated that he was Egypt's legitimate leader 98 times in 45 minutes. What his audience did not realize was that this was not the arrogance of power (or the vanity of a fool), but a well-bred Brother who trusted that what God decrees, men could never undo.

But what Egypt witnessed during this fateful summer was not men thwarting Heaven's design, but rather a bewildered population questioning – possibly for the first time – what Islamism really meant. This was the first instance of a Muslim public struggling to decouple Islam and Islamism. Two reasons animated this popular attempt: secular and religious. As citizens, they were appalled by the Brotherhood's incompetence in government; and, as Muslims, they were outraged by how their religion was manipulated to explain away this incompetence. In a word, many began to suspect that Brothers flaunted Islam to excuse their bankruptcy and lurking authoritarianism. They saw Islamists no longer as god-fearing underdogs striving for power to implement Islam, but as another breed of politicians using Islam to justify their power. And the Brotherhood's aggressive rhetoric added fuel to the fire.

The religious zeal that Morsi's election had inspired was not taken seriously at first. Egyptians were amused to learn that their president was the long-awaited liberator of Jerusalem, destined for a lead role in Armageddon. They scoffed at superstitions that Morsi was reincarnated from the time of the Prophet, and that carrying his picture down to the grave would sail one safely through purgatory. But then there were also frequent denunciations of critics as enemies of Islam; bands of Islamists trying to monitor social piety; suspicious release of militants; calls for holy war against Shi'ites in Syria; and other questionable acts. It turned out, however, that what Egyptians saw during Morsi's 1-year tenure was a drop in the ocean. On the eve of the June 30, 2013 uprising, Islamists camping outside Rab'a al-'Adawiya mosque no longer had the luxury of keeping their thoughts behind closed doors. They were forced to air their views from the stage to whoever was there to listen (Islamists and curious visitors). Al-Jazeera Egypt managed an almost uninterrupted live broadcast from the sit-in, and the juiciest parts went viral in the form of YouTube videos. So, for 40 nights, unsuspecting Egyptians received a crash course in Islamist ideology. And what they saw steeled their will to rebel. They witnessed religious condemnation of opponents; threats of eternal damnation in every prayer; comparisons with biblical and Prophetic battles; claims that angels descended on the Islamist sit-in; sacred visions reassuring the faithful of the coming victory; rumors that the country's transitional president was a closeted Jew, and that the Pope was behind the plot to remove Egypt's first Islamist president; and displays of Brotherhood children marching with coffins and white shrouds to express their readiness for martyrdom. Overall, Egyptians had a rough introduction to the Brotherhood's ideology of divine empowerment. And their initial response was to feel betrayed. The Brothers' well-crafted discourse on public service gave way to what sounded like the hallucinations of a millenarian cult. Islamists were suddenly recast as a heretical sect that must be violently flushed out of the Muslim community.[29]

The result was a blanket endorsement for repression. In a few months, over 10,000 members were detained, including the entire leadership of the Brotherhood (with only a handful escaping to Gaza, Doha, Istanbul, and London). And on December 25, 2013, for the first time in its turbulent history, the Brotherhood was designated a terrorist organization. The future remains unclear. Many Brothers are determined to fight on (peacefully for most, but violently for some) in what they believe to be the final chapter in their divine empowerment. Others decided to withdraw and refocus on attaining the level of piety necessary to win the next round through divine grace. Yet none seem to suspect the validity of religious determinism – a testament to its ideological resilience and the effectiveness of the cultivation process that sustains it.

In fact, in a letter from the now-imprisoned Morsi to his son Osama, the ousted president still insisted that divine help was imminent: "that not only will [I] return to office, but that victory will be total" (Solomon 2014). And a year after the Brotherhood's downfall, the movement's official website carried an article by Guidance Bureau member 'Abd al-Rahman al-Bar with the rousing title: "A Trial that will End in Resounding Victory" (*Ibtila' yantahi bi nasr mubin*). The Brotherhood luminary reasserted the claim that divine empowerment follows tribulation, and that victory first requires sorting out the truly faithful: "What is happening is no more than a test . . . that will soon be over, with the faithful rewarded with divine grace." According to God's unchanging laws, he maintained, "The most patient [believers] are the ones eligible for victory . . . regardless of material indicators to the contrary." Al-Bar concluded by assuring Brothers that: "no matter how hard oppressors try to harm them . . . once they turn to God, He will immediately grant them victory."[30]

In other words, the significance of the heady events of 2013 is not in their potential impact on the Brotherhood's ideology – which apparently emerged undented – but rather in the potentially paradigmatic shift in the Muslim popular psyche. Brothers were no longer simply perceived as the most eager among the believers, as men of God deserving public sympathy and protection from pernicious autocrats. Many Egyptians have now begun to view them as an ideological clique with an unorthodox (perhaps even distorted) version of Islam – a groundbreaking development for Islamists in Egypt and beyond.

5

Islamism in Egypt and Beyond

Youssef al-Qaradawi commemorated the seventieth anniversary of the founding of the Brotherhood with a book that began: "The Muslim Brotherhood is not only the largest Islamist movement. It is also the mother of all Islamist movements. It is the origin and the essence ... Other movements that derive their name from Islam are [little more than] successors, extensions, or dissenters" (1999: 30). This echoed a previous self-congratulatory note written by the third general guide, 'Umar al-Telmesani, that: "Every Islamist movement began by learning the principles of the Muslim Brotherhood, and then deviated to the left or to the right" (2008: 356). It is true that the Brotherhood invented Islamism and continued to represent it in its most pristine form. But other Islamists, including Brotherhood affiliates, struck their own path to adapt to local contexts. So let us consider, in this final chapter, Brotherhood-inspired groups in Egypt, Brotherhood branches in the Arab world, and fellow travelers in Turkey and Iran. The aim is not to examine these movements in any detail, but to offer snapshots highlighting how they parted company with the mother organization.

The first Brotherhood chapters, in Palestine, Libya, the Levant, and the Sudan, have become embroiled in civil strife. Those who negotiated a working arrangement with their monarchs, in Jordan, Morocco, and Kuwait, are integrating themselves ever more closely with the ruling elite. The most successful models, in Tunisia and Turkey, have reached the pinnacle of power and are struggling to stay there. The Brotherhood's European-based International Organization (al-Tanzim al-Dawli), established in the 1980s to coordinate its loose network of branches in 76 states, has risen to fame after the 2011 Arab uprisings. And the Shi'ite-inspired Khomeinism – the mirror image of Sunni Islamism – is striving to reform itself and break its international isolation, even as its acolytes in Lebanon and Bahrain are losing ground.[1] But let us begin close to home with other Egyptian Islamists.

Egyptian Dissidents: Reformers and Militants

The effectiveness of the Brotherhood's cultivation process was such that it has never suffered a major dissent in its 85 years of existence. There were numerous individual resignations, but not a single notable split. When high-profile members left, they blamed administrative corruption, organizational autocracy, or differences in priorities and strategies. None of them, from Ahmad al-Sukkari in 1947 to 'Abd al-Mon'im Abu al-Fotouh in 2012, questioned the ideological premises of Islamism. Even embittered defectors, such as Tharwat al-Khirbawi, would only lash out against paranoid leaders and Masonic practices, rather than providing a systematic ideological critique. There seemed, however, to have been one exception – though its credibility evaporated after 2011 – which was the case of al-Wasat (the Center) Party.

The student activists who became Brothers in the 1970s believed that the movement could best secure electoral gains by forming a political party. After years of haggling, the general guide authorized Abu al-'Ela Madi, an engineer, and 'Essam Sultan, a lawyer, to draft a proposal. The two former activists took the task to heart, drafting a party manifesto in the early 1990s, only to be turned down by a Guidance Bureau that did not want to provoke the regime by appearing too aggressive. On the spur of the moment, the frustrated bunch that was involved in the project decided to apply for a party license anyway. They were immediately cashiered from the Brotherhood on embezzlement charges (Madi 2007).[2]

Left to their own devices, the dissidents now sought a new ideological project for their embryonic party.[3] After searching in vain among Islamists for an intellectual of some stature, they decided to outsource. They first knocked on the doors of sympathizers, such as the journalist Fahmi Howeidy (2006), the criminal lawyer Muhammad Selim al-'Awwa, and the judge and lay historian Tariq al-Bishri. Most were kind enough to offer some useful suggestions on how Islamism could function in a pluralist democratic society.[4] But, despite their general endorsement, there was nothing concrete they could provide.

Pressed by potential supporters to lay down exactly what this new centrist platform was, Madi produced a 2005 volume entitled *Ru'iat al-Wasat fei al-Siyasa wa al-Mujtama'* (The Centrist Vision in Politics and Society). The book recycled old op-eds and interviews, and defined centrism loosely as an ideology that holds that "moderation, centrism, and justice" are the best course. Its main legacy, however, was the introduction of the new party not as an Islamic party, but as a 'civil party with an Islamic reference point' (*marji'iya*) – a formulation later adopted by the Brotherhood's 2011 party (Madi 2005: 12–13).

What could this possibly mean? Madi began by drawing comparisons with Christian democrats and Christian socialists in Europe, who invoked religion in politics. But, as the founder of al-Wasat went on, it became obvious that he did not know much about these parties beyond their names. Madi then explained that, since Islam endorses freedom, equality, property, and consultation, we could infer that it also endorses democracy, citizenship, welfare, capitalism, human rights, etc. (2005: 98). Yet this rendered centrism as little more than a blanket endorsement of Western concepts – as long as they did not violate the Islamic framework, which is not very clearly defined. So, in response to why non-Muslims should accept Islam as their reference point, for example, Madi argued nebulously that just as Islam binds Muslims because it is their religion, it binds non-Muslims because it is their civilization (2005: 98–108). Obviously, a more coherent system of ideas was yet to be articulated.

Fortunately, two non-Islamist intellectuals offered to help – and, ironically, both held doctoral degrees in literature. The first was Professor 'Abd al-Wahhab al-Mesiri, author of a two-volume study on secularism, and the first Arabic encyclopedia on *Jews, Judaism, and Zionism*. The other collaborator, oddly enough, was a Christian by the name of Rafiq Habib, who was infatuated with the Islamic civilization as a historical phenomenon, though he, naturally, did not believe in Islam. Together they provided the manifesto for what was called the Centrist Trend (Tayyar al-Wasat), which – as the name implies – presented a more moderate version of Islamism: tolerant of diversity, and politically engaged. What were the features of this new project, that merited renaming the party al-Wasat al-Jadid (New Center) in 2004? Al-Mesiri's contribution was an eloquent preface to the party program. But his dense prose and abstract philosophy did not really lend itself to practical implementation. Rafiq Habib tried harder, presenting what was supposed to be a radical critique of Western modernization's chief invention: the modern state. Habib's goal was to offer an authentic alternative, inspired by Islamic history and values (2001: 10–11). The starting point in his model was to place the family at the center of society. Unlike in the West, in Habib's viewpoint, it is the family (rather than the church, school, media) that socializes individuals. This is why Muslim society could never be standardized, like modern Western ones, but rather consisted of a mosaic of families and small communities. Accordingly, rather than a central state, Islamic politics should be practiced not through political parties, but through civic groups, such as families, tribes, sects, guilds, unions, etc. (Habib 2001: 17–19, 52–3). These civic groups collectively represent the nation, rather than the state. And the state should be the nation's guardian, rather than its master. What is needed is a "privatization of government," Habib concluded (2001: 98–100, 186–8). Two things were immediately apparent: first, far from liberating himself from Western theory, Habib's 'authentic' model was an amalgam of liberal state theory and totalitarian corporatism; the second and more important problem was that his proposals rang hollow in a country too far down the road of centralized modernization (at least three centuries).

None of this really mattered eventually because, as the Brotherhood rightly predicted, the government refused to sanction the new Islamist party, and it was only after the 2011 revolt that al-Wasat Party became legal. Curiously enough, the moment it acquired a formal existence, the party returned to the fold, playing second fiddle to the Brotherhood's main party and wholeheartedly supporting Brothers in parliament and the presidency. Advocates of centrism no longer saw any differences between them and the Brotherhood, and the Brothers, on their part, chose to forgive and forget about the embezzlement charges. Difference disappeared to the point where Rafiq Habib, the Wasat's primary ideologue, was appointed deputy leader of the Brotherhood's Freedom and Justice Party.

But, in contrast to this immaterial defection, the Brotherhood's accommodation with Egypt's autocrats inspired a much more radical alternative: militant Islamists (sometimes referred to as *jihadists*). Militants studied the Brotherhood's Special Order experiment and internalized Qutb's advocacy for a pious vanguard, and reached a much simpler conclusion than the Brothers: instead of transforming society to establish the Islamic state from below, why not undermine rulers right away through violence. They recognized, of course, that the regime had formidable military and security forces, but still hoped that a concerted campaign of violence would eventually weaken its grip. Brothers were not, one could say, alien to political assassinations and bombings. And they did support armed resistance in places like Palestine, Afghanistan, Kashmir, and later Chechnya. But they never adopted violence as an official strategy. By the mid-1970s, however, Islamist militants saw the Brotherhood's gradualism as cowardice, and their reliance on divine intervention as abhorrent fatalism.

Building on Qutb's claim that non-Islamists are, for all practical purposes, infidels, militants considered them fair game: they could be killed, their property destroyed, their wealth confiscated, their women enslaved, and so on. By the same token, non-Islamist wives must be divorced; parents and friends must be disowned; and jobs must be relinquished; and some even insisted on boycotting non-Islamist mosques and food. The time for persuasion was over. Whatever militants decreed must be enforced at gunpoint. Abiding by Islamic codes should not be a matter of choice: once someone embraces Islam, he or she must act accordingly (Yunis 2012: 319–21). The day Prophet Muhammad conquered Mecca and established the rule of Islam, the principle of tolerating half-hearted compliance was abolished – as commanded in the verse known among Orientalists as the verse of the sword.

Brothers had to respond. Second General Guide Hassan al-Houdeibi presented the main counterargument in his 1977 pamphlet *Du'a la Quda* (Missionaries Not Judges). The crux of his defense was that excommunicating society, as a whole, does not imply excommunicating each of its members. In other words, while society *en bloc* might be in a state of pagan ignorance (*jahiliya*), this did not necessarily apply to the individuals within it. Militants remained undeterred by this pedantry.

Like Brothers, they attempted to model their strategy after the first Muslim generation, who had rejected the false religion of their contemporaries, fled away to a remote location to organize their ranks, and then turned to waging holy war. Fittingly, therefore, the militant pioneer Shukri Mustafa asked his followers to 'excommunicate and migrate' (*takfir wa higra*), i.e. abandon their families, jobs, and neighborhoods, and move to deserted locations where they could create parallel communities and prepare themselves for *jihad*. Shukri, an agricultural engineer, had been locked up with the Brothers between 1965 and 1971, and was married to a Sister, but he decided in prison that the Brotherhood's social reengineering strategy was hopeless, and that a radical change was urgently needed. His Muslims' Group (*Jama'at al-Muslimin*) proved to be a brief affair. Lawsuits from the families whose sons and daughters had absconded forced the government to pursue the militant preacher. In a desperate move, Shukri's men kidnapped Muhammad al-Dahabi, an esteemed cleric and former minister of endowments, to be able to negotiate with the government, and, when rebuffed, decided to execute him in July 1977. The government's reaction was swift: in a few months, Shukri's followers were rounded up, and he and four ringleaders were executed.

The mantle passed immediately to the Islamic Jihad (*al-Jihad al-Islami*), which – as its name implies – skipped the excommunication and migration phases, and jumped straight to action. In 1980, Muhammad 'Abd al-Salam Farag, yet another engineer, published the infamous tract "al-Farida al-Gha'iba" (Absent Obligation), arguing that Islam was already established (i.e., no need to start all over again, as Qutb and Shukri argued), but Muslims had abandoned one of its main obligations: holy war. Wasting no time, Farag conceived a plot to assassinate President Sadat and spark an insurgency. He succeeded in the first part (and was duly hanged in 1982), but the security forces crushed the insurgents in a few days. Nonetheless, his ideas lived on, partly owing to the zeal of one of those convicted in the assassination case: a medical student named Ayman al-Zawahri.

Qutb had frequented al-Zawahri's household as an Arabic tutor, and Ayman's maternal uncle, Mahfouz 'Azzam, was Qutb's lawyer. The martyred Islamist and his views thus shaped the young Zawahri's mind, according to his comrade Muntasir al-Zayat (2003). In "Fursan taht Rayat al-Nabi" (Knights Under the Prophet's Banner), Zawahri wrote: "some thought that the execution of Sayyid Qutb had dealt a fatal blow to Islamism. But below the apparently calm surface, Qutb's beliefs were opening new horizons for the Islamist movement" (2001: 12). And in "al-Hassad al-Mur" (The Bitter Harvest) – Zawahri's scathing rebuke of the Muslim Brotherhood – Brothers were accused of ignoring Qutb's radical conclusions to protect their own skin (1991: 130). They were also guilty of subjecting God's will to votes and referendums – something he reminded Brothers of, following their failed bid in 2013. In Zawahri's words:

O Brother! The nation's representatives are gods that demand worship, O Brother! Those who elect them and accept their legislations are infidels who have substituted God with human-gods. Islam forbids nomination for democratic legislative councils ... Islam forbids participating or voting in these councils ... anyone who participates in these democratic creations is an infidel that must be killed ... Anyone who claims to be a Muslim democrat, or a Muslim that believes in democracy is an infidel that must be killed. It is as implausible as being a Muslim Christian or a Muslim Jew.

(1991: 21)

Following Qutb's execution, the 15-year-old Zawahri and his brother Muhammad created their first clandestine group: the Ma'adi cell (named after the Cairo suburb they grew up in). It was student-based and did little more than read Qutb's writings. Then, in 1974, it merged with other militant cells to create the Islamic Jihad. Because he was fluent in English, al-Zawahri was designated media spokesman for the 300 defendants in the Sadat assassination case (Zayat 2003). Video footage of the opening day of the trial, on December 4, 1982, shows the defendants, locked up in a zoo-like cage set in the middle of Cairo's Exhibition Grounds. They were chanting and praying. "Finally, the camera settles on Zawahri, who stands apart from the chaos with a look of solemn, focused intensity" (Wright 2002). At a signal, everyone fell silent, and al-Zawahri cried out:

> Now we want to speak to the whole world! Who are we? Why [did] they bring us here, and what [do] we want to say . . . We are Muslims who believe in our religion, both in ideology and practice, and hence we tried our best to establish an Islamic state and an Islamic society . . . We are not sorry for what we have done for our religion, and we have sacrificed, and we stand ready to make more sacrifices! We are here – the real Islamic front and the real Islamic opposition [as opposed to the Muslim Brotherhood].
>
> (quoted in Wright 2002)

Zawahri served a three-year sentence, and in 1987 made his way to Afghanistan. He had visited the war-torn country twice before, in 1980 and 1981, with Muslim Brotherhood aid convoys. This time his mission was to establish a secure base for the Islamic Jihad group outside Egypt. And once he met the Wahhabi millionaire, Osama bin Laden, he became "bin Laden's mind" (Zayat 2003). Wahhabism, conceived in the eighteenth century and adopted by al-Saud tribe, was not an ideology, but an ultra-orthodox version of the Hanbali School of jurisprudence. Doubtless, the literalist Muslims of Saudi Arabia, and later the Afghani religious students known as the Taliban, were quite receptive to militant views, but it was al-Zawahri who converted many of them from bigots to ideologues.

After the 1989 Soviet pull-out from Afghanistan, Zawahri and bin Laden held a war council at the town of Khost to consider the future of the hardened fighters who now had too much time on their hands. They resolved to create an international network of militants out of the database (*qa'dat al-bayanat*) developed to keep track of the Afghan war participants – hence, the name of the new group: al-Qa'da.[5] The goal was to send these seasoned veterans back to their countries to topple secular regimes. In that sense, the wave of violence that overtook Egypt between 1992 and 1997 (costing the lives of 1,200 people) was not unique; similar campaigns were unfolding in Somalia, Yemen, Libya, and Algeria. Zawahri's operators targeted intellectuals, politicians, officers, religious minorities, and tourists. In 1992, Zawahri and bin Laden moved to Sudan to be closer to the action. This allowed Zawahri, for instance, to cross the borders to Somalia in October 1993 and mastermind the attack on the US Special Operations team, the ill-famed 'Black Hawk Down' incident. The following year, Zawahri travelled tirelessly across Europe to establish recruitment bases in England, France, Germany, Spain, Italy, and Belgium, and sent envoys as far as the Philippines and Argentina. It was also rumored that he made a secret visit to the United States, sometime in the mid-1990s, scouting New York, California, and Texas, and locating fundraisers (Bodansky 2001: 99–105; Wright 2002). The powerful pair were expelled from their Sudanese safe haven after al-Qa'da's spectacular bombings in Saudi Arabia (in 1995 and 1996), and resettled in Kabul under the protection of the Taliban.

Their decade-long adventure in the Arab world made it obvious that Arab regimes were more resilient than al-Qa'da had originally suspected. The reason why they were so invincible, Zawahri concluded, was because the West bolstered them. Hence, a groundbreaking decision was made to reorient global terror from the near enemy (Muslim rulers) to the far enemy (their Western supporters). And on February 22, 1998, the World Islamic Front for Jihad Against the Jews and the Crusaders (al-Jabhah al-Islamiyah al-'Alamiyah li-Qital al-Yahud wal-Salibiyyin) was inaugurated, stating in its founding document: "To kill and fight Americans and their allies, whether civilian or military, is an individual obligation for every Muslim who is able to do so in any country ... Every Muslim, who believes in [God] and asks for His forgiveness, is called upon to abide by [God's] order by killing Americans ... anywhere, anytime, and whenever possible" (quoted in Bergen 2001: 95–6).

The bombing of the US embassies in Kenya and Tanzania, in the summer of 1998, was the signal attack, followed by the assualt on the USS *Cole* off the shores of Yemen, in October 2000, and, of course, the spectacular September 11, 2001 attacks. Harking back to his Brotherhood-inspired ideological roots, Zawahri described the collapse of New York's Twin Towers as follows: "This was not just a human achievement – it was a holy act" (quoted in Wright 2002). As he later declared, Islamists "reflected God's own power ... He has given them knowledge and strength drawn from His own, and turned them from a scattered few into a power that threatens the stability of the new world order" (2001: 4).

Despite its global notoriety, however, al-Qa'da did not yet manage to politically outweigh the Brotherhood in Egypt – though militants effectively overshadowed Brothers in Somalia, Yemen, Algeria, and recently in Iraq, Libya, and Syria. In Islamism's home country, none-theless, militants continued to operate on the fringes of the Islamist camp. Some renounced violence and joined forces with non-militant fundamentalists (*salafis*), whose most popular strand, the Alexandrian al-Da'wa al-Salafiya, chaperoned al-Nur (the Light) Party in 2011. Others stuck to their ways, operating under the old banner of the Islamic Group (al-Jama'a al-Islamiya) under the leadership of 'Assim 'Abd al-Majid, Muhammad al-Zawahri (Ayman's brother), and others convicted in the Sadat assassination case. These militants temporarily buried their differences with the Brotherhood after the latter's rise to power in 2012, and offered their services to the deposed Brothers after 2013. This recent collaboration between Brothers and militants legitimized the Egyptian government's historic, and surely ill-considered, decision to declare the Muslim Brotherhood a terrorist organization on Christmas Day 2013.[6]

The balance of forces between the Brotherhood and al-Qa'da began to shift, however, in the wake of the 2011 uprisings, which, on the one hand, disproved Zawahri's thesis that Arab regimes cannot be destabilized from within, but, on the other hand, created a power vacuum (a black hole, if you like) that is now drawing in hordes of militants away from Western capitals to Egypt's Sinai Peninsula, Libya's eastern provinces, the Turkish–Syrian border, northern Iraq, and similarly inflicted zones. This reverse exodus back to the near enemy is likely to present Brothers with a serious challenge, and will perhaps tempt them to adopt a more militaristic tone to maintain their legitimacy in a redemarcated Islamist arena.

Brothers on the Run: Palestine, Syria, Libya

When Egypt's Brothers thought of expanding, they naturally turned to their immediate neighbors. They began organizing cells in the late 1930s, and by 1944 Brotherhood branches had opened up in Jerusalem and Damascus, followed by the Libyan chapter, five years later.[7] The Palestinian affiliate was always close to heart, since many Egyptian Brothers fought there during the 1948 war, and claim that if they had not been stabbed in the back by the Egyptian army, on orders from the British government, they would have defeated the Zionists. The establishment of Israel led to the scattering of Palestinian Brothers: West Bank members linked with the Jordanian chapter, and members of the diaspora joined their respective branches in the Arab world, Europe, Asia, and the Americas. The bulk of the Palestinian Brothers remained concentrated in Gaza. For years, their fidelity to the

Brotherhood's ideological strategy of building a new Muslim generation before contesting power guaranteed Israeli tolerance, and Israel
even allowed them to establish an Islamic University in Gaza. Contrary
to the leftist-nationalist militants that operated under the umbrella
of the Palestinian Liberation Organization (PLO), Brothers focused
on the personal sphere, and, despite Palestinian accusations and
Israeli atrocities, they persisted in their policy of "patience, religious
work, and ... political passivity" (Brown 2012: 116–17).

But the first Intifada, in December 1987, shook the Brotherhood's
quiescence to the core. As Gaza residents rose spontaneously against
Israel and rejected calls for de-escalation as defeatist, the Brotherhood
could no longer remain on the sidelines. Not leading the resistance
risked surrendering dominance to secular groups. Thus, the
Brotherhood reinvented itself through an armed wing: the Islamic
Resistance Movement (known by its Arabic acronym: Hamas – which
means 'enthusiasm'). But immediate resistance never fully squared
with the Palestinian Brothers' ideological beliefs. As far as they were
concerned, Jerusalem fell because Muslims had turned away from
their religion, and only when they returned to it would they earn the
divine right to liberate the sacred city and its blessed environs. This
is why their positions sometimes appeared confused. "Hamas was
not only flexible; it was ambiguous," one scholar noted; "Its leaders
showed a remarkable ability to feint in different directions without
fully committing to any of them ... Individuals did not necessarily
know what the movement would do – and perhaps would not even
know their own position – until a question was forced by events"
(Brown 2012: 119). So Hamas would, for instance, reject a peaceful
settlement, but sign a long-term armistice; it would deny the legitimacy of the 1993 Oslo Accords and the elections they prescribed, yet
take part in these illegitimate elections and eventually win in 2006;
and it would accept democracy, yet seize power by force in the
summer of 2007 on a (probably justified) suspicion that their rivals
planned to cheat them out of their gains. This hesitation even perme-
ated their face-saving armed resistance, which amounted to firing
poorly guided and ineffective missiles every once in a while, and
patiently enduring Israeli retaliation. Indeed, being on the receiving
end of Israeli attacks, whether full-scale operations (as in 2010, 2012,
and 2014) or targeted assassinations, is what mostly bolsters the
movement's legitimacy. With the hope that a Brotherhood government in Egypt would offer relief vanishing with the 2013 overthrow,
Hamas negotiated, in April 2014, a national unity government with
its secular rival, Fatah. Clearly, Palestinian Brothers could no longer
sit back and content themselves with cultivating a godly community.

They have become part of everyday Palestinian politics, and as such will have to devise and implement concrete policies.

Unlike Palestinians, Syrian Brothers have produced a prolific thinker: Sai'd Hawwa, the author of several notable works on Sufism, theology, and jurisprudence, a multi-volume exegesis of the Qur'an, and a large biography of the Prophet. Hawwa studied jurisprudence in Damascus under the first comptroller general[i] of the Syrian Brotherhood, Mustafa al-Siba'ie (who in turn was mentored by Banna in Cairo), and joined the movement in 1952, working as a school-teacher (like Banna and Qutb). Though he quickly became a senior leader, he still devoted most of his time to writing. Even though the unorthodoxy of his oeuvre limited it to Islamist circles, Hawwa tried his best to push beyond religious determinism. He offered, for instance, a rational recipe for progress, based on the full utilization of resources. This meant that his criticism of the West (or, conversely, his defense of Islamism) had to be grounded in objective criteria: for example, arguing that alcohol should be prohibited because of the material harms of intoxication, rather than its violation of religious law. He also defended Islam's superiority because it combined utilitarian policies with refined culture, regardless of any divine sanction (Hawwa 1988: 16–22). Nonetheless, Hawwa did not fully transcend his ideological roots, insisting that science alone produces heartless intellectuals; highlighting the centrality of brotherly love to any progressive project; and returning to the characteristic Islamist claim that it was straying away from divinity (*rabbaniya*) that was responsible for Muslim misfortunes (Hawwa 1988: 87, 97, 272).

Hawwa's intellectual excursions have been made possible by the Syrian Brothers' unique experience. Syria was much more traditional, decentralized, and politically fluid than Egypt in the mid twentieth century. Also, in contrast to Egypt, Islamists enjoyed little following, compared to communists and nationalists. For these reasons, Brothers functioned relatively unnoticed. This all changed when Hafez al-Assad consolidated power in 1970 by promoting members of his sectarian minority, the Alawites. Now, Brothers could present themselves as representatives of the "[Sunni] 'natural' majority against an upstart [Shi'a] minority . . . [or] the 'state of the masses' [against] the 'state of a clique'" (Ayubi 1991: 92). It was no longer Islamism versus secularism, but a popular democratic struggle against an uprising minority. Brothers organized demonstrations and (mostly commer-

[i] Reserving the title of 'general guide' for the Egyptian Brotherhood leader and referring to branch leaders as 'comptroller general' symbolically maintains the dominance of Egyptian Brothers.

cial) strikes, and the regime responded with massive arrests. The emboldened Brothers persisted in the hope that Syrians might rally to their cause – which they did not. Battered from all sides, Islamists regrouped in Hama for one last stand. In February 1982, tanks and artillery surrounded the city. The ensuing bombardment leveled entire neighborhoods, killing an estimated 10,000 people (Islamists raise the figure to 40,000). Brotherhood membership was now punishable by death, and the movement did not recover until 2011.

With the recent Syrian uprising, the weakened Brothers tried to mesh in with the insurgent Free Syrian Army, and the mostly secular revolutionary council. On the ground, however, seasoned global militants dominated the Islamist camp. After some soul-searching, exiled Syrian Brothers, under Comptroller General Muhammad Riad al-Shaqfa, announced in Istanbul, in the summer of 2013, the formation of the National Party for Justice and the Constitution (known by its acronym: Wa'd – which means 'promise'). To distinguish itself from Egypt's ill-fated Freedom and Justice Party, the Syrians devised membership quotas: one-third Brothers; one-third independent Islamists; and one-third nationalists. Secular Syrians were hardly convinced that Brothers would constantly securitize membership to maintain this pluralist division, while militant Islamists could hardly warm up to the Brotherhood's multi-sectarian platform. At present, the party relies on Turkish goodwill and has no effective presence inside Syria (Sayigh and Lefèvre 2013).

The Libyan Brotherhood is a much more humble affair. Following the disbanding and repression of Egyptian Brothers in 1948, a few dozen made their way to Benghazi, where they lived peacefully under the Sufi-based Senussi monarchy. When Colonel Gadhafi took power in 1969, the now insecure Brothers tried to formalize their organization and participate in the newfound republic. When they discovered that Libya's young tyrant meant to repress them, they packed up and left for Europe and the United States, renamed themselves the Islamic Group, and bided their time. Meanwhile, militants returning from Afghanistan, organized as the Libyan Islamic Fighting Group (LIFG), launched a failed insurgency in the eastern provinces between 1995 and 1998. Seeking to counterbalance the militants, Gadhafi's infamous son, Saif al-Islam, welcomed back moderate Brothers in the late 2000s. On the eve of the February 2011 revolt, however, the Libyan Comptroller General Suleiman 'Abd al-Qadir admitted that he had only a few hundred members inside Libya. Like their Egyptian counterparts, the Libyan Brothers' support for the uprising was at best lukewarm. In fact, they had advised the outgoing regime on how to absorb popular rage (Ashour 2012). Following Gadhafi's bloody end, their new comptroller general, Bashir al-Qutbi, organized Brothers into the Justice and Construction Party, and participated in the country's first free elections, only to come out second to the liberals. Much like the Syrian case, Brothers in Libya are wedged between secular and Islamist militias – and their best bet is to present themselves as a good compromise between the two.

Brothers under Monarchy: Jordan, Kuwait, Morocco

It would have been unconvincing for Brothers to claim that some of the monarchical Arab societies had strayed away from religion. The royal families of Jordan and Morocco, for instance, traced their pedigree to the house of the Prophet, and portrayed themselves as defenders of Islamic tradition. And in sheikdoms like Kuwait, monarchs ruled over an ostensibly conservative community, where Islamic values were upheld in public. In these three examples, the political order remained closest to the prevalent model in Islamic history: with an active monarch advised by tribal leaders and other notables. The *'ulama* were held in great esteem, and rulers went out of their way to express their deference to Islam. This is why Brothers in these settings entrenched themselves in the ruling structures, rather than attempt to challenge them from below.

In 1945, Hassan al-Banna met the men who would head the Jordanian and Kuwaiti chapters ('Abd al-Latif Abu Qura, and 'Abd al-'Aziz al-Mutawwa', respectively). Eight years later, the two chapters were concurrently established. In Jordan, Brothers received royal support for a host of domestic and geopolitical reasons, in addition to the traditional outlook of the Jordanian monarch. The king was concerned with the spread of Islamist militancy among Palestinian refugees at the hands of groups like the Islamic Liberation Party (Hizb al-Tahrir al-Islami), which was created in Jerusalem in 1953 by a man named Taqiy al-Din al-Nabhani, and carried out bloody operations around the Arab world, beginning with the attack on the Technical Military Academy in Cairo in 1974. Brothers offered a moderate alternative that the king hoped would dominate the Islamist arena. Yet the most significant threat to the Hashemite dynasty was the Nasser-backed socialist Arab forces bent on toppling reactive monarchies. In 1953, the Hashemite branch in Iraq crumbled under the pressure of this Arab Cold War, and Egypt and Syria were making explicit threats against Jordan. Worse still, in 1970, the Palestinian wing of this progressive movement almost succeeded in unseating King Hussein. It was only normal for the royal house to support the

Muslim Brothers as the avowed enemies of progressive nationalism. In short, Jordanian Brothers became "an essential component of the Hashemite regime" (Ayubi 1991: 95).

At first, the Brotherhood was registered as a religious society, but then it expanded into a general-purpose NGO called the Islamic Center in 1965. Its Comptroller General, Muhammad 'Abd al-Rahman Khalifa, was one of King Hussein's confidants. And, with the palace's permission, Brothers ran as independents during the first parliamentary elections, in the mid-1950s, and won 10 percent of the vote – which was impressive considering that most seats were reserved for tribal notables. A Brother, 'Abd al-Latif 'Uraibat, headed the Jordanian parliament for three years (1990–3), before being promoted to the Assembly of Notables (1993–7). In the 1970s, Comptroller General Ishaq al-Farhan served as education minister, and went on to head the University of Jordan. By the end of the 1980s, the Brotherhood had increased its share of seats to almost a third of parliament, with five Brothers joining the cabinet. When political parties were authorized, in 1992, Brothers were the first to register their Islamic Action Front (Jabhat al-'Amal al-Islami). And, in return, Brotherhood parliamentarians swallowed their resentment of the 1994 Jordanian–Israeli peace treaty, and preferred to absent themselves when it was being ratified than defy the palace.

Ironically, the Brotherhood's relationship with the royal family deteriorated because both proved quite successful: the Brotherhood became the most organized political force in the country, and the monarchy weathered decades of political storms. Now, Brothers hoped to increase their share by scrapping electoral laws that favored tribal over party politics. They boycotted the 1997 elections, saw their seats reduced substantially in 2003 and 2007 (probably as a royal reprimand), and retaliated by boycotting the 2010 elections (Brown 2012). On the other hand, the monarchy felt not only that it no longer needed the Brothers to counter progressive nationalism and Islamist militancy, but also that Islamism itself might be the new threat. As young King 'Abdullah watched Islamists sweep into power in the wake of the 2011 Arab revolts, he surely suspected that his throne might be the next target.[8]

Kuwaiti Brothers had for long been blessed with royal support for the same reasons as their Jordanian counterparts. Operating under the rubric of the Social Reform Society, Brothers won 12 percent of the vote in the first elected assembly in 1963 – though, like Jordan, most seats were reserved for tribal leaders. Brothers then pursued their cultural and educational initiatives quite freely, including partnering with the government to found the sharia-compliant

Kuwaiti Finance House. Careful not to offend the ruling al-Sabbah family, Kuwaiti Brothers temporarily suspended relations with the Cairo headquarters after Egyptian Brothers supported Saddam. In 1991, they established the Islamic Constitutional Movement (al-Haraka al-Dusturiyya al-Islamiya, known by its Arabic initials as Hadas). They added to their parliamentary presence two cabinet posts: religious affairs and commerce. Again, as for their Jordanian counterparts, political gains whetted the Kuwaiti Brothers' appetite, encouraging them to spearhead electoral reform campaigns to limit the share of tribal notables (Brown 2007). That being said, regime–Brotherhood tensions in Kuwait have been fairly mild, considering that the wealthy and stable Sabbahis are less anxious about their reign than the Hashemites.

Another notable difference is that Kuwait has produced an influential Brotherhood theoretician, of the stature of Syria's Sa'id Hawwa. Muhammad Ahmad al-Rashid, the penname of the Iraqi-born 'Abd al-Rahman al-'Ali, published the five-volume Islamist bestseller *Ihya' fiqh al-Da'wa* (Reviving Missionary Jurisprudence), which begins by expressing the author's fidelity to the Brotherhood's operating credo: "These homilies are not intellectual discussions on the relationship between Islam and modern socioeconomic doctrines. They are intended for the true believer, whose only concern is to cultivate his soul and tender his heart and build bridges with his brothers in order to guide the nation back to its religion" (Rashid 1993: 7). It is curious to note that, despite the radically different socioeconomic and political contexts, Rashid's work displays all the typical features of Islamism as conceived by Banna and Qutb – whom he quotes endlessly. There is the theological reading of history: for example, how Jews and infidels are repeating the strategy of Moses' Pharaoh, which is infecting society with sexual laxness, freethinking, and materialism to defeat faith (Rashid 1993: 54). There is the subscription to conspiracy theory: Jews and infidels are intent on discrediting the faithful, so "whenever you hear something bad about Islamist leaders, search for a conspiracy" (Rashid 1994: 198). There is the reification of the movement, elevation of obedience, and deflation of the weight of tangible plans: "Islamist activism is like prayer. Just performing it rewards you. You must be in step with your co-worshippers. You must follow the prayer leader without fuss, realizing that leading an Islamist movement is a religious act comparable to leading prayers" (Rashid 1994: 159–60). And there is the dismissal of the role of scholarship, religious or otherwise: "Those who claim that only scholars have the right to teach misunderstand the [sacred] texts. Knowledge consists of different components. If you know one of

them, you can relay it to others without having to learn the rest"
(Rashid 1993: 97–8). Expectedly, young Egyptian Brothers are
encouraged to read his work. Though when Rashid hazarded a critique of Islamist stagnation in the 1990s, his book was immediately
banned in Brotherhood circles.[9]

The Islamist experience in Morocco is similar to those under other
monarchies in terms of regime tolerance. But a major difference
relates to how Islamist forces were organized in the first place. The
Moroccan story is one of fusion and overlap. One organizational
chain begins with 'Abd al-Karim al-Khatib, whom Brothers count as
one of their own. He started out in the royalist Independence Party,
and resigned in 1957 when the party abandoned traditional elites and
sided with the urban bourgeoisie. He was rewarded with a number
of royal appointments, including a cabinet post (1960–3), and the
prestigious position of first ever speaker of parliament (1963–5).
Al-Khatib then founded the ultra-royalist Popular Democratic and
Constitutional Movement (MPCD) in 1967, and remained its leader
for life. He was therefore poised to help a struggling Islamist faction:
a social movement calling itself the Movement of Unity and
Reform (Harakat al-Tawhid wa al-Islah, MUR). Since the 1970s, the
Brotherhood-inspired MUR has sought to function as a political
party. After refusing to grant it permission to do so (in 1989 and
1992), the palace directed it to merge with al-Khatib's party in 1996
to form the Party for Justice and Development (PJD). Contrary to
the Egyptian case, and probably influenced by their namesake (the
Turkish Justice and Development Party, AKP), Moroccan Islamists
drew clear boundaries between their social and political wings.[10] And,
like AKP, it snubbed grand ideological projects, and remained focused
on practical policies, especially trade with the EU. The PJD participated in parliamentary elections, beginning in 1997, but its first
notable success came in 2002, when it increased its share from 4
percent to 14 percent of parliament (a percentage it maintained in
2007), prompting an invitation from King Muhammad VI to join the
cabinet. During this period, it demonstrated its compliance with
regime policies, voting for even the most controversial bills, such as
the anti-terrorism and personal status laws, both passed in 2003. This
eventually paid off, helping it secure a plurality of seats (with one-
third of the vote) in the election held in the wake of the Arab uprisings
in 2011, and it was thus charged with forming a coalition government
with three other parties, with Islamist leader 'Abd al-Illah bin Qirane
as prime minister (Wegner 2007).

Meanwhile, there was another Islamist movement whose work
overlapped with that of PJD, and that is the Justice and Benevolence

group (al-'Adl wal-Ihsan). Its founder, 'Abd al-Salam Yassin, was influenced by Hassan al-Banna's model. Like the Egyptian Brotherhood's founder, Yassin graduated from the Teachers' College (in Rabat in 1947) and spent two decades as a schoolteacher. He then published in 1971 a remarkable treatise promoting the Brotherhood's principle of the comprehensiveness of Islam, *al-Islam bein al-Da'wa wal-Dawla* (Islam between the Message and the State). And imitating Banna, he wrote a (100-page) letter calling King Hassan II and his ministers to embrace Islamism before they ruined the country. Expectedly, his 1974 letter, *al-Islam aw al-Tufan* (Islam or the Flood), landed him in prison – after a humiliating three-year stint in a mental asylum. After his release in 1987, Yassin's supporters coalesced around the slogan 'justice and benevolence', and functioned exclusively as a social (almost missionary) movement with a mystic streak. Although Yassin remained under house arrest between 1989 and his death in 2012, his movement became the largest in Morocco, and many of its members helped bolster the PJD through their votes – again a replication of the Turkish model of separating civil and political activism.

Brothers in Power: the Sudan

Brothers began work in the Sudan at a disadvantage. The Egyptian-educated Sudanese youth who organized the Brotherhood chapter in 1954 found it difficult to compete with the two large Sufi-based movements in place. Sufism carried Islam to Egypt's southern neighbor, which was neither conquered by Islamic armies nor attracted traditional scholars. The Mahdiya movement, which bore the brunt of resistance against British colonialism, evolved into a social current, al-Ansar, and later a political party as well, al-Umma. Sudan's other major Sufi order, al-Khatmiya, produced a rival party: the Democratic Unionist Party (DUP). The two great parties took turns ruling Sudan from its independence in the mid-fifties until the Brotherhood-supported coups of 1969 and 1989. The leader of the 1969 coup, Colonel Ga'far al-Numeiri, started out as a progressive Arab nationalist in the fashionable Nasserist mold. But he quickly discovered that it was the Sufi parties and the disruptive communists who really threatened his rule. He therefore allied himself with the seemingly non-threatening Islamic Movement (al-Haraka al-Islamiya), the Brotherhood's Sudanese affiliate.

Hassan al-Turabi, the group's charismatic leader, had studied law in London and Paris, receiving his doctorate from the Sorbonne. He was appointed justice minister, chief public prosecutor, and presidential foreign affairs advisor, while another Brother, Ahmad 'Abd al-Rahman, was named interior minister. In the 1970s, Brothers instituted government-endorsed Islamic financial houses that offered credit to the lower middle class and enterprising businessmen. But it only caused the government to sink deeper into debt. At the Brotherhood's bidding, Numeiri enacted sharia-based laws between 1983 and 1984, and recast the presidential appointment into a *bay'a* (Islamic oath of allegiance). The antagonized non-Muslim South saw this as an opportunity to resume its long battle for secession. At the same time, bread riots spread across Sudan, in protest against the regime's attempt to replace effective policy with ideology. Turabi now believed Sudan needed a firmer hand at the helm and tried to replace the president. His plot was uncovered, landing him and dozens of Brothers in prison in January 1985. This turned out to be a blessing in disguise, however, because when Numeiri's regime collapsed two months later, Brothers could claim they had defected beforehand.

When fresh elections took place in 1986, Brothers secured around a quarter of the votes to become the third-largest party, right behind the Sufi-inspired pair. A Brother was appointed speaker of parliament, and used his clout to prevent sharia laws being rescinded. Turabi returned to government, along with six other Brothers, and was promoted in 1988 to the prestigious post of foreign minister. Nevertheless, he aspired to absolute power. In a risky gambit, he began courting the army, complaining that his coalition partners were willing to grant autonomy to the South and weaken Khartoum's overall control through a misguided policy of federalism. When the time came, he and his Brothers resigned from government, and threw their weight behind Brigadier-General 'Umar al-Bashir's June 1989 coup. The Brotherhood, now going by the name National Islamic Front, controlled Sudan through what became called the Salvation (*Inqaz*) regime (Ayubi 1991: 107–12; Esposito and Voll 2001: 120–5). And to guarantee their freedom of maneuver, Sudanese Islamists made it clear to the mother organization in Egypt that they had to adjust their strategy to their local circumstances – a position justified, as always, by reference to the Prophetic experience (Turabi 1989: 81–5).

Turabi styled himself as supreme revolutionary guide, *à la* Khomeni. He welcomed comrades from around the world, including al-Qa'da leaders Osama bin Laden and Ayman al-Zawahri, and engineered a radical foreign policy that antagonized Western and Arab powers equally – especially after his involvement in the attempt on Mubarak's life in 1995. Needless to say, rapid Islamization in the North lit a fire under the rebellion in the South. Soon, Khartoum found itself isolated internationally (with Western sanctions and Arab petro-dollars drying up) and fighting a war it could not win domestically. It did not help that Turabi soon created a secretive organization, referred to as al-Tanzim (The Order), to follow the application of his policies in all government departments and civil associations. Reports by Turabi's commissars frequently led to detention and torture. And absolute power apparently went to his head, as he frequently marveled at his personal achievements as a unique model to be replicated by Islamists worldwide (Turabi 1989: 83).

Political disenchantment with the course pursued by the Brotherhood's increasingly megalomaniacal chief eventually led to a palace coup in 1999 by President Bashir and Turabi's second-in-command, 'Ali Osman Taha. The coup preserved the Islamist–military alliance, albeit shifting to a moderate, conciliatory policy at home and abroad – though rampant corruption and authoritarianism remained. To signal the change, the new Islamist leader dropped the 'Islamic' reference from the party's title, calling it instead the National Congress Party. And Turabi's life was now divided between prison and house arrest. Relations with Arab countries were soon normalized, but the alienating Brotherhood policies of the past aided the secession cause in the South, as Khartoum finally realized in July 2011. One last step remained to normalize Sudan's duopoly, which was to transform the Islamist party into a non-ideological ruling party under President Bashir. This occurred in November 2012, effectively dissolving Sudan's Brotherhood (Verhoeven 2013).

What is particularly interesting about the Sudanese case is how being involved in real-life politics made Brothers much less abstract and religiously deterministic in their thinking. It also revealed that Brotherhood politics could be very similar to secular totalitarian politics, as was obvious in their supporting of military and palace coups, violent repression of dissent, support for international belligerence, and, finally, political scheming and backstabbing. That being said, in a different context, Islamist performance in power could be much less disreputable, as in the case of Tunisia.

Islamists Sharing Power: Tunisia

The Tunisian case was distinguished from the very beginning by the radicalism of its secular regime. President Habib Bourguiba had been by far the most thoroughgoing secularist in the Arab world, comparable to the French and Turkish models at their most extreme moments. During his three-decade rule (1957–87), the president went beyond legal amendments (such as dissolving religious courts and confiscating endowments) to discouraging sacred practices (such as pilgrimage and fasting). Shortly before his overthrow, Sheikh 'Abd al-Fattah Muru and his fellow clerics at the historic Zaituna University (Tunisia's response to Cairo's al-Azhar) gathered up the courage to revive religious education. Muru linked up with a bright young philosophy professor by the name of Rashid al-Ghannoushi, who had started a Tunisian Qur'an Preservation Society amongst his students. Ghannoushi had graduated from Zaituna, and then went on to study philosophy at the University of Damascus, followed by a doctoral degree from Paris. He arrived at the Sorbonne in 1968 and from his small flat in the Latin Quarter witnessed first-hand the students' and workers' rebellion. This inspiring episode of popular defiance encouraged him to unite his efforts with Sheikh Muru, in the 1970s, to form the Islamic Movement Trend (MTI). Expectedly, Ghannoushi was imprisoned for most of the period between 1981 and 1988.

In November 1987, Zain al-'Abidin Bin 'Ali, a military officer who at the time was acting prime minister, removed his mentor, Bourguiba, in a bloodless coup. Parliamentary elections were held in April 1989, and the MTI won 17 percent of the vote, reinventing itself as a political party under the name of al-Nahda (Renaissance). Soon, however, Bin 'Ali's darker side emerged. In 1992, some 25,000 Nahda members were detained, forcing Ghannoushi into what turned out to be a two-and-a-half-decade exile. This second, longer European internship was even more intellectually significant than the first. Though he joined the Brotherhood's International Organization, Ghannoushi had always been critical of the mother organization in Cairo for aspiring towards absolute tutelage over society. He believed that even if Islam was comprehensive, it did not have to be represented by an all-purpose comprehensive organization. His reflections in Europe further convinced him that Islamists should divide their labor between independent groups in politics, civil society, finance, education, etc. He also cherished the fact that his party – which had indicatively dropped any reference to Islam in its title – not only embraced pluralism, but also drew on a variety of intellectual trends: religious and secular, fundamentalist and rational. Undoubtedly, this markedly open-minded perspective distinguished al-Nahda from other Islamist groups (Ayubi 1991: 115; Esposito and Voll 2001: 114). Equally significant, Ghannoushi's time in Europe helped him to ponder over some of the most contentious issues in Islamist politics, and to produce detailed tracts on human rights, the status of women, social justice, and global peace.

This made a great difference in al-Nahda's performance in the aftermath of Bin 'Ali's overthrow in 2011. Returning from a long exile, Ghannoushi pushed his party to form a working coalition with Tunisia's powerful labor unions, represented by the left-leaning Democratic Forum for Labor and Liberties (known as al-Takatul) and the liberal Congress for the Republic. Hamadi al-Jebali, editor of the Islamist newspaper *al-Fajr*, and 16-year political detainee, served as prime minister, along with the leftist Mustafa Bin Ja'far as chairman of the Constituent Assembly, and the liberal human rights lawyer al-Munsif al-Marzuqi as transitional president. Ghannoushi himself made sure al-Nahda did not demand the inclusion of sharia in the new constitution in order not to alienate his secular partners. Regardless of this and other remarkable moves, Islamist–secular relations in Tunisia cannot be described as unproblematic. Yet it is safe to say that they are no more problematic than rivalries in any other democracy – which in itself is a notable achievement.

Islamists at the Heart of the Fallen Caliphate

No other Muslim country had undergone a more thorough secularization than the seat of the Islamic empire in the 1920s. Fearful of the grip of the past, Mustafa Kemal, the Turkish apostle of Westernization, took no chances: he abolished the caliphate; sequestered religious endowments; undermined clerics; removed sharia laws; adopted Latin script; banned Islamic dress codes and the call for prayers; realigned Turkish history with that of the West; and reinvented Turks as modern European citizens. He then crowned his methodical campaign by entrusting the military with preserving the secular identity of his new republic. Faced with such adversity, Islamism in Turkey could at best aspire to merely normalize Islam's position within society.

The Kurdish-born Sunni scholar Bediüzzeman Sai'd al-Nursi began the process of damage control with a consciously apolitical and mild-tempered Sufi movement. Back in 1907, Nursi had presented Sultan Abdülhamid with proposals on how to reconcile Islamic principles with modern thinking. Ignored by the caliph, he turned his hope to the Young Turks' modernizing regime, which was instituted a year after he met the stubborn monarch. Nursi fought in World War I, and the trauma of defeat led him to support Mustafa Kemal and his mutinous officers. In fact, Nursi was the only cleric invited to address the revolutionary Grand National Assembly in 1922. But, after a short stint in Ankara, Nursi became disillusioned by the religious irreverence of the soon-to-be master of Anatolia and his coterie. Prudently though, Nursi recognized the futility of resisting the mighty waves of secularism, and advised his students to eschew political activism in favor of cultivating individual piety and producing a more capable Muslim generation – a strategy reminiscent of the Brotherhood's. Like Hassan al-Banna, he also presented his writings in the form of epistles – in this case: the Epistles of Light (*Risale-I Nur*) – and invited his followers to study them.[11] However, one needs to go beyond these superficial similarities to appreciate the distinctiveness of Turkish Islamism. Nursi was a Sufi scholar not an ideological doctrinaire; his epistles provided a rich treatment of the spiritual world not a set of political speeches and administrative instructions; his Nur movement (Nurcu) was conceived as a community of learning (*dershane*), rather than a tightly controlled organization; and his aim was to produce an 'intellectually able' (*entelektüel mümkün*) group that could strategize change, rather than a pious vanguard whose very existence would summon divine intervention.

Ironically, the ban on religious publications cemented the Nur movement by forcing its members to reproduce and translate (from Arabic) handwritten copies of the epistles and circulate them from door to door. As the republic moved to multi-party politics in the 1940s, the movement proved to be the most well-organized section of Turkish civil society. Faithful to the will of its spiritual leader, Nur members only lent support to political leaders who promoted Islam, without formally identifying, let alone joining, any particular party. This not only became the model for future Islamist activists, but it also made them flexible enough to weather the military backlashes that swept away political factions between 1960 and 1997. Nur votes and fundraising helped bring the Democratic Party to power in 1950, in the hope that its landowning elite would adopt a more sympathetic view towards Islam. And the party did, in fact, ease some of the secular restrictions, before it was overthrown by the May 1960 coup, two months after Nursi passed away (Mardin 1989; Abu-Rabi' 2003).

Afterwards, Nurcu adherents (an estimated 6 million members by the end of the twentieth century) became more institutionalized, establishing branches across Turkey and abroad, yet never coalescing into a hierarchical organization that could be repressed. Its example inspired similar groups: the most visible and politically influential being the Gülen movement, which clustered around the Anatolian schoolteacher Fethullah Gülen. This new group was really an evolution, rather than an extension, of the Nur movement. Its founder subscribed to Nursi's ideas, but then combined them with modern

Western philosophy to produce a religious ideology that supported a powerful nationalist state, a free market economy, and, most importantly, a justification of Turkish secularism. In other words, this neo-Nurcu group reformulated Islam in a way that appealed to both the Kemalist establishment and Islamist activists. Its much praised 'Turkish–Islamic synthesis' was thus credited with finally establishing a *modus vivendi* for the country's religious population, nationalist military, and secular elite. Underlying its marked pragmatism, however, were formidable organizational resources, including a media empire, with a prominent daily (*Zaman*), a public relations company, an array of educational institutions (300 high schools, 7 universities, and dozens of dormitories and summer camps), all funded by a giant business network and homegrown financial institutions. This was the intellectual and financial infrastructure that produced the 'golden generation' – Gülen's rendition of Nursi's 'intellectually able group', which was responsible for the electoral triumphs of the Welfare Party (Refah Partisi, RP) in 1997, and the Justice and Development Party (Adalet ve Kalkınma Partisi, AKP) in 2002 (Esposito and Yavuz 2003; Yavuz 2013).

On the political front, the democratic space provided by the 1960 coup makers allowed Necmettin Erbakan, an engineering professor and admirer of the Egyptian Brotherhood, to create Turkey's first Islamist party: the National Order Party (Milli Nizam Partisi, MNP). Dissolved by the 1971 coup for violating the secular character of the republic, Islamists regrouped – in what would become a recurring pattern – in another party: the National Salvation Party (Milli Selâmet Partisi, MSP). This time, Islamists not only contested parliamentary elections (winning 12 percent of the vote in 1973, and 9 percent in 1977), but also managed to secure a foothold in the cabinet. Islamists increased their political share following the 1980 anti-communist coup. Though their party was again disbanded, the coup leaders relied on Islamists to purge communism once and for all. Erbakan thus returned with the new and more vigorous Welfare Party (Refah Partisi, RP), and succeeded in joining, then leading, a coalition government. The secret to the Islamist success was twofold. On the one hand, it represented the middle ground in a violently polarized society. Islamists distinguished themselves from the left by emphasizing free enterprise; from the right by preaching social equality; and from both by offering a cross-class cultural identity. On the other hand, Islamists capitalized on their first-rate grassroots to provide welfare to thousands of new urban migrants: food, healthcare, casual employment, cheap credit, and temporary shelter. Both of these were typical Islamist strategies, but Refah became more successful than other movements because the military, which dominated the Turkish regime, had little interest in government, whereas the authoritarian political elites in the Arab world did. Refah therefore advanced unopposed, increasing its share of the national vote from 8 percent in 1987, to 17 percent in 1991, to an impressive 21 percent in 1995. And in June 1996, Erbakan became the first Islamist prime minister in the history of the republic.

Unfortunately, the dizzying success tempted Islamists to do too much too quickly. They immediately set about packing the bureaucracy with their followers; diverting savings to Islamist holding companies; campaigning to reinstitute sharia; promoting religious education and Sufi orders; and brandishing a militant rhetoric, such as Erbakan's defiant remark that Islamists would remain in power either through normal channels or by shedding blood. More dangerously, Refah thought it could now clip the wings of the military – a fatal miscalculation, as it turned out. The high command forced Erbakan to resign in the summer of 1997, and shortly afterwards Refah was dissolved (Heper and Güney 2000: 638–45). In a curious historical coincidence, both Morsi in Egypt and Erbakan in Turkey assumed power in June, and were ousted by generals the following June. But, unlike their Egyptian counterparts, Turkey's Islamists accepted their political defeat and decided to live to fight another day. It is true that this was not the first coup (although the previous two were directed against right-wing authoritarianism and communism, not Islamism). It is also true that they had for long honed their skills to survive in Turkey's political quicksand. But ideological differences were crucial. Turkish Islamists were practical politicians who understood that gain and loss in politics were subject to power calculations. Their Egyptian comrades saw their success as a sign of divine favor, and were therefore shaken to the core by the reversal of fortune.

So, rather than wasting time examining what cosmic shift might have caused their downfall, Turkish Islamists simply regrouped in yet another political party, the Virtue Party (Fazilet Partisi, FP), and secured 15 percent of the votes in the 1999 elections. When banned again in 2001, the rump of the party followed Erbakan into what turned out to be his last and weakest party, the Felicity Party (Saadet Partisi, SP), which performed poorly in national elections, falling from 2.5 percent in 2002 to a negligible 1.24 percent in 2011 – the year Erbakan passed away. Most of the young cadres, however, preferred to beat a new path away from their mentor – adopting the slogan 'We have changed' in the 2002 electoral campaign. They believed that Islamism's social base should expand beyond the agricultural class and the urban petite bourgeoisie to Turkey's most

dynamic socioeconomic sector: Anatolia's medium-sized manufac-
turer-exporters – the so-called 'Anatolian tigers' – who adopted an
inspiring Weberian view of the relationship between Islam and capitalism. Again, in contrast to Egyptian Brothers, Turkish Islamists
thought strategically in terms of durable social alliances, rather than
rely on religious dogma combined with sporadic provision of welfare
to the poor (especially before elections). The young political dissidents also saw the need to substitute Islamism as an ideology with
conservative democracy – a catch-all label meant to present the party
as a unique synthesis between everything that Turks cherished (Yavuz
2003).

In 2001, adherents to this new platform formed the Justice and
Development Party (Adalet ve Kalkınma Partisi, AKP). In contrast to
the ailing leaders of most Turkish parties (including Erbakan), the
founders of AKP were young, energetic, media-savvy, and particularly
attentive to business interests, including the bid to join the EU. Recep
Tayyip Erdogan, AKP's charismatic leader, came from Istanbul's
underprivileged Kasımpasa neighborhood. He studied economics at
Marmara University, played soccer semi-professionally, and became
an Islamist grassroots organizer from the 1980s. His working-class
background, his rough character (tuned through years on the soccer
field), and his street activism distinguished him from other members
of the political elite. At the age of 40, he became mayor of Istanbul
(1994–8), where he managed to rapidly improve the city. The party's
second-in-command, Abdullah Gül, came from the business-oriented
Anatolian city of Kayseri, and held a doctorate degree in economics.
Between them, the leading pair secured a large constituency stretching
from popular classes to aspiring businessmen.[12] In 2002, AKP became
the first Islamist party to govern without a coalition since the republic's embrace of multiparty politics six decades before. It meteoric rise
continued, with its share of parliament seats increasing from 34
percent in 2002,[13] to 47 percent in 2007, to a landslide 50 percent
in 2012. Equally significant was the election of a party member to
the presidency, despite the fierce resistance of secular parties and the
misgivings of the top generals. This was again the first time since the
1940s that the president (Gül) and prime minister (Erdogan) belonged
to the same party (Tugal 2007: 9–11).[14]

A decade-long rule allowed AKP to perform tasks beyond the
reach of its predecessors. Most critically, it reduced chances for
another military intervention through constitutional amendments,
trials of officers involved in past coups, and entrenching itself ever
more closely with Washington and Brussels. It then led a paradigmatic shift from Turkey's conventionally isolationist and defensive

foreign policy to what became known as 'neo-Ottomanism' (*Osmanlicaler*), an active and assertive foreign policy geared to establishing Turkey as a global power in its own right. Unlike their anti-intellectual contemporaries in Egypt, AKP based its foreign policy shift on a coherent new doctrine, Strategic Depth (*Stratejik Derinlik*), and appointed its brilliant architect, the renowned international relations professor, Ahmet Davutoglu, foreign minister.[15] Domestic success and geopolitical ambition encouraged Erdogan to throw his weight behind other Islamist movements, especially the Palestinian Hamas, Syrian Brothers, and the mother of all Islamist movements: the Egyptian Muslim Brotherhood.

It is likely, however, that AKP has overshot its mark. Indicators of its leader's hubris became rife starting from the summer of 2013: from his ham-fisted suppression of popular protests around Gezi park, to his imperialistic rage against the officers who ousted his Brotherhood friends in Egypt, to his misguided attempt to bring the Gülen movement under AKP control, to his frequent references to a global conspiracy against him, and, finally, to his refusal to investigate corruption charges against his ministers and family members. Nonetheless, Turkish Islamism remains an instructive example of adaptation to secular, multiparty politics, as well as pursuing level-headed policies at home and abroad. What its detractors complain about is hardly unique to Islamist movements: after all, few successful politicians could remain immune to the arrogance of power.

Shi'a Islamism

The minority status of Shi'ites (a little over 10 percent of Muslims) guaranteed their overall historical quiescence. This was theologically justified by the messianic doctrine of occultation (*ghaiba*), which instructed Shi'ites to resign to their fate pending the return of their Hidden Imam, and to take refuge in the practice of dissimulation (*taqqia*) to conceal their true beliefs when outnumbered. So, even when they settled safely in the Persia of the Safavids in the sixteenth century, *mullahs* remained deeply conservative. It is commonly alleged that Shi'ite clerics have more influence than their Sunni counterparts because they claim infallibility and tax their followers directly. This is true only in theory. Practically speaking, both Sunni and Shi'a Muslims are required to emulate (*taqlid*) the positions of qualified scholars (*mujtahids*). And just as no single Sunni authority could oblige Muslims to follow him, Shi'a believers get to choose which of their many 'infallible' clerics they prefer to follow. In addition, the donations and endowments received by Sunni clerics are no less substantial than the tithe (*khums*) collected by their Shi'a brethren. What this means is that, despite institutional and theological differences, there is nothing fundamentally different about the relationship between scholars and followers in the Sunni and Shi'ite worlds. Nor have modern Shi'ites managed a higher level of piety than Sunnis. Iran's legendary Islamist revolutionary 'Ali Shari'ati had in fact accused his compatriots of spiritual poverty, and provided a devastating critique of their deviation from the path of Islam's founding generation – just as Banna and Qutb had done before (Shari'ati 1988). In other words, Shi'a Islamists were no less concerned about the eroding influence of modern secularism and political bankruptcy than their Sunni neighbors. And, indeed, a handful of clerics featured in social protests from the end of the nineteenth century onwards. But the overwhelming majority of the *mullahs* in the shrine city of Qum (Iran's religious education center) were no more politically engaged than those of Cairo's al-Azhar. Up until the very end of the Iranian Revolution, the critical mass within the clergy, represented by the most senior authority Ayatollah Shariatmadari, never demanded the overthrow of the monarchy (though they did ask the Shah to respect the constitution), and never called for the establishment of an Islamic republic. And the most senior authority in the Shi'ite world, Ayatollah Kho'i of the Iraqi seminary in Najaf, distanced himself from the revolutionary trend in Iran.

Ruhollah Khomeini was therefore every bit as unorthodox as Hassan al-Banna.[16] They both believed that saving Islam required breaking out of its centuries-old pattern; they were both exultantly charismatic; and they both infused their cause with a mystic aura. There were, however, substantial differences. To start with, Khomeini never shied away from admitting he had to break sharply with existing traditions, while Banna was careful to present his work as an extension of the past. This was particularly significant since Khomeini, in contrast to Banna, was an accredited Islamic scholar (*ayatollah*). Secondly, Khomeini always defied authority, whereas his Egyptian counterpart (and his followers) preferred to negotiate with it. Compared to Banna's mild letters to the Egyptian monarch and his ministers, when Reza Shah, the coup leader who instituted the Pahlavi dynasty in the 1920s, presented a package of secular measures, Ayatollah Khomeini penned an outrageous tract, *Kashf al-Asrar* (Uncovering the Secrets), which stated: "All the orders issued by the dictatorial regime of the bandit Reza Khan have no value at all. The laws passed by his parliament must be scrapped and burned. All the idiotic words that have proceeded from the brain of that illiterate soldier are rotten and it is only the law of God that will remain and resist the ravages of time" (quoted in Algar 2001: 53–4) – little wonder that his son and successor, Muhammad Reza, exiled the hotheaded *mullah* in the mid-1960s.

Yet the most important difference, of course, was that Khomeini was a revolutionary strategist and conspirator of a caliber unseen since Lenin. Islamists in Egypt and Iran rose to power on the back of revolutionary waves not of their making. But Khomeini was a master of timing, waiting patiently until revolutionary action had cleared the path before asserting his authority. He was also a tough negotiator, keeping the pressure on the old political and military–security elite until he could derive the necessary concessions. He was shrewd enough to feint political detachment and promote a liberal and a leftist to the presidency and the premiership, respectively, until he was ready to sweep them aside. And, unlike the Egyptian Brothers, Khomeini did not believe that good intentions guaranteed him divine favor. He understood that if he failed to outmaneuver his opponents through vigilance and cunning, nothing would save him.[17] Khomeini recruited dynamic young *mullahs*, such as future President Hashemi Rafsanjani, to manage a large network of followers that could quickly be converted into revolutionary committees (*komitehs*) when the time came. He also asked him to enlist the support of Islamist and leftist guerrillas that had already been operating in Iran for years (Rafsanjani 2005: 34–64).

Last but not least, Khomeini had actually been working, since the 1960s, on a concrete model for his Islamic state. His new order had a supreme jurist, aided by an assembly of clerics, reigning above the entire system as the representative of the Hidden Imam (the concept of *velayat-el faqih*) – a previously unthinkable formulation in Shi'ite thought; democratic power-sharing in the legislative and executive branches, within the limits set by the jurists; a revolutionary guard of professionals (*Pasdaran*) and volunteers (*Basij*), complemented by morality patrols (*Hezbollahis*), to permanently parallel formal military and police forces; a populist economic policy geared towards the disadvantaged (*muztad'afin*); and a belligerent foreign policy that pulled no punches from the very first day (Khomeini 1981). Not only that: Khomeini had also created a clandestine Islamic Revolutionary Council, a full year before the Shah's overthrow, to compile a list of trustworthy candidates for various government posts (from ministers to mayors) once the revolution triumphed; to prepare a detailed oil policy for the new regime; and to draft an Islamist constitution, which was eventually adopted in October 1979 (Rafsanjani 2005: 213–21).

One cannot fail to notice here how Khomeini's ideas echoed Banna's principle of the comprehensiveness of Islam, and Qutb's claim that, since absolute sovereignty over the world belongs to God, people cannot be allowed to make choices that violate His will. But in contrast to the founders of the Egyptian Brotherhood, he set little store by producing a model society, or even a model vanguard whose steps are guided by God's grace. Khomeini believed in methodical scheming, and then striking hard and fast at the right time before one's opponents knew what hit them. Egypt's Brothers believed in buying time by appeasing opponents and peddling aimlessly in politics until divine empowerment was at hand.

Khomeini's death in 1989 coincided with the election of his chief lieutenant Hashemi Rafsanjani as president. The latter embarked on what Asef Bayat (2007: 10–12) described as the 'post-Islamist' turn, i.e., Islamist attempts to normalize their rule after the energy and zeal of the founding period had been exhausted. Not only the realities of power, national and geopolitical, but daily pressures from citizens and activists to deliver, compelled Islamist revolutionaries to give up on the Romantic crusade of fashioning the ideal Muslim community and igniting a worldwide revolution. The ebbs and flows of this difficult process have been linked to presidential elections, with the appointment of reformer Muhammad Khatami (1997–2005), followed by the reactionary tenure of Mahmoud Ahmadinejad (2005–13), and then a reverse to reform with Hassan Rouhani. It is not clear whether the Islamist republic will adapt fast enough or collapse under pressure. Undoubtedly, though, it will end up far from what Khomeini had originally conceived.

Conclusion: The End of Islamism?

In January 2011, the month of the Egyptian revolt, I published my first analysis of the power relations between the Muslim Brotherhood and the state. I concluded that, despite their inroads into society, the Brotherhood's political strategy always relied on "the regime's tacit consent" and left the movement "helpless against regime repression" (Kandil 2011: 56). This conclusion proved tragically accurate two years later when the military toppled the first Brotherhood parliament and government. Back then, my aim was to understand *why* the Brotherhood's strategy was so ineffective. In this book, I address the more complicated question of *how* this strategy was first formulated, sustained, and imbued in the minds and hearts of members. And the starting point, I argue, is religious determinism.

Examining the cultivation of Brothers, the building of their society, the construction of their ideology, and their historical evolution in Egypt and beyond, leads me to conclude that Islamism is, at bottom, an ideology that attributes worldly success to religious devotion. And it supports this claim by an unorthodox interpretation of Islamic revelation and history. According to Brothers, sharia is not just a set of duties imposed on Muslims in this life in hope of reward in the next, but also a tool for worldly accomplishments. Islamic history is not the history of ordinary people who happen to be Muslims, but an illustration of divine power in action. In the Brotherhood's viewpoint, only passive believers rest their hope on otherworldly salvation, and only the faithless search for material causality in history. A godly community could summon support from beyond; and Brothers therefore aspire to produce one.

Of course, obliterating the boundaries between the here and the hereafter is not uncommon among the religious. And those who think comparatively will instantly recognize traces of what is referred to here as religious determinism in many other sects (puritans and evangelicals come to mind), millenarian cults, and even well-intentioned individuals who believe that, in general, good things happen to good people. But Islamism, as propounded by the Brotherhood, is where this concept receives its most systematic treatment. And while religious determinism is not the only ideological theme that permeates the Brotherhood, it is prioritized here because it is the most general and enduring theme, and, more importantly, the one with the greatest impact on the movement's overall political strategy.

One of religious determinism's byproducts is the discouragement of adherents from developing concrete solutions to real-life problems. Islamism is therefore a perfect example of ideology, in Mannheim's (1936) sense of the term; it is as a set of abstract propositions incongruous with reality. Unless they become effectively immersed in everyday politics, as was the case outside Egypt, Islamists strive primarily for spiritual revival. They integrate themselves in local communities, run for elections, and develop their wealth in order to bring about this religious transformation – a project they aim to achieve gradually, almost by stealth, rather than share with their skeptical compatriots.

The absence of plausible alternatives weakened the Brotherhood's hand in the power struggle that led to its ousting in 2013. Even if Brothers were prevented from achieving progress on the ground by old-regime forces, the presence of a credible agenda for the future would have galvanized public support, and made an Islamist defeat more difficult. Here Therborn's distinction between mobilizing and governing is crucial:

> The key figures in processes of ideological mobilization are not theoreticians and writers of books, but orators, preachers, journalists, pamphleteers ... however, an important distinction must be made between, on the one hand, ideological mass mobilization for political change and, on the other, the problems of successfully defending and consolidating a victorious revolution. In the process of breaking up a regime in crisis, the weight of immediate action and single-minded devotion is paramount. But after a revolution, the degree of articulation ... [and] strength of ... theories and programmes crucially determines the fate of the ... classes that have been mobilized – for these are their only assets ... during the construction of a new society.
>
> (1999: 119)

Counter-revolution, Therborn concludes, becomes possible only when old-regime members win over large sections of the population by proving that the new rulers simply cannot deliver (1999: 121).

That being said, only a harsh critic could accuse Islamists of deliberately distorting Islam. Nor is this, of course, simply a huge misunderstanding. The truth of the matter is: Islamism, like any other ideology, owes more to the historical conditions in which it was conceived than its advocates would like to admit. An ideology that developed at such an abysmal point in Islamic history – with the caliphate collapsing irreversibly, and Muslim lands being carved up between frighteningly superior powers – would naturally seek hope in divine deliverance. Those who found it hard to provide powerless Muslims with a realistic plan to catch up with the rest of the world (as nationalists later tried and failed) had to urge them to perfect the only thing they could really master, the only thing they had not yet been dispossessed of: personal piety.

Since the early 1990s, several doomsday predictions have loomed over the future of Islamism. Olivier Roy (1994) dismissed Islamists on account of their failure to come up with more than religious rhetoric with no impact on politics or society. Gilles Kepel (2006) speculated that Islamism had run its course: its initial attempt at social reengineering was aborted, and its recent turn to militancy failed to attract Muslim support. Asef Bayat (2007) similarly saw Islamism in decline, but was hopeful that post-Islamists could finally transcend their narrow faith-based agenda to develop a broad appeal for social rights and liberties. As this book made clear, Islamists are not in the habit of following the work of Western academics, and so, naturally, none of these gloomy prophecies affected them in the least. But the extraordinary events that transpired in Egypt over the summer of 2013 are bound to leave their mark. After an eight-and-a-half-decade cultural campaign, Brothers believed they had won the hearts and minds of Egyptians. Nothing could convince them that 'the people' – or, at least, so many of them – could ever reject them. They were not alone in this belief. Dozens of news reports and research papers have reassured them that the 'politics of piety' would be the trump card in any free power contest.

But Islamism, which was born in Egypt in 1928 at the hands of a primary schoolteacher in a sleepy provincial town on the Suez Canal, faced the first popular uprising against it – also in Egypt. This was not an anti-Islamist coup of the Algerian, Turkish, or Pakistani variety. Although the revolt would have certainly been aborted without military support, the fact remains that millions of Muslims voted with their feet against Islamist rule, refusing to be either threatened by divine wrath or patronized by religious appeals; they refused to endorse the Brotherhood's conflation of Islamism and Islam. What happened in Egypt was a sudden disruption in the public view of the Muslim Brotherhood. And considering that Islamists in Egypt and beyond are, in one way or another, varieties of this ideological group, this public change of heart is bound to have worldwide repercussions.

To conclude, Islamism, the ideology that abolishes the boundaries between this life and the next, found itself, in 2013, face-to-face with the iron curtain that separates the two. And whether Brothers will now attempt to knock it down by force, or return to nurturing their piety to be able to cross it effortlessly in the future, understanding where Brothers stood before this fateful summer is essential to any discussion about their future prospects.

Appendix: A Note on Theory and Method

Following Mann (1986), Thompson (1990), Skocpol (1994), and Therborn (1999), I am chiefly interested in how organizations employ ideas in macro-level power struggles. My main concern in this book, therefore, is how Islamism as an ideology influenced the Muslim Brothers' performance in the struggle that ended their rule in 2013. But while most political sociologists highlight how ideology empowers actors, I am also concerned with how it constrains them. Even if ideology is little more than a weapon in the arsenal of various power actors, the type of weapon certainly restricts strategy. And even if ideology is socially determined in the first instance, it soon comes to constitute reality, and, as such, directs behavior. To fully appreciate the structuring role of ideology, I turn to Bourdieu (1990), Therborn (1999), and Foucault (2000), who demystify power relations within organizations by recasting them as structured spaces of dominant and subordinate positions.

Bourdieu grounds ideas and practices in specific fields of power where actors defend or enhance their ideal and material interests.[1] If ideological movements are conceived as fields of power, one can investigate how they act both as 'structuring structures' and 'structured structures', thus regulating members' behavior without explicit rules – something Bourdieu playfully compares to "conductorless orchestration." This occurs through endowing members with self-evident, taken-for-granted beliefs (*doxa*) and practical dispositions (*habitus*) that reproduce the field (1990: 59). Foucault regards this disciplining process as *objectification*, and explains how generating and governing new subjectivities cannot be achieved "without knowing the inside of people's mind, without exploring their souls, without making them reveal their innermost secrets" – what he refers to at one point as "pastoral power" (2000: 333). Therborn transcends Foucault by insisting that ideological movements do not just produce subjects, but perform two simultaneous processes: subjection and qualification. Disciplining technologies both produce subjects and qualify them to perform new roles, including the role of agents of political change (1999: 17, 46). Taken together, Bourdieu illustrates how ideological movements operate as autonomous, self-reproducing fields of power; Foucault underlines how they produce new social types through knowledge-based disciplining techniques; and Therborn adds, quite crucially, that these new ideological subjects are also qualified to carry out political change.

So, in a sense, this book is not concerned with what ideology is, but rather with what it does and how. It treats ideology as a subject-producing process that structures the thoughts and temperaments of members through a matrix of discursive and non-discursive processes. An ideological movement, from that perspective, is essentially the field of power within which these processes unfold. But this book also introduces the concept of an ideology's 'central organizing principle.' As incoherent as they are, and as malleable as they can be in the hands of skilled operators, ideologies certainly exercise a gravitational pull. They may be stretched to fit changing situations – but to a limit, lest they lose their efficacy. Indeed, every major ideology retains a basic core: an umbilical cord that holds its members together. If that is severed, the ideological movement loses its claim to logical and moral superiority and devolves into a network of interests.[i] Examining the role of ideology in real-life struggles therefore requires understanding how this central theme structures the thought and action of both leaders and followers. Religious determinism, I argue here, is Islamism's key concept, and the Egyptian Muslim Brotherhood is the movement that first invented, embodied, and exported it. To arrive at a full understanding of what religious determinism is and how it functions, I apply a method designed to gauge Islamist ideas, organization, and practices in equal measure.

My method builds on Foucault's insight that institutional power relations only reveal themselves in action – when domination counters resistance. In his words, resistance is the "chemical catalyst [that]

---

[i] A religious ideology, for instance, cannot renounce divinity and still hope to maintain the loyalty of its supporters. Fascists might postpone war, but cannot embrace pacifism. Capitalists might accept regulation, but cannot relinquish private property.

bring[s] to light power relations, locate[s] their position, and ... methods" (2000: 329). Even though Foucault generally advocates that power is invisible to its subjects, he does concede that individuals can recognize and resist those instances of power closest to them. In these immediate "struggles against subjection," individuals defend their individuality and links to others by questioning the "knowledge, competence, and qualification" of those who seek to classify and separate them through "secrecy, deformation, and mystifying representations" (Foucault 2000: 330–1). Dominant actors, in turn, cannot simply purge troublemakers. A power relation, Foucault reminds us, is a partnership, "an ensemble of actions which induce others and follow from one another" (2000: 337). The forces of order therefore contain resistance through inciting, seducing, constraining, forbidding. Instead of confronting resistance, they govern it by structuring its field of action (Foucault 2000: 341). Therborn (1999: 82–3) similarly describes how ideological movements counter resistance through affirmations and sanctions, whether discursive (indoctrination, censorship, excommunication) or non-discursive (rituals, promotion, marginalization). I show how Brothers use these techniques to secure internal order – techniques of the Foucauldian stock, such as hierarchical observation, normalizing judgements, and even formal examinations, as well as those listed by Therborn.

Bourdieu is also interested in studying institutional power relations – famously quipping that the "real is the relational" – and believes that hierarchies are preserved through shaping the cognitive, moral, and corporal dispositions of subjects (Bourdieu and Wacquant 1992: 97). He is particularly concerned with how power strategies contend within the field of power – or "battlefield" as he originally conceived it (Bourdieu and Wacquant 1992: 17). He identifies three such strategies: conservation strategies, to maintain dominant positions; succession strategies, to make these positions available to others; and subversion strategies, to challenge the order of domination (Bourdieu 1991: 98–9). I explore all three: how Brotherhood leaders reproduce domination; how loyal members toe the line to move up the organizational ladder; and how dissidents question the foundations of this order.

But how can an outsider become sufficiently familiar with a closed society like the Brotherhood to uncover practical dispositions and subtle disciplining techniques? One of the challenges of participant-observation is that subjects could hardly forget that the participant is also an observer. With a movement that conceals many of its ideas, a straightforward ethnography is simply impossible. I was therefore forced to devise an innovative way to combine the merits of ethnomethodology with the requirements of knowledge. The solution was to use field notes as the basis for interviews, rather than as a direct source. Without assuring my informants that I would not quote anything from my field notes, they would not have been completely at ease. But without my notes, I would not have known which questions to pose whenever I decided to wrap up the project.

The research began in 2006 with a handful of interviews with leading Islamist figures, and a revisiting of Islamist literature, including some 30 memoirs and published writings, as well as secondary sources. This was supplemented by a 6-year regular attendance at a Brotherhood mosque in California, and hours of audio/video indoctrination materials (sermons, podcasts, and recorded interviews). This was helpful, but insufficient. The breakthrough occurred when I was informally asked, in the summer of 2008, to lecture on ideology to a group of inquisitive Brothers. Weekly lectures were organized at the house of a Brother during the months I spent in Cairo, with 30 attendants on average. This bonding period allowed me to study them closely over the next five years – and our relationship was considerably intensified during the 2011 revolt. It was also during this time that tell-all memoirs and testimonies became available.

Months into Morsi's presidency, it became obvious that the Brotherhood's days in power were numbered. In March 2013, I returned to Egypt to conduct over 40 interviews, some with members of my original crowd, and others with Brothers they knew.[ii] I initially began with a purposive sample to capture a variety of experiences through including members from different genders, age groups, social backgrounds, and organizational experiences. But after the first round of interviews, I moved to snowball sampling, asking interviewees to nominate others who were different from them. Cross-referencing helped minimize bias and untypical positions. Informal data gathering from people who came across Brothers in various personal and professional capacities was also useful. Equally informative were three focus group sessions, during the Brotherhood's time in power (December 30, 2012); on the eve of the gathering rebellion against them (March 27, 2013); and after the violent clearing of the sit-ins (September 3, 2013).

My informants were also kind enough to supply me with documents from their personal archives, such as training manuals for group prefects, the all-important cultivation curriculum, internal memos, resignation and prison letters, and personal correspondence.

[ii] Some allowed me to use their full names, and others their first, middle, or last name, or a nickname.

This was complemented by a review of voting records and public opinion surveys furnished by a variety of national and international agencies. Finally, I had the opportunity to witness Brotherhood exchanges first-hand, on the street, through social media, and in private meetings, during the turbulent summer of 2013. This all helped me identify the multi-faceted process that sustains the Brotherhood's core ideological concept: religious determinism.

In the following tables, I shed some light on those I relied on for primary information, including demographic data (Table 1), and organizational affiliation (Table 2).

Table 1

Age	Gender	Occupation	Status	Urbanness
20–40 years: 29	Male: 70	Businessman: 13	Upper class: 11	City: 48
40–60 years: 28	Female: 7	Cleric: 4	Middle class: 47	Countryside: 29
60–80 years: 20		Engineer: 14	Popular classes: 19	
		Housewife: 3		
		Journalist: 3		
		Lawyer: 9		
		Medic: 7		
		Natural sciences: 5		
		Schoolteacher: 4		
		Social scientist: 9		
		Manual worker: 4		
		Other: 2		

Table 2

Contribution	Type of affiliation	Length of affiliation	Family relations
Interviews: 42	Member: 33	3–10 years: 11	Born into Brotherhood: 13
Memoirs: 17	Devotee: 15	10–20 years: 26	Married or related to
Unpublished	Dissident: 17	20–40 years: 28	Brotherhood family: 25
documents: 14	Outsider: 12		Unaffiliated: 27
Published work: 38			
Audio/video			
materials: 15			
Sermons: 2			

Acknowledgements

This book really belongs to the interviewees. It is their lives that I struggled to make sense of – and I hope to have done them justice. I mark out three for special recognition: Shatla arranged a number of critical interviews; Rida provided invaluable documents; and Tariq and his family did both. Sherif al-Abd and Adham al-Khouli were not interviewed, but helped organize key interviews. My warmest gratitude, however, goes to Khaled Mahmoud, who inspired the whole project.

On the professional level, I first discussed this research with Professors Perry Anderson and Bahgat Korany, and their enthusiasm was contagious. Professor Rogers Brubaker offered penetrating critiques of a shorter version. Professor John Thompson encouraged me to write it up and continued to push me forward. And Professor Michael Mann was, as usual, generous with his support.

I was fortunate to receive feedback on this project from various audiences at Oxford University, Kings College London, the University of California at Los Angeles and Irvine, as well as colleagues and students at Cambridge University.

As always, this work would have been infinitely more difficult to conclude without the understanding and affection of my wife and children.

Notes

Introduction

1 Khadija Khairat al-Shatir's pronouncement from in front of her father's prison was uploaded on August 27, 2013 on www.youtube.com/watch?v=QsZsVM7kwes.

2 Brotherhood propagandist Safwat Hegazi proclaimed on stage in Rab'a, on July 24, 2013, that Friday would bring a divine miracle and Morsi would be back in office the next day.

1 Cultivating the Brother

1 In the early 1980s, the Egyptian government controlled only 6,000 of the country's 46,000 mosques. A couple of decades later, the ratio increased dramatically: out of 170,000 mosques, the Ministry of Religious Endowments administered just under 30,000 (Yohannes 2001: 261). Unmonitored mosques are open ground for recruitment to various causes, including Islamism.

2 A Brother (*akh*) advances through five ranks of membership: assistant (*musa'id*); affiliate (*muntasib*); organized (*muntazim*); working ('*amil*); and warrior (*mujahid*).

3 Geographically, the Brotherhood is divided, in ascending order, into family, branch, region, province, and finally sector. Egypt is divided into three sectors: Greater Cairo in the center, the Nile Delta in the north, and Upper Egypt in the south. In terms of provinces, the Brotherhood follows the government's administrative division of Egypt into 27 governorates. Each province is then divided into regions, which in

Brotherhood lexicon refers to neighborhoods with 40 to 100 full members. There are about 300 regions in total, and each controls a variable number of branches. In terms of organizational governance, *shura* (consultation) councils are elected for each level of the hierarchy (above the family) to express Brothers' opinions and help form a General *Shura* Council, which legislates, appoints an Executive Office, and elects the Guidance Bureau and General Guide. In addition to geographical and occupational units, Brothers are enlisted in specialized committees, such as finance, legal affairs, sports, etc. These also assume a pyramidal structure, with a central committee overseeing affiliates at regional and branch levels, and reporting to the highest executive and legislative bodies.

4   Some interviewees have participated in these meetings in Kuwait, Saudi Arabia, Canada, the US, and the UK.

5   At the beginning of his activist career, the Brotherhood's founder would deliver 5-minute speeches in about 20 cafés each night. He also visited 3,000 of Egypt's 4,000 villages, rather than concentrating on urban centers (Qaradawi 2000: 30). He said he targeted the less religiously observant and intellectually inclined because he did not want to preach to the converted (Banna [1948] 1990: 61).

6   For exegesis, the Brotherhood recommends Qutb ([1966] 1980); for jurisprudence, Sayyid Sabiq's *Fiqh al-Sunna*, which was commissioned and prefaced by Banna himself, as well as brief studies by Qaradawi; for the life of the Prophet and his Companions, and Islamic history in general, there is Muhammad al-Ghazzali's *Fiqh al-Sira*, and the lengthy volumes by Raghib al-Sirgani and 'Ali al-Sallabi. Even the history of the Brotherhood itself could only be learned from accredited sources, such as Mahmoud 'Abd al-Halim's four-volume study, *Al-Ikhwan al-Muslimun: Ahdath Sana'at al-Tarikh*.

7   The pillars are: comprehension; loyalty; action; *jihad*; sacrifice; obedience; perseverance; devotion; brotherhood; and trust. The first pillar is explained in 20 points, and the rest much more briefly.

8   By 2013, the Teachings had been interpreted by 20 Brothers. Some of them belonged to the founding generation ('Ali 'Abd al-Halim); most were religious scholars (Qaradawi, Ghazali, 'Abd al-Mon'iem Ahamd Ti'elab); a few were regular members (Goma'a Amin); and others were Brotherhood leaders in Syria, Iraq, Yemen, Lebanon, Jordan, and the Sudan (Tag al-Din 2013: 69–74).

9   A primary example here is *Al-'Awasim min al-Qawasim*, by thirteenth-century jurist Abu-Bakr ibn al-'Arabi.

10   Al-Azhar University is one of the Islamic world's oldest and most prestigous centres of Islamic learning.

11   This is repeated in Qur'an lesson 14, which discusses the verse: 'Indeed, God has purchased from the believers their lives and their properties in exchange for Paradise' (9: 111).

12   The speaker was actually citing the beginners' curriculum ("Mabadi' al-Islam" 2003: vol. III, 268).

13 In fact, an entire book is devoted to the dark fate of those who leave the Brotherhood: Fatthy Yakan's "Al-Mutasaqitun 'ala Tarieq al-Da'wa" (Those Fallen by the Mission's Wayside).

14 The first bylaws were issued in 1945 and amended in 1948. They were replaced with new ones in 1978 and 1982. The latest version was ratified in 1990 and was amended in 2009 and 2010 (though rumor has it that it was also amended in 1992 and 1999). Internal pressure to access them by restive Brothers like 'Abd al-Mon'iem Mahmoud and Ibrahim al-Houdeibi (both interviewed in this work) leaked to outsiders. And Mahmoud eventually secured a copy and published it in *Al-Dustur* newspaper in 2008. The Guidance Bureau finally felt compelled to post them on the Brotherhood's official website in 2009. This was the first time that regular Brothers had seen the bylaws ("Istiqala" 2012; Houdeibi 2013; Mahmoud 2013).

15 Of these, 5 won seats during Guidance Bureau elections – Sa'ad al-Katatni (Menia), Sa'ad al-Husseini (Gharbia), Muhie Hamid (Sharqia), Muhammad 'Abd al-Rahman al-Morsi (Daqahlia), Usama Nasr (outskirts of Alexandria) – and 3 were elevated to the Bureau without elections when other members passed away or were imprisoned – Muhammad Morsi (Sharqia), Sabri 'Arafa al-Komi (Daqahlia), and Mahmoud Hussein (Asyut). Notably, the 2009 Bureau had an extra seat that the 16 designated in the bylaws.

16 The provincials were: Muhammad Badei' (Mahala), Muhammad Morsi (Sharqia), Sa'ad al-Katatni (Menia), Muhammad 'Abd al-Rahman al-Morsi (Daqahlia), Mahmoud Abu-Zeid (Daqahlia), Mahmoud Hussein (Asyut), Muhie Hamid (Sharqia), Sa'ad al-Husseini (Gharbia), 'Abd al-Rahman al-Bar (Daqahlia), Mustafa Ghoneim (Gharabia). City dwellers with a rural background were: 'Essam al-'Erian (from the suburbs of Giza), Osama Nasr (from the suburbs of Alexandria), Rashad al-Bayumi (who lives in Cairo but was raised in and frequently returns to Suhag), and Mahmoud 'Ezzat (a Cairo resident linked to Daqahlia). And urban members were: Mahmoud Ghuzlan (Cairo), Khairat al-Shatir, and Goma'a Amin (Alexandria) (Tammam 2012: 84–6).

17 There have been several works on Qutb's life and his ideological influence (Moussalli 1992; Euben 1999; Calvert 2011; Toth 2013). Yet the most impressive, by far, remains Sherif Yunis' (2012) intellectual biography.

18 In working as schoolteachers, they are both following in the footsteps of the movement's first and second founders, and hoping to shape the minds of pupils according to Islamist doctrine (Nada 2012: 176).

19 Details of their names and occupations can be found in Sabbagh (2012: 95).

20 The Brotherhood claims that it does not have a database with the educational backgrounds of its members for security reasons. An interviewee, who had been with the Brotherhood since the 1970s, confirms that they have just circulated application sheets for members to fill out

in order to begin building such a database (Sharif 2013). All interviewees agreed – citing personal knowledge – that the percentage of social scientists is negligible.

21 Of course, the students of natural science targeted here are mostly skilled technicians, not the Avicenna, Galileo, Darwin, Einstein, or Hawking types.

22 Brotherhood clerics were the first of their kind: countering secular infringements on religion by dabbling in political and social theory – something Muslim clerics scarcely attempted before. Scholars, from the sociologist Ibn Khaldun to the medic Avicenna and the mathematician Khawarizmi, did not justify their secular findings using religion, and jurists and theologians rarely made assumptions about the secular world. Islamism changed all that. Nonetheless, the Brotherhood did not treat its clerics as intellectuals by proxy. When any of them crossed the line, Brothers pulled no punches. For example, when Qaradawi criticized the Guidance Bureau in 2009, Bureau member Mahmoud Ghuzlan (2009a) published an open letter repudiating him in the harshest terms – basically accusing him of parroting ill-informed opinions.

23 A quarter of a decade later, Muhammad Habib, deputy general guide, saw America through the same lens during his visit: "Western society in general, and America in particular, lives in moral chaos" (2012: 82).

24 Undeterred, Nada insisted two years later, in his memoirs, that Shi'ites were just another school of Islamic jurisprudence, not heretics (Nada 2012: 120).

25 This substantiates Mitchell's (1993: 40) suspicion – in the most informative history of the Brotherhood in English – that the founders "deliberately generalized" the idea of *al-nizam al-Islami* (Islamic order).

26 Brothers were probably right: the movement's most frequent dissenters were lawyers – those who most resemblance social scientists. Prominent examples include 'Essam Sultan, Mukhtar Nuh, and Tharwat al-Khirbawi. One of the younger dissidents was the Alexandrian lawyer 'Abd al-Mon'iem Mahmoud, who created the first blog by an Egyptian Islamist, *Ana Ikhwan* (I am a Brother), to present his views freely. However, Brothers had to accept lawyers as a necessary evil, since non-Islamist court lawyers could not be trusted. Social scientists, in contrast, could be dispensed with.

2 Building the Brotherhood

1 Another volume of the cultivation curriculum cites the longer verse: 'You will not find people who believe in God and the Last Day having affection for those who oppose God and His Messenger, even if they were their fathers or their sons or their brothers or their kindred' (Qur'an 58: 22, in "Madkhal" 1997: 182).

2 Televized interview posted on April 23, 2013 on www.youtube.com/ watch?v=ClyvyzCe2Cg.

3 The following script is patched together from slightly different versions, as recorded in the interviews.

4 In the Teachings, 'Companionship' (*al-suhba*) is the thirteenth tenet of the first pillar of the oath of allegiance.

5 Muhammad 'Abdullah al-Khatib posted "Ja' al-Haq wa Zahaq al-Batil" (Right has Prevailed and Wrong has been Vanquished) on April 17, 2013 on www.fj-p.com/article.php?id=56271.

6 In the Sisterhood, the stress is mostly on the parental side. Sanaa' Farghali (2013), the experienced cultivator, considered herself a mother to all the girls under her supervision.

7 Another famous work is Ahmad Ra'if's *Al-Bawaba al-Sawda'* (The Black Gate). But, besides books wholly devoted to prison episodes, any of the memoirs of older Brothers contain sections on their prison tours.

8 www.ikhwanonline.com/Article.aspx?ArtID=83916&SecID=391.

9 This refers to Qur'an 11: 42–3: 'And it sailed with them through waves like mountains, and Noah called to his son who was apart [from them], "O my son, come aboard with us and be not with the disbelievers." He said, "I will take refuge on a mountain to protect me from the water." [Noah] said, "There is no protector today from God's decree, except for those whom He gives mercy." And the waves came between them, and he was among the drowned.'

10 The video was uploaded on May 23, 2011. The date of the lecture is not defined: www.youtube.com/watch?v=xm5dL5SQE4E.

11 Veteran cultivator 'Abd al-Bar refers to wives reporting on their husbands for illicitly communicating with females through chat rooms and mobile phones, or watching pornography ("Taqrir" 2007).

12 Annual subscriptions and donation are required by article 5 of the Brotherhood's General Order. The annual contribution is divided as follows: 5 percent membership fee; 1 percent aid for detainees and their families; 1 percent for the Palestine fund; and 3 percent as a voluntary contribution, which all except the most needy feel obliged to pay through peer pressure.

13 The state television interview with Muhammad Badei' was first broadcast on May 29, 2013 and posted on https://www.youtube.com/watch?v=svprMpBkLd8&feature=player_embedded.

3 Forging the Ideology

1 A claim made by Brotherhood cleric Jamal 'Abd al-Hadi in Rab'a al-'Adawiya, on July 1, 2013, and uploaded on https://www.youtube.com/watch?v=3oOaAbsqVcg. Preachers like Safwat Hegazi repeated claims about a cosmic sign that would herald Morsi's return, and recounted holy dreams on stage.

2   Although Brothers sometimes note the importance of striving through material means (*al-akhz bei al-asbab*), they do so mostly to appeal to materialist-minded outsiders (Muslims and non-Muslims alike). In truth, "they do not place much store in *asbab* (means), but rely ultimately on *baraka* (divine blessing)" (Khalid 2013).

3   Of course, the general claim that if someone does good things, good things happen to him or her has always been part of the popular psyche. But it was meant to apply to individuals not groups or nations. In fact, many other staples of Muslim popular wisdom contradict this claim, such as "al-mu'min musab" (believers are [always] victims [of trials and tribulations]). Likewise, popular religion embraces Sufi miracles (*karamat*) enthusiastically without implying that saintly miracles could have a transformative political effect on an entire society.

4   The fuller definition, presented in the Teachings, is a bit more obscure and notably ineloquent: "Islam is a comprehensive order that deals with all aspects of life: it is a state and homeland or a government and nation; it is morality and power or mercy and justice; it is culture and law or science and judiciousness; it is finance and wealth or earning and richness; and it is holy struggle and a mission or an army and doctrine; just as much as it is true faith and correct worship" (Banna [1949] 1993: 305).

5   http://islamstory.com/ar.

6   "Hawl al-Makhraj min Azmat Masr" (On the Way Out of Egypt's Crisis) was posted on April 2, 2012 on http://islamstory.com/ar.

7   The author holds a copy of the pamphlet.

8   This topic is fully covered in Qur'an lessons 18–22 ("Turuq" 2002: vol. I, 103–43).

9   Interestingly enough, this mentality spilled over into Islamists' professional world. Professor Isma'il, a longtime member of the faculty of medicine in one of Egypt's biggest universities, interacted with dozens of Brotherhood physicians. What struck him most was that no matter how talented they were, Brothers showed little enthusiasm for examining their successes with an eye towards systematizing them in a rational and communicable fashion: "It is like the difference between a mechanic and an engineer. They regarded their success as a form of blessing that can hardly be rationalized" (Isma'il 2013).

10 Muhammad Abdullah al-Khateeb posted "Ja' al-Haq wa Zahaq al-Batil" (Right has Prevailed and Wrong has been Vanquished) on April 17, 2013, on www.fj-p.com/article.php?id=56271.

11 I attended both Friday sermons in January 2009 and November 2012.

12 I attended this lecture, which was delivered on March 7, 2011 in Cairo's El Sawy Cultural Wheel under the title of "al-Thawra al-Masriya" (The Egyptian Revolution).

13 Uploaded on August 11, 2013 on www.youtube.com/watch?v=jn5kMv DspH4.

14 Uploaded on August 8, 2013 on www.youtube.com/watch?v=NUiKD9 DHoNk.

15 Sirgani's '*Al-Ahzab am Uhud* ([Battle of] The Trench or Uhud') was posted on July 21, 2013 on http://islamstory.com/ar.

16 Uploaded on August 27, 2013 on www.youtube.com/watch?v=QsZs VM7kwes.

17 Posted on the Brotherhood's website in September 2011 as part of the coverage of the general guide's visit, www.ikhwanonline.com/print .aspx?ArtID=90846&SecID=210.

18 Sacred visions constitute the third tenet (out of 20) of the pillar of Comprehension, which is, in turn, the first pillar (out of 10) of the oath of allegiance in the Teachings.

19 Uploaded on June 20, 2013 on www.youtube.com/watch?v=1_eoIWk NcFc.

20 Uploaded on July 9, 2013 on www.youtube.com/watch?v=X0aRvFq Eysw&sns=em.

21 A more elaborate version is provided in the third pillar of the Teachings (Banna [1949] 1993: 308–10).

22 Asef Bayat (2007: 14) probably provided the best description of this strategy: "Through their cultural production – establishing new life-styles and new modes of thinking, being, and doing things – movements may be able to recondition and *socialize* states and political elites into the society's sensibilities, ideals."

23 "The starting point for most of the discussions of property is the orthodox view that all property belongs to God . . . [and that] human beings are simply trustees placed in charge by God to ensure His property is used fruitfully and in a morally commendable way" (Tripp 2006: 58).

24 Islamists' economic confusion usually causes them to serve the domi-nant interests. The best example is Islamic banking. Islamists originally intended for it to embody their high moral principles, but "Far from representing an alternative to the capitalist economic system, it [became] a full player within it, offering to its customers a distinctive way of making a profit [without moral scruples]" (Tripp 2006: 199).

25 In truth, the only time Machiavelli made an explicit reference to this principle, he attributed it to a corrupt priest in his 1518 play, *Mandragola*.

4 The Slow Rise and Rapid Fall from Power

1 The Ayyubids needed to reestablish Sunni dominance and purge Shi'a scholars and practices from Egypt, as well as rally Muslims in Egypt and the Levant to fight Crusaders. The Mamluks, as a caste of foreign warriors newly converted to Islam, needed to legitimize their rule, partly through holding the *'ulama* in great esteem, or at least pretending to. Accordingly, many illustrious scholars rose to dominance during these successive dynasties. Examples include Ibn 'Abd al-Salam, Ibn Bint

al-'Aaz, al-Nawawi, al-Subki, and Ibn al-Qayyim. This was also the golden age of Sufi saints, such as al-Shazli and al-Naqshabandi.

2   As with other traditional intellectuals, according to Gramsci (1971: 7), religious scholars' historical continuity and special qualifications inspired a certain *esprit de corps* that made them autonomous. The most that religious scholars aspired for, as recorded in Ibn Taymiyya's thirteenth-century *al-Siyasa al-Shar'iyah* (Legitimate Politics), was "close collaboration between the two fundamental classes of the state: the emirs and the *'ulama*, the sword and the book" (Zubaida 2005: 91–100). But, in practice, Islamic law developed as a "system of socio-moral legitimacy outside the state structures" (Esposito and Voll 2001: 9). Or, as Zubaida conclusively put it: "political power was separated from lawmaking" (Zubaida 2005: 78; see also Ghalioun 1993: 97; Hallaq 2005: 208). This is why Muslim jurists did not produce a coherent political theory. When they bothered to address politics at all, it was either to enumerate the preferred traits of the legitimate ruler, as in al-Mawardi's *al-Ahkam al-Sultaniya* (Principles of Rule), or to advise rulers on how to govern effectively without violating sharia, as in al-Juwayni's *al-Ghiathi* (The Savior), both written in the eleventh century. The best accounts of the professionalization of religious scholarship and its complicated interaction with politics are Zubaida's *Law and Power in the Islamic World* (2005), and Hallaq's *Authority, Continuity, and Change in Islamic Law* (2005). For a more detailed historical treatment, see Cook (2004) and Crone (2004). The most recent take is Ziadeh's (2013) elaborate study of the evolving relationship between scholars and rulers in Egypt, the Levant, and the Ottoman caliphate.

3   One can cite here the resounding condemnation of the influential eighteenth-century historian al-Jabarti for how *'ulama* had become "seduced by the world and abandoned ... knowledge" (cited in Ziadeh 2013: 134).

4   It was only natural that capitals close to the center of the Islamic empire felt a greater need to match Western modernization than peripheral ones.

5   Prominent examples include the Constantinople-based Ibrahim Muteferriqa and Mahmoud Ra'if (who published in the 1760s and 1790s, respectively). The latter was distinguished by being the first (though by no means the last) Muslim to publish a treatise in French. Another went as far as proclaiming that France was the world's bosom, and that it fed all the world's sociopolitical and cultural currents (Ziadeh 2013: ch. 3).

6   The first student, 'Uthman Nur al-Din, was sent to France in 1809, and the first full delegation followed in 1826. By 1840, 'Ali's vanguards had transmitted their modern education to another 9,000 students. From then onwards, the flow of students receiving higher education in Europe (and later America) and bringing it back home never ceased.

7   By 1875, the number of Christian missionary schools was double that of public schools. The ratio was particularly skewed for girls' schools,

with 29 missionary schools to only 3 public schools. A 1945 census counts 233 missionary schools, divided as follows: 157 French, 39 English, and 37 American. Equally significant was the number of Westerners teaching in Cairo's first modern university. During its first eight years of operation, 138 European professors in law, social sciences, and humanities were appointed (Sabbagh 2012: 51-52). Azhar tried to reform itself to absorb this dizzying transformation in the educational field, but its modest reforms fell short (for details see Hassan 2006: 158–68).

8 This intellectual trend was quickly noted by scholars such as Adams (*Islam and Modernism in Egypt*, 1933), and Gibb (*Modern Trends in Islam*, 1947), and received its most fulfilling treatment in Hourani's *Arab Thought in the Liberal Age* (1962). Other important studies include Kerr (1966), Awad (1969), Binder (1988), and Kurzman (2002).

9 Liberal icons dominated politics (Ahmad Lutfi al-Sayyid, Sa'ad Zaghloul), social reform (Qassim Amin, Houda Sha'rawi), and culture (Taha Hussein, Tawfiq al-Hakim, Ahmad Amin), followed by nationalist intellectuals (Mustafa Kamil, 'Abd al-Rahman al-Raf'ie), communists (Salama Moussa), and even fascists (Ahmad Hussein). In 1907, the Muslim world's first secular parties were created in Egypt: the nationalist Watani party, and the liberal Ummah party.

10 'Abduh's (2002: 7) call, "We must understand that although religion itself is a divine matter, its advocates are men, with all their greed, lust for power, and other shortcomings," rang hollow for those grounded in Islamic tradition. Inspired by the Protestant Reformation, 'Abduh seemed to have forgotten that Islamic sciences evolved at the hands of scholars spread around learning centers, rather than through a central authority that claimed infallibility, as did the medieval church. His Kantian encouragement for each believer to think for himself ('Abduh 2002: 64) negated Islam's longtime tradition that the ignorant should either take the time to learn or follow those who did. It also contradicted the fact that any community of knowledge develops "standards of role performance that are not accessible to all members of a society" (Berger and Luckmann 1967: 74), and the Qur'an's (9: 122) instruction that, since "not everyone can or should become a specialist" in religious sciences, one group must "dedicate itself to knowledge . . . [and] act as a reference point" (Zubaida 2005: 20).

11 'Ali 'Abd al-Raziq's 1925 bombshell, *Al-Islam wa Usul al-Hukm* (Islam and the Principles of Governance), questioned the religious origins of the caliphate. Taha Hussein's Cartesian *Fei al-Shi'r al-Jahili* (On Pre-Islamic Poetry), published the year after, took a few shy steps towards a textual analysis of the Qur'an, and his 1938 *Mustaqbal al-Thaqafa fei Misr* (The Future of Culture in Egypt) invited Egyptians to embrace their Western Mediterranean heritage rather than their Arab one. Hussein went on, along with Ahmad Amin, to publish revisionist histories of Islam. And Muhammad Hussein Heikal produced in 1933 an innovative portrait of the Prophet, *Hayat Muhammad* (Muhammad's

Life), highlighting his human traits. During the same period, Salama Musa published his 1927 *Bein al-Yawm wal-Ghad* (Between Today and Tomorrow), calling for the wholesale adoption of the European culture. Even the sympathetic 'Abd al-Raziq al-Sanhouri, Egypt's foremost legal scholar, proclaimed in the 1930s that Islamic jurisprudence had stagnated to the point where it could no longer govern society, and that a unified Islamic caliphate had proved historically impossible (Sanhouri 2010).

12 Sa'id al-'Ashmawi, Farag Fouda, and Jamal al-Banna (Hassan al-Banna's youngest brother) are typical examples of the first group, and Muhammad Arkun, Talal Assad, and Nasr Hamid Abu Zied exemplify the second.

13 Equally shocking, this article was published by the mainstream daily *al-Ahram*, on May 17, 1934, not some obscure newspaper (Diyab 1987: 94).

14 Qutb received an MA from Wilson's Teachers' College, complemented by independent seminars in Colorado State University. He also visited cosmopolitan centers (New York, San Francisco, Los Angeles).

15 Before his conversion, Qutb had been impressed by Brotherhood cleric Muhammad al-Ghazali's writings on Islam's economic values, and produced a short tract on *Al-'Adala al-Ijtima'iya fei al-Islam* (Social Justice in Islam), in 1948, though he had not yet shaken off his secular worldview (Yunis 2012: 147).

16 Banna was assassinated on the street by a police officer on February 12, 1949. Qutb was first detained briefly in March 1954, then again in November, when he was handed a 15-year prison term (starting July 1955). He was released on probation for health reasons in May 1964, but was soon picked up again (in August 1965) and accused of plotting to overthrow the regime. Qutb was hanged on the morning of August 29, 1966. Given Qutb's lifelong radical temperament, it is unlikely that he only embraced extremism due to torture.

17 It is generally agreed that 'Umar ibn 'Abd al-'Aziz was the reviver of the first Islamic century; Muhammad ibn Idris al-Shafe'i of the second; and Abu Hamid al-Ghazali of the fifth.

18 In fact, Sayyid Qutb published an open letter urging the coup leaders to establish a just dictatorship, and ignore old-regime liberals (Moussalli 1992: 32).

19 Brothers later alleged they had been negotiating with the British on Nasser's behalf, but the minutes of meetings, as recorded by the British, show otherwise (Kandil 2011: 28-9).

20 The second founder drew inspiration from the distant past, but according to his best biographer he really represented the culmination of the Romantic elitism of Egypt's modern intelligentsia (Yunis 2012: 16). As Yunis explained, the nineteenth-century educated middle class felt powerless vis-à-vis landlords and ignorant peasants, and placed their hope in controlling the state and transforming society from above (Yunis 2012: 145).

21 In a 2009 interview with the Egyptian daily *al-Masri al-Youm*, General Guide Mahdi 'Akif confessed that State Security provided him with a list of districts to run in. The regime wanted to demonstrate to post-9/11 America the dangers of pursuing their democracy-promotion campaign. And the Brothers saw no harm in cooperating with security agents to gain more seats in parliament (Gallad et al. 2009: 11).

22 See Kandil (2012) for the complex institutional interactions that led to Mubarak's overthrow.

23 Mubarak and his security apparatus had been charged with murdering protesters during the 2011 revolt. A court sentenced him to life in prison on flimsy evidence (because security officers refused to supply any), and so he was released on appeal, and thereafter harassed with petty corruption charges, which he skirted one after the other. On the eve of Morsi's election, an independent commission was set up to reinvestigate Mubarak's original crime. Six months later, on December 2012, it produced a detailed report that incriminated the old tyrant and his security associates. The contents were leaked to the *Guardian* and the Egyptian daily *al-Shorouk*. Morsi's trusted prosecutor general announced that shocking arrests were imminent, and that revolutionary justice was on the way. Then nothing happened.

24 Polls and surveys were conducted by Al-Ahram Center for Political and Strategies Studies (ACPSS) in partnership with the Danish–Egyptian Dialogue Institute (DEDI) between August 2011 and November 2012.

25 The Brotherhood had initially promised not to nominate anyone for the presidency. Then it decided to put forward its chief strategist, Khairat al-Shatir, but he was deemed ineligible because he failed to rescind a past conviction for money-laundering. So, instead, the Brothers opted for Morsi, who had been recruited during his doctoral studies in Southern California, sat in parliament between 1995 and 2005, and was elected to the Guidance Bureau in 2009 based on his reputation as an organizational yes-man.

26 ACPSS–DEDI survey conducted in November 2012.

27 Monthly surveys were conducted by the Egyptian Center for Public Opinion Research (Bassera): http://baseera.com.eg/baseera.

28 "One Year After Morsi's Ouster, Divides Persist on El-Sisi, Muslim Brotherhood," Pew Research Center (Washington, May 2014).

29 Egyptians were positively livid about foreign correspondents warning against brainwashing by official propaganda. Citizens on the receiving end of Islamist violence did not get their views from television. Those who personally identified their Brotherhood neighbors leading violent raids against the residents of Manyal, Bein al-Sarayat, Bulaq, and Ramses could hardly believe Islamist claims that these were security-hired thugs. When viewers turned to the media, it was to follow Islamist speeches in Rab'a, not what anti-Islamists had to say. The government had always described its enemies as terrorists, but citizens never paid heed – this time, they did. Egypt's naturally suspicious citizens would never have believed their government when it cried "Wolf!"

30 'Abd al-Rahman al-Bar's *Ibtila' yantahi bi nasr mubin* (A Trial that will End in Resounding Victory) was posted on www.ikhwanonline.com/ Article.aspx?ArtID=188927&SecID=363 on June 10, 2014.

5   Islamism in Egypt and Beyond

1 Wahhabi Islam in Saudi Arabia, Abu al-'Ala' al-Mawdudi's Islamic Group (*Jamaat-e-Islami*) in Pakistan, and the Afghani Taliban that have been inspired by both will not be covered here because they have no ideological affiliation with the Muslim Brotherhood. Also, countries where militant groups have eclipsed Brothers, such as Algeria, Yemen, and Somalia, will not be discussed.

2 Ahmad al-Sukkari, the Brotherhood's first dissenter, was a close friend of Hassan al-Banna, yet when he exposed financial irregularities in movement accounts, he was denounced as an attention-seeker and a spy for the liberal Wafd Party (Sabbagh 2012: 203).

3 The founders applied for licenses in 1996, 1998, 2004, and finally received one after the 2011 revolt.

4 One of their most representative contributions is the 2001 collection entitled *Ru'a Islamiya Mu'asira* (Contemporary Islamic Views), which was edited by al-'Awwa. The best analysis of their work in the English-speaking world is Raymond Baker's (2003) *Islam without Fear: Egypt and the New Islamists*.

5 Cooley (2000), Bergen (2001), Wright (2007), and Gerges (2011) provide well-researched accounts of the alliance of Qutb-inspired Egyptian militants and Afghan war veterans to form al-Qa'da. And the memoir of Ayman Sabri Farag (2002), the Egyptian militant who served in Afghanistan, and Zawahri's old comrade Montasir al-Zayat (2002) offer valuable first-hand accounts.

6 The General Bureau denies such an alliance. But former deputy general guide, Muhammad Habib, and several other former leaders, including 'Amr 'Umara and Ahmad Ban, publicly acknowledged this tactical alliance and urged Brothers to rescind it (*Al-Shorouk*, March 16, 2014, p. 6; *Al-Ahram Weekly*, March 22, 2014, p. 5). Nageh Ibrahim, a founder of the militant Islamic Group, added that, despite historic differences, "The Muslim Brotherhood and Al-Qaeda became very close, and there was an alliance and cooperation between them. Perhaps one reason for this was the kinship or in-law connection between the head of the former president's office and Ayman Al-Zawahri … There was also a phone call between Morsi and Ayman Al-Zawahri in which the latter insisted on certain measures at Al-Azhar … [Their] organizational structures never intertwined. There was a convergence of interests" (quoted in *Al-Ahram Weekly*, March 20, 2014, p. 3, http://weekly.ahram.org.eg/News/5743/17/Mapping-the-Brotherhood.aspx).

7   Brothers state in their official history that their first branch outside Egypt was formed in 1933 in Djibouti. But it has been the work of a few young men who studied in Cairo, and little has been heard about it since (Mahmoud 1999).

8   The insecure monarch had also expressed his concern with the spread of Shi'a Islamism from Iran to Iraq, Bahrain, Syria, and Lebanon – what he referred to as the new Shi'ite crescent.

9   Sameh 'Eid remembers his astonishment at hearing prefects instruct Brothers to read all of Rashid's works, except for *al-Masar* (The Path), because it was misleading ('Eid 2013: 199; Rida 2013 had the same experience).

10 After several rounds of debate between 1998 and 2000, a *Document of Complementarity* was adopted that stated that PJD and MUR would consult and cooperate but remain essentially separate, with one tackling politics, and the other devoted to religious vocation.

11 Nursi's prolific writings (mostly in Arabic) include an exegesis of select verses of the Qur'an, in addition to a voluminous compilation of religious commentaries, fragmented reflections, memoirs, and the long speeches he insisted on improvising and delivering in person during his numerous trials (see Nursi 1996).

12 Perry Anderson correctly highlights AKP's surprising popularity among the lower classes despite its faithful adoption of "a neo-liberal regimen with the fervour of the convert" (Anderson 2009: 449). This popularity could be partly explained by Erdogan's crushing native charisma, his humble origins, common man's piety, traditional Turkish machismo, and plain-talking populism, which all combined to create a powerful personality cult. However, it was not all a matter of charisma: AKP did actually try to provide "neo-liberalism with a human face," combining respect for market forces with systematic efforts to alleviate poverty and improve public services (Önis 2007: 24).

13 The Turkish 1980 constitution decrees that parties that receive less than 10 percent of the vote cannot enter parliament, and the votes they received are to be reallocated among the winners. This threshold rule meant that AKP's 34 percent win was eventually bumped up to give control over 60 percent of parliament seats.

14 The most comprehensive analysis of AKP is Yavuz (2006).

15 The Strategic Depth doctrine, first published in 2000, explained how strategic depth is predicated on geographical and historical depth, and outlined in great detail how Turkey could benefit from both.

16 Keddie admitted that all those who outranked Khomeini considered him a misguided populist innovator (Keddie 1981: 210). Cronin said that, compared to his peers – past and present – he was "entirely exceptional" (Cronin 2010: 266). And Rajaee put it more bluntly: "[Khomeini's ideas] ran contrary to traditional Muslim political thought [among Shi'ites], the established practice in the seminaries, and even the position he himself had taken before"; they were nothing less than "a paradigm shift" (Rajaee 2007: 90–1).

17 The classic comparison between Egyptian and Iranian Islamists remains Asef Bayat's 'Revolution without Movement, Movement without Revolution: Islamist Activism in Egypt and Iran, 1960s–1980s', first published in 1998 in *Comparative Studies in Society and History*, and republished in his 2007 book.

Appendix: A Note on Theory and Method

1 Although the practical logic of Bourdieu's actors is pre-reflective, unlike Mann's (1986: 3) purposive actions, he maintains an important distinction between the practical logic of actors, and the theoretical logic – available to scholars – which discerns the drives and consequences of practices (Bourdieu 1977: 9).

Bibliography

Islamist Memoirs

Abu al-Fotouh, 'Abd al-Mon'eim. 2010. *Shahid 'ala Tarikh al-Haraka al-Islamiya, 1970–1984* (Witnessing the History of the Islamic Movement, 1970–1984). Cairo: Dar al-Shorouk.

'Abd al-Hadi, Fatima. 2011. *Rihlati ma'a al-Akhawat al-Muslimat: Min al-Imam Hasan al-Banna ela Sujun Abd al-Nasser* (My Journey with the Muslim Sisterhood: From Imam Hassan al-Banna to Abd al-Nasser's Prisons). Cairo: Dar al-Shorouk.

Al-'Ashmawi, Hassan. 1985. *Muzakirat Harib (Memoirs of a Fugitive)*. Beirut: Dar al-Fatah lel-Tiba'a wal-Nashr.

Al-Banna, Hassan. [1948] 1990. *Muzakirat al-Da'wa wal-Da'iya* (Memoirs of the Message and the Advocate). Cairo: Al-Zahra' lel-'Ilam Al-'Arabi.

'Eid, Sameh. 2013. *Tagribti fei Saradib al-Ikhwan* (My Experience in the Corridors of the Brotherhood). Cairo: Maktabat Jazeera al-Ward.

Farag, Ayman Sabri. 2002. *Zekriat Arabi-Afghani* (Memoirs of an Arab-Afghani). Cairo: Dar al-Shorouk.

Fayez, Sameh. 2013. *Janat al-Ikhwan: Rihlat al-Khuruj min al-Jama'a* (The Brotherhood's Paradise: Exodus from the Movement). Cairo: Dar al-Tanweer.

Al-Ghazali, Zeynab. 1999. *Ayam min Hayati* (Days of My Life). Cairo: Dar al-Tawzi' wal-Nashr.

Al-Gindy, Anwar. 2001. *Hassan al-Banna al-Da'iya wal-Imam wal-Mujadid al-Shahid* (Hassan al-Banna: The Martyred Missionary, Leader, and Reviver). Beirut: Dar al-Qalam.

Habib, Muhammad. 2012. *Zikrayat: 'An al-Hayat, wal-Da'wa, wal-Siyasa, wal-Fikr* (Memories: On Life, the Call, Politics, and Thought). Cairo: Dar al-Shorouk.

Hammuda, Hussein Mohamed Ahmad. 1985. *Asrar harakat al-zubat al-ahrar wa al-Ikhwan al-Muslimeen* (Secrets of the Free Officers' Movement and the Muslim Brothers). Cairo: Al-Zahraa lel-'Ilam al-Arabi.

Hatthout, Hassaan. 2000. *Al-'Aqd al-Farid, 1942–1952: 'Ashar Sanawat ma'a Hassan al-Banna* (The Unique Decade, 1942–1952: Ten Years with Hassan al-Banna). Cairo: Dar al-Shorouk.

Al-Houdeibi, Hassan. 1973. *Al-Islam wa al-Da'iya* (Islam and the Advocate). Cairo: Dar Al-Ansar.

Al-Khirbawi, Tharwat. 2012. *Sir al-Ma'bad* (The Temple's Secret). Cairo: Dar Nahdat Misr.

Nada, Youssef. 2012. *Min Dakhil al-Ikhwan al-Muslimin* (From Inside the Muslim Brotherhood). Cairo: Dar al-Shorouk.

Al-Qaradawi, Youssef. 2000. *Al-Sheikh al-Ghazali kama 'Araftuh: Rihlat Nisf Qarn* (Al-Sheikh al-Ghazali As I Have Known Him: Half-a-Century's Journey). Cairo: Dar al-Shorouk.

Qutb, Sayyid. 1999. *Tifl fi al-Qariyah (A Child in the Village)*. Cologne (Germany): Al-Kamel Publishers.

Rafsanjani, Akbar Hashemi. 2005. *Hayati* (My Life). Beirut: Dar al-Saqi.

Al-Telmesani, 'Umar. 2008. *Omar al-Telmesani*. Cairo: Halal el-Nashr wal-Tawzi'.

Al-Zayat, Montasir. 2002. *Ayman al-Zawahri kama 'Araftuh* (Ayman al-Zawahri As I Knew Him). Cairo: Uli al-Nahi lel-Intag al-'Elami.

Published Writings and Interviews

'Abduh, Muhammad. 2002. *Al-Islam bin al-'Elm wa al-Madania* (Islam between Knowledge and Civilization). Cairo: Al-Haiy'a al-Masriya al-'Ama lel-Kitab.

Abu-Khalil, Haitham. 2012. *Ikhwan Islahiun* (Reforming Brothers). Cairo: Dar Dawawin.

Ahmad, Labiba. 1934. *"Risala" (Letter) Al-Ikhwan al-Muslimun* (March 1, 1934).

Amin, Gum'a. 2005. *Awraq min Tarikh al-Ikhwan al-Muslimeen* (Papers from the History of the Muslim Brothers). Cairo: Dar al-Tawzi' wal-Nashr.

Al-'Awwa, Muhammad Selim (ed.). 2001. *Ru'a Islamiya Mu'asira* (Contemporary Islamic Views). Kuwait: Al-'Arabi Book.

Al-'Awwa, Muhammad Selim. 2006. *Fi al-Nizam al-Siyasi le al-Dawla al-Islamiya* (On the Political Order of the Islamic State). Cairo: Dar al-Shorouk.

Al-Banna, Hassan. [1949] 1993. *Majmu'at Rasa'il al-Imam al-Shahid Hasan al-Banna* (The Martyred Imam Hasan al-Banna's Collection of Epistles). Cairo: Al-Maktaba al-Tawfiqiya.

Al-Bishri, Tariq. 2008. *Qira'a fei al-Fikr al-Siyasi lel-Haraka al-Islamiya* (Reading into the Political Thought of the Islamist Movement). Cairo: Markaz al-'Elam al-'Arabi.

Al-Fakharani, Ahmad. 2013. "Sameh Fayez: Tarbiya al-Ikhwan tatruk Tashuhat Nafsia uas'ab mahwuha" (Sameh Fayez: The Brotherhood's Cultivation Leaves Psychological Damages that Can Hardly Be Removed). *Al-Masry al-Youm* (Cairo: May 7, 2013).

Al-Gallad, Magdi, Fouad Charles al-Masry, and Ahmed al-Khatib. 2009. "Mahdi 'Akef fei awal hiwar sahafi ba'd azmat al-insihab" (Mahdi 'Akef in his First Newspaper Interview Following the Withdrawal Crisis). *Al-Masry Al-Youm.* (Cairo, October 24, 2009, p. 11).

Al-Ghazali, Muhammad. 1981. *Dustur al-Wihda al-Thaqafiya bein al-Muslimin* (Constitution for Muslims' Cultural Union). Cairo: Dar al-Shorouk.

Al-Ghazali, Muhammad. [1954] 1998. *Qaza'if al-Haq* (Barrage of Righteousness). Cairo: Dar al-Shorouk.

Ghuzlan, Mahmoud. 2009a. "Risala Maftuha ella al-Doctor Youssef al-Qaradwi" (Open Letter to Dr Youssef al-Qaradawi). *Al-Masry al-Youm* (Cairo: November 1, 2009).

Habib, Rafiq. 2001. *Al-Umma wal-Dawla: Bayan Tahrir al-Umma* (The Nation and the State: A Manifesto for National Liberation). Cairo: Dar al-Shorouk.

Hawwa, Said. 1988. *Kai la Namdi Ba'idan 'an Ihtiyagat al-'Asr* (So We Do Not Stray Far from the Needs of the Age). Beirut: Dar al-'Emad.

Al-Houdeibi, Hassan. 1977. *Du'a la Quda* (Missionaries Not Judges). Cairo: Dar al-Tawzi' wal-Nashr.

Al-Houdeibi, Muhammad Ma'mun. 1997. *Al-Siyasa fei al-Islam* (Politics in Islam). Cairo: Dar al-Tawzi' wal-Nashr.

Khomeini, Ruhollah. 1981. *Islam and Revolution: Writings and Declarations of Imam Khomeini (1941–1980).* North Haledon, NJ: Mizan Press.

Madi, Abu al-'Ela. 2005. *Ru'iat al-Wasat fei al-Siyasa wa al-Mujtama'* (The Centrist Vision in Politics and Society). Cairo: Maktabat al-Shorouk al-Dawliya.

Mahmoud, 'Abd al-Halim. 1999. *Al-Ikhwan al-Muslimeen: Ahdath Sana'at al-Tarikh* (Muslim Brothers: Events that Made History). Cairo: Dar al-Da'wa.

Mahmoud, 'Abd al-Halim. 2005. *Manhaj al-Islah al-Islami fei al-Mujtama'* (The Islamic Reform Approach to Society). Cairo: Maktabet al-Usra.

Mahmoud, 'Ali 'Abd al-Halim. 1994. *Fihm Usul al-Islam* (Comprehending the Fundamentals of Islam). Cairo: Dar al-Tawzi' wal-Nashr.

Medhat, Marwa. " 'Abu Baraka: Al-Inqilab 'ala Morsi Shirk bei-Allah" (Abu Baraka: The Coup against Morsi is [a form of] renouncing God's unity). *Al-Watan* (Cairo: July 20, 2013).

Nursi, Said. 1996. *Risale-I Nur Külliyatı I-II* (Epistles of Light Volumes I–II). Istanbul: Nesil.

Al-Qaradawi, Youssef. 1999. *Al-Ikhwan al-Muslimun* (Muslim Brothers). Cairo: Maktabat Wahba.

Qutb, Sayyid. [1954] 1992. *Dirasat Islamiya* (Islamic Studies). Cairo: Dar al-Shorouk.

Qutb, Sayyid. [1966] 1980. *Fei Zilal al-Qur'an* (In the Shadows of the Qur'an), 9th edition. Cairo: Dar al-Shorouk.

Qutb, Sayyid. [1966] 1982. *Ma'alim fei al-Tariq* (Signposts). Cairo: Dar al-Shorouk.

Qutb, Sayyid. [1953] 2001. *Al-Islam wa al-Salam al-'Alami* (Islam and Universal Peace). Cairo: Dar al-Shorouk.

Al-Rashid, Muhammad Ahmad. 1993. *Ihya' fiqh al-Da'wa, kitab 1: al-Muntalaq* (Reviving Missionary Jurisprudence, Book 1: The Induction). Beirut: Mu'asast al-Risala.

Al-Rashid, Muhammad Ahmad. 1994. *Ihya' fiqh al-Da'wa, kitab 2: al-'Awa'iq* (Reviving Missionary Jurisprudence, Book 2: The Obstacles). Dubai: Dar al-Muntalaq.

Al-Sabbagh, Muhammad Sabri Salim. 2012. *Al-Ikhwan al-Muslimun 'ala Tariq al-Nagah* (Muslim Brothers on the Path of Salvation). Cairo: Dar Oktub.

Sanhouri, 'Abd al-Raziq. 2010. *Al-Din wal-Dawla fei al-Islam* (Religion and State in Islam). Cairo: Magalat al-Azhar.

Shari'ati, 'Ali. 1988. *Religion versus Religion*. Chicago: Kazi Publications.

Tag al-Din, Muhammad Saad. 2013. *Ayuha al-Ikhwan, men Antum? Hasan al-Banna Mujadid Qarn am Za'im 'Esaba?* (O Brothers, Who Are You? Hasan al-Banna: the Century's Reviver or a Gang Leader?). Cairo: Dar al-Tawzi' wal-Nashr.

Al-Telmesani, 'Umar. 1981. *Ba'd ma 'alamani al-Ikhwan al-Muslimin* (Some of What the Muslim Brotherhood Taught Me). Cairo: Dar al-Tawzi' wal-Nashr.

Ti'elab, 'Abd al-Mon'iem Ahmad. 1991. *Al-Bay'a: Sharh Risalat al-Ta'alim* (Oath of Allegiance: Explaining the Teachings Epistle). Asyut (Egypt): Matba'at al-Sharqawi.

Turabi, Hassan. 1989. "Al-Bu'd al-'Alami lel-Haraka al-Islamiya: Al-Tajriba al-Sudaniya" (The International Dimension of the Islamist Movement: The Sudanese Experience). Pp. 75–98 in *Al-Haraka al-Islamiya: Ru'iya Mustaqbaliya: Awraq fei al-Naqd al-Zati* (The Islamist Movement: A Future Vision: Papers in Self-Critique), edited by 'Abdullah al-Nafisi. Cairo: Maktabat Madbouli.

'Umara, Muhammad. 2006. *Ma'alim al-Mashru' al-Hadari fei Fikr al-Imam al-Shahid Hasan al-Banna* (Features of the Civilizational Project in the Thought of Martyred Imam Hasan al-Banna). Cairo: Dar al-Tawzi' wal-Nashr.

'Uwda, 'Abd al-Qadir. [1953] 1988. *Al-Islam wa Awda'na al-Qanuniya* (Islam and our Legal Order). Beirut: Mu'asasat al-Risala.

'Uwis, 'Abd al-Halim. 2010. *Falsafat al-Tarikh: Nahu Tafsir Islami lel-Sunan al-Kawniya wa al-Nawamis al-Ejtima'iya* (Philosophy of History: Towards an Islamic Interpretation of the Cosmic Laws and the Social Rules). Cairo: Dar al-Sahwah.

Unpublished Documents

"Istiqala Musababa" (Justified Resignation). Presented on March 8, 2012. (Muhammad Sai'd 'Abd al-Bar).

"Al-La'iha Al-Dakhiliya Le-Gama'it al-Ikhwan al-Muslimeen" (The Bylaws of the Muslim Brotherhood). First drafted in 1945, and amended in 1948, 1951, 1978, 1982. Latest version ratified in 1990, and amended in 2009 and 2010.

"Mabadi' al-Islam" (Islamic Principles), Vols. I–III. 2003.

"Al-Madkhal fei al-Tarbiya" (Introduction to Cultivation). 1997.

"Mashru' al-Nahda" (Renaissance Project). 2012.

"Mubadarat al-Ikhwan al-Muslimeen hawl Mabadi' al-Islah fei Masr" (The Muslim Brotherhood's Initiative on the Principles of Reform in Egypt). 2004.

"Muqarana bein Ghazwat al-Ahzab al-Qadima wa al-Haditha" (Comparing the Old and New Battle of the Parties). Pamphlet circulated in January 2013.

"Al-Nizam al-'Am Lel-Ikhwan al-Muslimeen" (The General Order of the Muslim Brotherhood). First drafted in 1982, and amended in 1994.

"Sallimli 'ala al-Manhaj: Kartha mein Fasl Wahid" (Greetings to the Curriculum! A Tragedy in One Act), circulated on January 3, 2010. (Anonymous playwright).

"Taqrir bisha'n al-Tarbiya" (Report on Cultivation). Presented to the Guidance Bureau on February 15, 2007. (Muhammad Sa'id 'Abd al-Bar).

"Turuq al-Tadris al-Haditha" (New Education Methods), Vols. I–II. 2002.

Yakan, Fatthy. "Al-Mutasaqitun 'ala Tarieq al-Da'wa" (Those Fallen by the Mission's Wayside), http://islamstory.com/ar.

Al-Zawahri, Ayman. 1991. "Al-Hassad al-Mur" (The Bitter Harvest), www.almaqdese.com.

Al-Zawahri, Ayman. 2001. "Fursan taht Rait al-Nabi" (Knights Under the Prophet's Banner), www.almaqdese.com.

Online and Audio/Video Materials

'Abbas, 'Alaa al-Din. 2008. "Intiqam al-Ikhwan al-Muslimeen" (Revenge of the Muslim Brotherhood), Ikhwanonline.com.

Al-Bialy, Ahmad. 2011. "Dar al-Ikhwan" (The Brotherhood's House), www.domiatwindow.net/article.php?id=6802.

Ghuzlan, Mahmoud. 2007. "Maza na'ni bei Shi'ar: Al-Islam hwa al-Hal" (What Do We Mean by the Slogan: Islam is the Solution?), Ikhwanonline.com.

Ghuzlan, Mahmoud. 2009b. "Mara ukhra, Nahnu wa al-Shia" (Again, Us and the Shi'ites), Ikhwanonline.com.

Al-Khatib, Muhammad Abdullah. 2013. "Ja' al-Haq wa Zahaq al-Batil" (Right Has Prevailed and Wrong Has Been Vanquished), www.fjp.com/article.php?id=56271.

Muheb, Sheikh. Friday sermons in a Southern California mosque attended by the author between September 2006 and June 2012.

Muslim Brotherhood's Domestic and International Bylaws and General Order www.ikhwanonline.com/Article.aspx?ArtID=58497&SecID=211.

Nada, Youssef. 2009. "Nahnu wa al-Shia" (Us and the Shi'ites), Ikhwanonline.com.

Al-Sirgani, Ragheb, http://islamstory.com/islam-history.

Personal Interviews

'Abd al-Bar, Muhammad Sa'id (Cairo, April 5, 2013).

'Abd al-Fattah, Seif (Cairo, April 2, 2013).

Abu al-Fotouh, Abd al-Mon'iem (Cairo, December 17, 2006).

Abu al-Magd, Kamal (Cairo, December 27, 2006).

Ahmad (Cairo, March 24, 2013).

Alfy (Cairo, September 21, 2013).

Al-Bishri, Tariq (Giza, January 10, 2007).

Deif, Ahmad (Giza, March 30, 2013).

Al-'Erian, 'Essam (Cairo, December 21, 2006).

Farghali, Sanaa' (Sixth of October City, March 29, 2013).

Hani (Giza, March 23, 2013).

Al-Houdeibi, 'Alia (Sixth of October City, April 1, 2013).

Al-Houdeibi, Ibrahim (Cairo, March 18, 2013).

Howeidy, Fahmi (Giza, December 25, 2006).

Ibrahim, Sa'd al-Din (Cairo, October 19, 2003).

Isma'il (Al-Ein al-Soukna, March 30, 2013).

Jamal (Giza, March 26, 2013).

Khalid (Giza, May 13, 2008; Giza, September 21, 2013).

Lotfi, Sarah (Sixth of October City, March 29, 2013).

Madi, Abu al-'Ela (Cairo, January 3, 2007).

Mahmoud, 'Abd al-Mon'iem (Oxford, May 15, 2013).

Malik, Muhammad (Cairo, April 2, 2013).

Mikkawi (Cairo, March 27, 2013).

Radwan (Sixth of October City, March 22, 2013).

Rami (Sixth of October City, June 28, 2013).

Rida (Giza, March 23, 2013).

Sameh (Giza, March 19, 2013).

Sami (Sixth of October City, April 9, 2013).

Samir, Ahmad (Giza, April 9, 2013).

Shafiq (Giza, March 23, 2013).

Shahin, 'Emad al-Din (Cairo, March 25, 2013).

Sharif (Giza, April 7, 2013).

Al-Sharif, Ashraf (Oxford, May 16, 2013).
Shatla (Giza, March 19, 2013).
Tag al-Din, Muhammad Sa'd (Cairo, March 29, 2013).
Tariq (Giza, March 23, 2013).
Wahba (Sixth of October City, March 22, 2013).
Walid (Cairo, March 27, 2013).
Yasser (Giza, March 19, 2013).
Youssef (Sixth of October City, March 22, 2013).
Yunis, Sherif (Cairo, March 27, 2013).
Al-Zayat, Muntasir (Cairo, October 12, 2003).

Secondary Sources

Abu-Rabi', Ibrahim (ed.). 2003. *Islam at the Crossroads: On the Life and Thought of Bediüzzaman Said Nursi*. New York: State University of New York Press.
Adams, Charles. 1933. *Islam and Modernism in Egypt: A Study of the Modern Reform Movement Inaugurated by Muhammad 'Abduh*. Oxford: Oxford University Press.
Algar, Hamid. 2001. *Roots of the Islamic Revolution in Iran*. New York: Islamic Publications International.
Anderson, Perry. 2009. *The New Old World*. New York: Verso.
Ashour, Omar. 2012. "Libyan Islamists Unpacked: Rise, Transformation, and Future." Doha: Brookings Institute.
Awad, Lewis. 1969. *Tarikh al-Fikr al-Hadith fei Masr* (History of Modern Thought in Egypt). Cairo: Dar al-Hilal.
Ayubi, Nazih. 1991. *Political Islam: Religion and Politics in the Arab World*. London: Routledge.
Baker, Raymond William. 2003. *Islam Without Fear: Egypt and the New Islamists*. Cambridge, MA: Harvard University Press.
Bayat, Asef. 2007. *Making Islam Democratic: Social Movements and the Post-Islamist Turn*. Stanford: Stanford University Press.
Benin, Joel. 1988. *Workers on the Nile: Nationalism, Communism, Islam, and the Egyptian Working Class, 1882–1954*. Princeton: Princeton University Press.
Bergen, Peter L. 2001. *Holy War Inc.: Inside the Secret World of Osama bin Laden*. New York: Simon & Schuster.
Berger, Peter L., and Thomas Luckmann. 1967. *The Social Construction: A Treatise in the Sociology of Knowledge*. New York: Anchor Books.
Binder, Leonard. 1988. *Islamic Liberalism: A Critique of Development Ideologies*. Chicago: University of Chicago Press.
Bodansky, Yossef. 2001. *Bin Laden: The Man Who Declared War on America*. Roseville, CA: Prima Publishing.
Bourdieu, Pierre. 1977. *Outline of a Theory of Practice*. Cambridge: Cambridge University Press.

Bourdieu, Pierre. 1990. *The Logic of Practice*. Cambridge: Polity.

Bourdieu, Pierre. 1991. "Genesis and Structure of the Religious Field." *Comparative Social Research* 13: 1–43.

Bourdieu, Pierre and Loïc J. D. Wacquant. 1992. *An Invitation to Reflexive Sociology*. Chicago: University of Chicago Press.

Brown, Nathan J. 2007. "Pushing Toward Politics: Kuwait's Islamic Constitutional Movement." Washington, DC: Carnegie Endowment for International Peace.

Brown, Nathan J. 2012. *When Victory Is Not an Option: Islamist Movements in Arab Politics*. Ithaca, NY: Cornell University Press.

Calvert, John. 2011. *Sayyid Qutb and the Origins of Radical Islam*. Cairo: American University in Cairo Press.

Collini, Stefan. 2006. *Absent Minds: Intellectuals in Britain*. Oxford: Oxford University Press.

Cook, Michael. 2004. *Commanding Right and Forbidding Wrong in Islamic Thought*. Cambridge: Cambridge University Press.

Cooley, John K. 2000. *Unholy Wars: Afghanistan, America, and International Terrorism*. New York: Pluto Press.

Crone, Patricia. 2004. *God's Rule: Government and Islam: Six Centuries of Medieval Islamic Political Thought*. New York: Columbia University Press.

Cronin, Stephanie. 2010. *Soldiers, Shahs, and Subalterns in Iran: Opposition, Protest, and Revolt, 1921–1941*. New York: Palgrave Macmillan.

Diyab, Muhammad Hafez. 1987 *Sayyid Qutb: Al-Khitab wal-Ideologiya* (Sayyid Qutb: Discourse and Ideology). Cairo: Dar al-Thaqafa al-Jadida.

Esposito, John L., and John O. Voll. 2001. *Makers of Contemporary Islam*. Oxford: Oxford University Press.

Esposito, John L., and Hakan Yavuz. 2003. *Turkish Islam and the Secular State: The Gülen Movement*. Syracuse: Syracuse University Press.

Euben, Roxanne L. 1999. *Enemy in the Mirror: Islamic Fundamentalism and the Limits of Modern Rationalism: A Work of Contemporary Political Theory*. Princeton: Princeton University Press.

Foucault, Michel. 2000. *Power*. New York: The New Press.

Gerges, Fawaz. 2011. *The Rise and Fall of Al-Qaeda*. Oxford: Oxford University Press.

Ghalioun, Burhan. 1993. *Al-Dawla wa al-Din: Naqd al-Siyasa* (The State and Religion: A Critique of Politics). Beirut: Arab Institute for Research and Publications.

Gibb, Hamilton A. R. 1947. *Modern Trends in Islam*. Chicago: University of Chicago Press.

Gramsci, Antonio. 1971. *Selections from the Prison Notebooks*. New York: International Publishers.

Hallaq, Wael B. 2005. *Authority, Continuity, and Change in Islamic Law*. Cambridge: Cambridge University Press.

Hallaq, Wael B. 2013. *The Impossible State: Islam, Politics, and Modernity's Modern Predicament*. New York: Columbia University Press.

Hammuda, 'Adil. 1999. *Sayyid Qutb: Min al-Qariyah ila al-Mashnaqah* (Sayyid Qutb: From the Village to the Scaffold). Cairo: Dar-Qeba.

al-Haramin al-Juwayni, Imam. 2011. *Al-Ghiathi* (The Savior). Jeddah: Dar al-Menhaj.

Hassan, Amaar 'Ali. 2006. *Al-Islah al-Siyasi fei Muhrab al-Azhar wal-Ikhwan al-Muslimeen* (Political Reform in the Sanctuary of Azhar and the Muslim Brothers). Cairo: Markaz al-Qahira le-Dirasat Huquq al-Insan.

Hefner, Robert W. (ed.). 2005. *Remaking Muslim Politics: Pluralism, Contestation, Democratization.* Princeton: Princeton University Press.

Heper, Metin, and Aylin Güney. 2000. "The Military and the Consolidation of Democracy: The Recent Turkish Experience." *Armed Forces & Society* 26 (4): 635–57.

Hourani, Albert. 1962. *Arab Thought in the Liberal Age, 1798–1939.* Oxford: Oxford University Press.

Kandil, Hazem. 2011. "Islamizing Egypt: Testing the Limits of Gramscian Counterhegemonic Strategies." *Theory and Society* 40: 37–62.

Kandil, Hazem. 2012. *Soldiers, Spies, and Statesmen: Egypt's Road to Revolt.* London: Verso.

Keddie, Nikki R. 1981. *Roots of Revolution: An Interpretive History of Modern Iran.* New Haven: Yale University Press.

Kepel, Gilles. 2006. *Jihad: The Trial of Political Islam.* 4th edition. London: I. B. Tauris.

Kerr, Malcolm H. 1966. *Islamic Reform: The Political and Legal Theories of Muhammad 'Abduh and Rashid Rida.* Berkeley: University of California Press.

Kurzman, Charles. 2002. *Modernist Islam, 1840–1940: A Sourcebook.* Oxford: Oxford University Press.

Mann, Michael. 1986. *The Sources of Social Power, Vol. I: A History of Power from the Beginning to A.D. 1760.* Cambridge: Cambridge University Press.

Mannheim, Karl. 1936. *Ideology and Utopia: An Introduction to the Sociology of Knowledge.* New York: Harvest Book.

Mardin, Serif. 1989. *Religion and Social Change in Modern Turkey: The Case of Bediüzzaman Said Nursi.* New York: State University of New York Press.

Mitchell, Richard P. 1993. *The Society of the Muslim Brotherhood.* Oxford: Oxford University Press.

Mitchell, Timothy. 1988. *Colonizing Egypt.* Cambridge: Cambridge University Press.

Moussalli, Ahmed S. 1992. *Radical Islamic Fundamentalism: The Ideological and Political Discourse of Sayyid Qutb.* Beirut: The American University of Beirut Press.

Önis, Ziya. 2007. "Conservative Globalism at the Crossroads: The Justice and Development Party and the Thorny Path to Democratic Consolidation in Turkey." *Mediterranean Politics* 14 (1): 21–40.

Rajaee, Farhang. 2007. *Islam and Modernism: The Changing Discourse in Iran.* Austin: University of Texas Press.

Roy, Olivier. 1994. *The Failure of Political Islam*. London: I. B. Tauris.

Sayigh, Yezid, and Raphaël Lefèvre. 2013. "Uncertain Future for the Syrian Muslim Brotherhood's Political Party." Washington, DC: Carnegie Middle East Center (December 9).

Shahin, Emad. 1998. *Political Ascent: Contemporary Islamic Movements in North Africa*. Boulder, CO: Westview Press.

Skocpol, Theda. 1994. *Social Revolutions in the Modern World*. Cambridge: Cambridge University Press.

Solomon, Ariel Ben. 2014. "Muslim Brotherhood Continues to Struggle against Regime." *The Jerusalem Post* (May 21).

Tammam, Husam. 2012. *Al-Ikhwan al-Muslimin: Sanawat ma Qabl al-Thawra* (The Muslim Brotherhood: Pre-Revolt Years). Cairo: Dar al-Shorouk.

Therborn, Göran. 1999. *The Ideology of Power and the Power of Ideology*. London: Verso.

Thompson, John. 1990. *Ideology and Modern Culture*. Cambridge: Polity.

Toth, James. 2013. *Sayyid Qutb: The Life and Legacy of a Radical Islamic Intellectual*. Oxford: Oxford University Press.

Tripp, Charles. 2006. *Islam and the Moral Economy: The Challenge of Capitalism*. Cambridge: Cambridge University Press.

Tugal, Cihan. 2002. "Islamism in Turkey: Beyond Instrument and Meaning." *Economy and Society* 31 (1): 85–111.

Tugal, Cihan. 2007. "NATO's Islamists: Hegemony and Americanization in Turkey." *New Left Review* 44: 5–34.

Verhoeven, Harry. 2013. "The Rise and Fall of Sudan's Al-Ingaz Revolution: The Transition from Militarized Islamism to Economic Salvation and the Comprehensive Peace Agreement." *Civil Wars* 15 (2): 118–40.

Wegner, Eva. 2007. "Islamist Inclusion and Regime Persistence: The Moroccan Win–Win Situation." Pp. 75–92 in *Debating Arab Authoritarianism: Dynamics and Durability in Nondemocratic Regimes*, edited by Oliver Schlumberger. Stanford: Stanford University Press.

Wright, Lawrence. 2002. "The Man behind Bin Laden: How an Egyptian doctor became a Master of Terror." *The New Yorker* (September 16, 2002).

Wright, Lawrence. 2007. *The Looming Tower: Al-Qaeda's Road to 9/11*. London: Penguin.

Yavuz, Hakan. 2003. *Islamic Political Identity in Turkey*. New York: Oxford University Press.

Yavuz, Hakan (ed.). 2006. *The Emergence of a New Turkey: Democracy and the AK Parti*. Salt Lake City: University of Utah Press.

Yavuz, Hakan. 2013. *Towards an Islamic Enlightenment: The Gülen Movement*. Oxford: Oxford University Press.

Yohannes, Okbazghi. 2001. *Political Economy of an Authoritarian Modern State and Religious Nationalism in Egypt*. London: The Edwin Mellen Press.

Yunis, Sherif. 2012. *Sayyid Qutb wa al-Usuliya al-Islamiya* (Sayyid Qutb and Islamic Fundamentalism). 2nd edition. Cairo: Al-Hay'a Al-Masriya al-'Ama lel-Kitab.

Ziadeh, Khaled. 2013. *Al-Katib wa al-Sultan: Min al-Faqih ela al-Muthaqaf* (The Author and the King: From the Jurist to the Intellectual). Beirut: Al-Dar al-Masriya al-Lebanoniya.

Zubaida, Sami. 2005. *Law and Power in the Islamic World*. New York: I. B. Tauris.

Index